Then, now and Always

A Winston's Wish publication
Copyright © 2004
Julie A Stokes – Winston's Wish

Published January 2004
ISBN 0-9539123-5-3

British Library Cataloguing in Publication Data
A catalogue record of this title is available from the British Library.

Edited and produced by Portfolio Publishing, 01732 824715
Designed by Heidi Baker

Winston's Wish
The Clara Burgess Centre
Bayshill Road
Cheltenham GL50 3AW

Family Line: 0845 20 30 40 5
Guidance and information for families of bereaved children and professionals supporting bereaved children

Phone: 01242 515157 (general enquiries)
Fax: 01242 546187
Website: www.winstonswish.org.uk
E-mail: info@winstonswish.org.uk

Charity registration number 1061359

Then, now and Always

Supporting children as they journey through grief:
a guide for practitioners

Julie A Stokes

For Cónor, Kate and Matt –
then, now and always …
no matter what.

Acknowledgements

It is with thanks to many, many people that *Then, Now and Always* has materialised, largely because it has been written from a wealth of experience, gained throughout the past decade. For that experience I would like to acknowledge **all** the inspiring people I have worked with over that time. Indeed the boundless creativity and wisdom of the Winston's Wish staff, volunteers, trustees and other professional colleagues will inevitably mean that the book becomes instantly out of date! But that is a good thing and reflects the effervescence of this rapidly expanding field.

At times producing the book has resembled pushing a honey-coated boulder up a hill. I am therefore completely indebted to 'the magnificent seven' (Allyson, Di, Hazel, Heidi, Helen, Kat and Sally)*. Individually they have demonstrated that many sticky hands made lighter work and collectively they have ensured that the book has become a reality. Particular thanks to the editorial team for their tireless scrutiny of the manuscript, for their wise suggestions and for their patience with me when I simply did not want to hear about any more changes. Many of the good things about this book are due to their perseverance and all of the mistakes are mine.

I remain inspired by Barbara Monroe for being such a clear strategist and dedicated ambassador for the Childhood Bereavement Network and for providing an insightful Preface, and by Professor Danai Papadatou for her collaborative professionalism in building global networks and for her very thorough peer review of this book. Thank you to trainee health psychologist Lindsey Wood for her invaluable help with the references, to Jemma Hogwood for her careful proof reading and also to the patient Calouste Gulbenkian Foundation, in waiting for their grant to bear fruit. Sincere gratitude to John Ritchie who came equipped with a personal understanding of childhood bereavement coupled with an entrepreneurial capacity which has enabled much of the content of the book to become a reality in terms of services for families.

The Afterword has kindly been written by our wise Chair, Dame Janet Trotter, whose discerning encouragement consistently gives me both stability and reassurance when navigating the unpredictable world of organisational development.

And finally, my wondrous family – especially Ronan, Cónor, Kate and Matt – for their generous support with my work and for reminding me, just when I needed reminding, that writing a book is, and always should be, only a small part of one's life.

*See editorial team and contributors below.

Editorial team

Helen Martins, Portfolio Publishing
Allyson McCulloch, Family Services Manager, Winston's Wish
Sally McIlwraith, Quality Assurance Manager, Winston's Wish
Hazel Millar, Director of Family Services, Winston's Wish
Di Stubbs, Helpline and Web Co-ordinator, Winston's Wish

Contributors

Katrina Alilovic, Counselling Psychologist, Winston's Wish (Chapter 7)
Hazel Millar (Chapter 13)
Jenny Miller, Training Consultant (earlier draft of Chapter 5)
Barbara Monroe, Chair, Childhood Bereavement Network (Preface)
Di Stubbs (Chapter 9)
Dame Janet Trotter, Chair, Winston's Wish (Afterword)

We would like to thank everyone who has shared their thoughts, stories, ideas and personal journeys in this book. In most cases, names have been changed to protect confidentiality. Thanks also to everyone who allowed their photos or artwork to be used and to those who took part in photoshoots.

Inside this book...

Preface

Sharing the journey

The past two decades have witnessed increasing interest in, and awareness of, the needs of bereaved children, young people and their families. Robust and painstaking programmes of research such as the Harvard Child Bereavement Study and Grace Christ's work at the Sloan Kettering Hospital in New York are beginning to illuminate the factors which influence outcome and children's developmental needs. We now know that there are costs, often long term, associated with allowing children's grief to remain hidden and unsupported. More recently this growing interest and the associated theoretical insights have begun to be matched by the development of specialist children's bereavement support services. The Childhood Bereavement Network (www.ncb.org.uk/cbn) in the UK has over 200 organisational and individual members who endorse its 2002 belief statement that 'all children have the right to information, guidance and support to enable them to manage the impact of death on their lives'.

The Childhood Bereavement Network is supporting the development of a consistent, proactive, national system of basic support services that are accessible to all children and their carers, whoever they are and wherever they live. A few, particularly those who are for some reason already vulnerable or at risk, will need on-going therapy. All have a right to access appropriate information and support. Central to this vision is a model of community-based, preventive, non-stigmatising, supportive care. Winston's Wish has been running such a programme for over 10 years and this volume distils for service providers, interested professionals and students the essence of its experience, its skills and its methodically developed and evaluated structures and systems. This book is much needed. There is of course no single recipe for provision, and services will always need to be configured in the light of local needs, priorities and resources. However, here is a well-referenced 'how to' manual of interventions – a map of possibilities with strong theoretical underpinning.

The contents capture key elements in delivering services to bereaved children, covering core aspects of the Winston's Wish programme from involving families in assessment, to memory work and weekend camps, including telephone and internet support and work with schools. Also covered are difficult issues such as specialist groups for families bereaved by suicide and therapeutic interventions in complicated grief. Case studies are used throughout to clarify and illuminate. There is a wealth of detail but clarity of message always remains at the forefront. Good intentions are not sufficient to achieve quality standards. The author emphasises the importance of appropriate skills and training, support and supervision and a systematic infrastructure of regularly monitored, evaluated and reviewed policies and methodologies.

The tone throughout is one of respect and empowerment and the ethos that of health promotion, rather than an illness model. Children will experience loss. This book offers a structured approach to supporting them and their families and locates that support firmly in a social context. We know that children revisit and reinterpret their loss experiences over time and that they will need on-going support from their families, friends, schools and communities as they do so. This book illustrates the possible development of resilient and supportive communities, rather than focusing on a model of 'expert' therapy for those designated to be at risk. The message is one of optimism. Children and young people, and those close to them, can confront and respond to the changes in their lives brought about by bereavement and in doing so learn profoundly important lessons to take with them as they move through life.

Barbara Monroe
Chief Executive, St Christopher's Hospice
Chair, Childhood Bereavement Network
Director, Candle Project

Introduction

The opportunity to make a difference

There are moments when you suddenly know that you are completely out of your depth. Driving in snow, chemistry A-level, baking a soufflé, understanding a balance sheet. I have had many such moments, but there is one such moment which came a decade ago that proved to be a turning point that has led me on a personal journey, searching for some answers.

Peter was 11 years old. He was a clever, articulate boy, eager to start at grammar school. His mother's recurrence of cancer was not part of the family's plan. It was a nightmare for everyone. Everyone assumed that Peter would have understood that his mother's skeletal body signalled her imminent death. The day before she died, when she was already in a coma, his dad asked me if I would talk to Peter. He was concerned that Peter had not 'brought the subject up' himself. Eager to support dad, I sat on Peter's bedroom floor while he fiddled with a *Star Wars* Lego set. I asked him what he thought about mum's illness. He said: 'It's taking longer than I expected'. My momentary composure was turned on its head when he then said: 'I hope she'll be up again soon'. I am sure he could see that I was visibly taken aback. And he became visibly agitated when I tentatively said: 'Peter, you do know that mum's illness is very serious – the doctors think she will die soon'. His eyes filled up and then his face became contorted with anger. 'Why … why are *you* telling me this – where's dad?'

Had we all unintentionally let Peter down by this subtle, yet utterly effective form of exclusion?

As a palliative care professional I found myself hopelessly out of kilter with the vision Peter held for his family. He believed his mum was getting better.

And anyone familiar with the needs of a bereaved child will recognise just how out of touch we all were in understanding Peter's needs. The next day I completed an application for a Winston Churchill Travelling Fellowship to visit child bereavement services in Canada and the United States. Fortunately, the application was successful and in July 1992 I set off to see how other services could respond to children coping with a family death. Those services were a wonderful inspiration. As Churchill declared: *'With opportunity comes responsibility'*. So, moved and inspired by the child bereavement services I saw on my study trip, I came back to the UK later that year and set up a service for children whose parent or sibling had died. As soon as the service was advertised, we began to realise that bereavement in childhood was not rare. This gave us the opportunity to make a difference. As time passed, it also became our responsibility to listen – and listen very carefully – to thousands of bereaved children, their parents and representatives from their communities. The 10-year journey we have travelled with bereaved families has led to the on-going evolution of a service we call 'Winston's Wish'.

The service was originally set up to meet the needs of bereaved children in Gloucestershire. Right from the start, we received enormous support from the local community to deliver our services. While direct services are still available for families in Gloucestershire, our nationwide programme of support for families now includes a telephone helpline and interactive website, with other services for families who live outside Gloucestershire available through statutory or privately funded referrals.

Winston's Wish aims to offer a comprehensive portfolio of services, many of which are described in this book. Our experience continues to grow through the provision of direct services underpinned by a strong commitment to research and development. We also offer tailor-made training and consultancy services for those working with bereaved families and those keen to set up a grief support service in their own area.

'Churchill' quickly metamorphosed into 'Winston' – a bear – who became the mascot of an exclusive 'club' that everyone would prefer not to join. We say that it is Winston's 'wish' that every bereaved child should receive the help they need to cope with the death of someone important in their lives.

Trying to realise our vision has, at times, been exhausting and difficult to achieve. But our 10-year journey has taken us forward step by step. It has given us greater clarity, and the confidence to begin to answer the question: *'How can a child bereavement service understand and meet the needs of children and the communities in which they live?'*

Ten years ago bereaved children were often referred to as 'the forgotten mourners' (Smith 1999). As Barbara Monroe explains in her Preface, there is a growing network of child bereavement services emerging across the UK. Now, the vision is no longer beyond reach – but there is still much to do. We hope this book will assist others who are also in the process of developing services for bereaved children. Equally, we expect it will stimulate further debate to enable us all to learn from each other's experience.

We have organised the book into the following structure:
- **Chapters 1 and 2** describe the ways in which the services provided by Winston's Wish have evolved, and consider how interventions are developed based on an understanding of current bereavement theory and research findings.
- **Chapters 3 to 11** describe the range of interventions which fit together to encompass a community-based child bereavement service.
- **Chapters 12 and 13** explore how an organisation can structure itself, embed itself into a nurturing community, while also attending to crucial service evaluation issues.

As adults, we want to educate our children that all lives have significance and worth. If a life ends then everyone, regardless of their age, has the right to mourn. Child bereavement services face a pioneering opportunity – to ensure that this basic principle is extended to all children in our communities nationwide.

Winston's Wish started out equipped only with free bears from a herbal shampoo company and a lot of goodwill from a National Health Service (NHS) palliative care team. However, we found that there are riches greater than money. We found these riches in the generosity of people prepared to give their time, energy and creativity, and in their genuine desire to make a difference when a childhood journey is suddenly forced to change direction.

Like any journey it is reassuring to have fellow travellers. My sincere thanks to everyone who has played their unique part in making Winston's 'wish' a reality, and in making our journey so eventful and rewarding. I especially want to say a heartfelt 'thank you' to all the bereaved families, from whom we learn something new every day.

Finally, I find myself reflecting on two people I have never met in person: my maternal grandmother (another Julie – not by coincidence) and Maureen, my only maternal aunt. Both died when they were far too young, leaving my own mother a bereaved child whose journey would never be smooth and who, even some 60 years later, still feels the pain of well-meaning exclusion. Future generations deserve better.

Julie Stokes
Consultant Clinical Psychologist
Founder and Chief Executive, Winston's Wish

'Losing a father as a child makes you feel incredibly disadvantaged emotionally. There isn't that person willing you on, there to help you. No-one there to rebel against or draw things from. You become horribly self-reliant, and you grow up quicker in one sense, and never grow up in another.'

James Dyson

'To "companion" bereaved children means to be an active participant in their healing ... you allow yourself to learn from their experiences. You make the commitment to walk with them as they journey through grief.'

Alan Wolfelt (1996)

Chapter One

A community-based child bereavement service

The Winston's Wish approach

Holding on, while letting go ... helping families to build a bridge between the past and a new future.

In this chapter, we describe the ways in which the services provided by Winston's Wish have evolved. A community-based approach is explained, and the range of services briefly described as experienced through the eyes of Tom, a 9-year-old bereaved child, his family and the community in which he lives.

'The death of a
parent is one
of the most
fundamental losses
a child can face.'

Worden 1996

Understanding death for families with children

Whether sudden or expected, few life events have a greater impact on families than the death of a family member. The ways in which families make sense of, and cope with their grief vary greatly. Everyone's bereavement journey will be unique.

But grief is normal – and necessary – and needs to be acknowledged, not bottled up or covered up. Grief is not an illness – nor is it something you simply 'get over'. Society tends to imagine a family death as so devastating for children that they should be completely protected – or the opposite, that children are so resilient that they will simply bounce back without any support. In our experience bereaved children do absolutely experience the pain and bewilderment of grief. However, with the help of supportive adults they can also heal, learn and grow into individuals who know both the tenderness and torment of developing the skills of resilience at a young age.

The needs of young children are still frequently overlooked, often fuelled by the notion that childhood is a time to be protected from harsh realities. But all children are curious about death and are likely to be deeply affected by the loss of someone close. The concept of death becomes increasingly concrete for most children as they move into adolescence, when the reality of death can cause chaos and confusion (Christ 2000).

Children don't always have the language or understanding to express how they feel. Finding safe and creative ways to help children express their feelings after the death of someone important in their lives is vital. Equally important is the ability of others to listen to children's stories relating to the death – and, by listening, to validate the children's experiences of grief.

Bereaved children need to feel comfortable expressing all feelings and thoughts associated with grief – such as anger, sadness, guilt and anxiety – and to be helped to find appropriate ways to do this.

Community-based child bereavement services are about PREVENTION. As Schuurman (2003) highlights: 'Without the right conditions for healing, children and teens will carry these emotional wounds into the rest of their lives. We know that children who have a parent die are at risk. They are more likely than other children to experience higher levels of depression; an increase in health problems and accidents; poorer school performance; more anxiety and fear; lower self esteem;

Everyone's
bereavement journey
will be unique.

a destructive belief that all events in their lives are beyond their control; and less optimism about succeeding later in life'. In her book, Schuurman provides validation for the experiences of adults who were bereaved as children. Such evidence makes a strong case for the services outlined in this book.

The scale of the need

Many countries around the world collect reliable data about the frequency of bereavement in childhood. Some countries, for instance, use demographic and health surveys to estimate prevalence rates of parental deaths, while others use different measures. Prevalence rates in the USA indicate that 6.1% of adolescents between the ages of 13 and 17 have experienced the death of a parent (74% death of a father, 25% death of a mother and 1% both parents). These figures come from the Social Security Administration, which is responsible for distributing death benefits to families where a parent has died (Ayers et al 2003).

Our estimates suggest that two children under 18 are bereaved of a parent every hour of every day in the UK, adding up to almost 20,000 newly bereaved children a year. An analysis based on data from the Office for National Statistics (Meltzer et al 2000) estimates that 3% of 5 to 15-year-olds have experienced the death of a parent or sibling: this equates to 255,000 young people in the UK. Kiernan (1992) looked at bereaved children aged 16 and found that 5.5% of UK children had experienced family disruption through the death of a parent. Harrison and Harrington (2001) estimated the risk of parental death by the age of 16 was 6% in the UK. These estimates are broadly comparable to rates in the USA, bearing in mind the differences in the type of bereavement and age group affected. Other countries quote much higher figures, for example 14.8% in Mozambique (Ayers et al 2003).

Whatever the exact figures are, the numbers are huge and the need to offer proactive support for such a major life event is compelling.

Our estimates suggest that two children under 18 are bereaved of a parent every hour of every day in the UK, adding up to almost 20,000 newly bereaved children a year.

Figure 1: Realities for grieving children
- All children and young people grieve.
- Grieving is a long-term process.
- Children and young people revisit their grief and frequently construct a changing relationship with the person who has died.
- Younger children will need help in retaining memories which facilitate a continuing bond.
- Children express their grief differently to adults.
- Children cannot be protected from death.
- There are clear developmental differences between children and young people in the understanding, experience and expression of grief.
- A child's grief occurs within a family and community context and will be influenced by significant adults.

A thorough analysis of the myths, realities and challenges surrounding children, adolescents and death is presented in an expanded statement from the International Working Group for Death, Dying and Bereavement (1999).

Developing a proactive approach to bereavement care

It was our intention to develop a community-based child bereavement service and to construct it carefully using foundations which embrace basic assumptions stemming from the existing literature (see Figure 1).

In accepting these assumptions we wanted to develop a service which was about 'understanding and helping' rather than 'treatment and curing'. We believe it is about translating knowledge into appropriate services which are valued by the child, their family and community. We wanted it to be about well-grounded action – theoretically informed and based on solid research and practical solutions. Our understanding of grief reflects the premise that grief is a natural, healthy, predictable set of responses to loss. It supports the definition by Weiss (2001: p47) which proposes a theory of 'grief as a response to loss of a relationship of attachment ... the severe and prolonged distress to the loss of an emotionally important figure'.

Corr et al (2000) provide a helpful framework to understand the various ways in which grief can manifest itself (see Figure 2).

Grief is a natural, healthy, predictable set of responses to loss.

Figure 2: The ways in which grief can manifest itself

- In *feelings* such as sadness, anger, guilt and self-reproach, anxiety, loneliness, fatigue, helplessness, shock, yearning, emancipation, relief or numbness.
- In *physical sensations* such as hollowness in the stomach, a lump in the throat, tightness in the chest, aching arms, over-sensitivity to noise, shortness of breath, lack of energy, a sense of depersonalisation, muscle weakness, dry mouth or loss of co-ordination.
- In *cognitions* such as disbelief, confusion, preoccupation, a sense of presence of the deceased or paranormal ('hallucinatory') experiences.
- In *behaviours* such as sleep or appetite disturbances, absent-mindedness, social withdrawal, loss of interest in activities that previously were sources of satisfaction, dreams of the deceased, crying, avoiding reminders of the deceased, searching and calling out, sighing, restless over-activity, or visiting places and cherishing objects that remind one of the deceased.

These are essentially physical, psychological (affective/cognitive) and behavioural manifestations of grief. Grief can also express itself in social and spiritual manifestations such as the following:

- In *social* difficulties in interpersonal relationships or problems in functioning within an organisation.
- In *spiritual* searching for a sense of meaning, hostility towards God or a realisation that one's value framework is inadequate to cope with the particular loss.

Each child is different and so is his or her experience of grief. However, as Shapiro (1994) clearly demonstrates, a child's grief is especially vulnerable to distortion by the 'needs, projections and instructions of adults'. Children perceive the world more literally than adults, and depend on adults for much of their information about a family death. 'The death of a family member generates circumstances in which adults, both protectively and consciously, as well as self-protectively and unconsciously, distort the information they give to their children about the nature and circumstances of the death or about their ongoing shared experience of grief.' (Shapiro 1994: p86)

'I think daddy will
come back for my
birthday.'

Amy, aged 4

Case study Anna (aged 3)

A mother arrived for a session with her 3-year-old daughter, announcing that Anna had been 'a real handful this week'. When she came in Anna immediately went to pick up Winston (a teddy bear) and sat on the floor, with her back turned. In previous sessions we had discussed how the mother could respond to Anna's frequent questions wanting to know where her dad had gone. Her mother felt she had answered her questions but wondered if Anna had really understood, so we agreed to try and initiate a discussion to clarify her understanding.

> **Practitioner:** *'Anna, where is your dad?'*
> **Anna:** *'He's dead'.*
> **Practitioner:** *'Where has he gone?'*
> **Anna:** *'To heaven'.*
> **Mum (whispering to practitioner):** *'See – I told you she knows'.*
> **Practitioner:** *'Where is heaven Anna?'*
> **Anna:** *'It's a better place'.*
> **Practitioner:** *'Do you know where that better place might be?'*
> **Anna:** *'London'.*

Anna had literally believed her granny when she told her: 'Don't worry, daddy has gone to a better place'. She was confused because it was also known in the family that Anna's dad 'took her everywhere', so why would he not share the 'better place' with her too, especially as she had decided it was 'not too far away' in London.

3 to 5-year-olds find it difficult to accept death
as permanent. They ask many questions and sometimes
crave quick solutions: 'Next time, get two daddies'.

3-5

When we begin to see the world through a child's eyes we can perhaps begin to understand why Anna and her mother both felt so frustrated and confused. A developmental perspective is crucial in enabling adults to understand and support a bereaved child (Christ 2000). The unwitting influences of the wider system on a bereaved child need to be carefully assessed: sometimes this can be done most effectively by adults who are more emotionally distanced from the child, and who can risk clarifying issues without needing to protect the child to the same extent. The following case study aims to capture the world through Tom's eyes following the sudden death of his father by suicide.

Case study   Tom (aged 9)

Tom is 9 years old. He lives at home with his parents and two sisters, aged 3 and 15. He is in Year 4 at a local primary school, where he has a number of good friends. Tom enjoyed a good relationship with his dad (Pete) – 'the boys' would often be seen playing rugby together and messing about mending things. However, over the past year Pete had become more distant and quiet, and would fly off the handle at small things. He was under a lot of pressure at work and extremely nervous about potential redundancy. Tom's dad kept these worries mostly to himself and eventually experienced a period of severe depression. He was signed off work, but he believed being off sick made him even more likely to be made redundant. One morning Pete left the house 'to pick up some shopping'. He did not return. At lunchtime, two policemen came to the door to explain that Pete had been found dead having fallen under a train. They explained sensitively that they believed his death was not an accident.

Having touched on the experience of his father's death through Tom's thoughts in Figure 3, the following Figure 4 demonstrates how a community-based service may accompany the family on the first three years of their bereavement journey.

'The first time I cried was several months later. I was at a friend's house after school. She wasn't feeling well and her mum brought her a glass of milk. Suddenly I realised that my mum was never going to do that again.'

Marion, bereaved aged 13

Figure 3: Making sense of death – reflections of a 9-year-old son, six months after his dad's death by suicide

Dad
'He was a great dad. The policemen said he didn't die in pain. Why did he do it? He must have forgotten about us for a moment.'

Mum
'I don't talk much about dad as it upsets mum. I hope she will be OK without dad.'

Dad's workmates
'They climbed three mountains in 24 hours and gave the money they raised to Winston's Wish.'

Older Year 6 boy
'James said my dad's picture was in the paper. He told me he was mangled by a train and his head was squashed.'

Sister (15)
'Emma and dad didn't get on that well – she get really angry sometime. I think she hates me. I'm not allowed in her bedroom.'

GP
'I keep getting pains in my tummy. Dr Shaw sees me to check that it is nothing bad. She sometimes asks how I'm getting on without dad. I don't say much.'

PlayStation 2
'It's wicked. I'm already on level 4!'

Estate agent
'He wants to sell our house. He has taken a picture of it and put it in the paper. I don't want to move. Why do things have to change?'

Dog
'Ben's my friend … he is always there.'

Grandad
'Pops died last year. He had a thing called cancer. He told me great stories.'

Head teacher
'Mr Green never mentioned it. Maybe he doesn't know my dad died? Or maybe he knows "how" he died and thinks it was a bad way to die.'

Class teacher
'Mrs Simms was kind to me. Her mum died when she was 12. We decided to tell my class together – they wrote me notes which arrived on the day of dad's funeral.'

Mates at school
'My mates are good fun, but they *never* talk about my dad. They moan about their dads because they are strict.'

Grandmother
'Granny is very, very upset all the time. She goes to dad's and pops' graves every day.'

Dad's boss
'Why did he make dad work so hard? He cried at the funeral.'

Neighbours
'They brought us home-made vegetable soup when dad died. Mum said they were kind, but I don't like vegetables.'

Vicar
'He asked me what I wanted to have at the funeral. We played dad's favourite song, and I wrote a poem which he read out. I keep a copy of it in my memory box so I don't forget.'

Sister (3)
'Lucy is too young to understand – she is lucky because she gets lots of hugs from everyone.'

Dad's rugby jumper
'I keep it under my pillow … it smells like dad. I miss him loads. *Why* did he do it?'

Best friend
'I spend lots of time at Sam's house now – gets me away from mum's friends who visit and ask me if I'm OK. I usually say yes.'

Figure 4: Sharing the journey – how can a child bereavement service understand and meet the needs of a child, their family and the community?

First year

February

Tom's father, Pete, dies when he jumps in front of a train. Tom's grandmother Jenny calls the *Family Line* two days after her son's sudden death by suicide. She had heard of Winston's Wish at a Women's Institute talk. Jenny has a 40-minute discussion with an experienced practitioner. They discuss funeral plans and her concerns about Lucy (3), Tom (9) and Emma (15) viewing their father's body. We agree to send an information pack to her daughter-in-law, Lynda. Lynda knew Jenny was calling, but didn't feel up to making the call herself.

Later that day, Tom's class teacher, Mrs Simms, phones to ask for guidance on how best to support Tom and his friends at school. We send our *school strategy* in the post and, as the school is local, we make an appointment to meet up with the teacher and head teacher after school the next day.

April

Two of our practitioners meet Lynda and the three children at their home to discuss how we may be able to help. This initial *assessment* lasts 2–3 hours and takes place around six weeks after Pete's death. The practitioners suggest the children collect mementos for their memory boxes and the family later decides to attend a residential group for families affected by suicide. This will be in four months. In the meantime, Lynda is offered six *individual sessions*, as she is struggling with agoraphobia and depression since Pete's death.

August

Tom, Emma and Lynda attend a *residential group* six months after Pete's death. They meet eight other families where suicide was the cause of death. (Lucy is looked after by her grandmother as she is too young to attend.) The family is later contacted to evaluate their experience of the residential group.

November

Lynda and Lucy attend a non-residential fortnightly group for parents with *pre-school* aged children.

December

The whole family and grandparents attend the *Christmas ceremony*. Afterwards 300 children and parents go to the theatre to watch a Christmas show.

March
Tom, Lucy and Lynda come to celebrate Winston's birthday (one of three annual *social-therapeutic events* to help families keep in touch). This year it is a trip on a steam train.

August
The family meets up with other families at the *summer fun day*. Lynda has tended to avoid going on holiday since Pete died so this is a good day out during the long school holidays.

September
Lynda and all three children attend *Camp Winston*. Having previously attended the group for families bereaved by suicide they now feel more comfortable reflecting on memories of dad rather than focusing on how he died. They also wanted to come as a complete family now that Lucy is older. On Camp Winston they meet 12 other families with 23 children altogether.

Third year

January
Lynda, Lucy and Tom continue to attend events, particularly enjoying the Christmas ceremony again. Lynda has enrolled for a college course. Tom has now settled at secondary school but has some special help provided for dyslexia. Emma is doing A-levels, and has left home to live with her boyfriend. She is hoping to be selected to train as a Camp Winston *volunteer* next year. Lucy, now 6, is settled at junior school and from time to time enjoys looking at her *memory box* which is filled with positive reminders of when dad was alive.

February
The anniversary of Pete's death is approaching. Lynda finds herself feeling really low. She calls the *Family Line* to talk about how she can get through the day.

June
Emma seems very preoccupied with her weight; mum is concerned and rings the *Family Line*. After a long discussion Emma is offered six *individual sessions*. Emma also regularly logs on to the *interactive website*, specially designed for 12 to 18-year-olds.

A grandparent or other person could also be included in the referral criteria if they had taken a particularly influential role in the child's life.

Developing a blueprint for service delivery

If we seriously want to consider the needs of a bereaved child like Tom, acknowledging that he exists as part of a wider system, then service delivery must be community based (see Figure 4). To respond to this complexity, service providers need to develop a comprehensive range of services which are flexible to meet individual needs. Importantly, this requires a considerable but invaluable investment of resources for each child.

As we began to evolve the service, the following issues quickly emerged and, after much soul-searching, we decided to be guided by the following principles:

A community-based service should be freely available to *any* child who has experienced the death of a parent or sibling.

Figure 5 provides an analysis of relatives who had died in families receiving a service over a two-year period (2001–02): 67% of the children referred have experienced the death of a parent.

For children under the age of 5, 75% of parental deaths are fathers and 25% are mothers. However, by the age of 16, 66% of parental deaths are fathers and 34% are mothers.

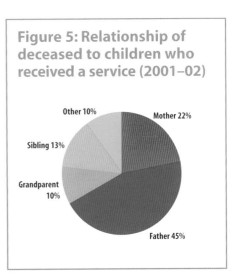

Figure 5: Relationship of deceased to children who received a service (2001–02)

Other 10%
Mother 22%
Sibling 13%
Grandparent 10%
Father 45%

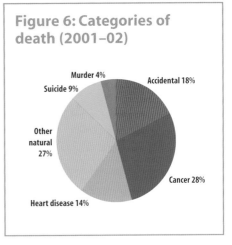

Figure 6: Categories of death (2001–02)

Murder 4%
Accidental 18%
Suicide 9%
Other natural 27%
Cancer 28%
Heart disease 14%

8

8% of children referred are under 5 years old. Very young children have particular needs to help them retain and build memories.

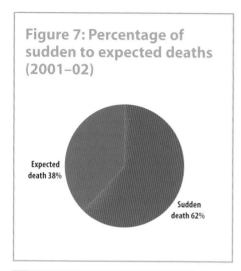

Figure 7: Percentage of sudden to expected deaths (2001–02)

Expected death 38%

Sudden death 62%

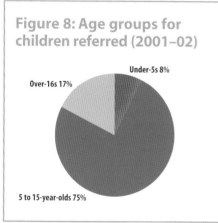

Figure 8: Age groups for children referred (2001–02)

Under-5s 8%

Over-16s 17%

5 to 15-year-olds 75%

A grandparent or other person could also be included in the referral criteria if they had taken a particularly influential role in the child's life. An example would be a grandad who picked the child up from school every day to support a single parent in paid employment.

Whenever possible the *cause* of death should not be relevant to service delivery. The hospice movement is noted for its capacity to pioneer new services. Not surprisingly, many hospices have developed excellent services for the children of hospice patients who have died. Indeed, Winston's Wish was started by a palliative care team based at Gloucestershire Royal Hospital. However, after two years it became clear that a significant number of the deaths (60–70%) that we were dealing with were not connected to palliative care. The deaths were often sudden (for example, suicide, road traffic accidents (RTAs), heart attacks) as distinct from the expected deaths arising from chronic conditions (for example, cancer, motor neurone disease, multiple sclerosis and so on). Figure 6 shows the causes of death affecting children who received a service in 2001–02: 28% of the deaths were related to a cancer diagnosis, 18% accidental death (of which 66% were RTAs), 14% heart conditions, 9% suicide and 4% murder/manslaughter.

'I knew mum had an illness and that it was called cancer, but the doctor didn't tell me she would die from it!'

Peter, aged 11

Figure 9: The Winston's Wish programme of direct support

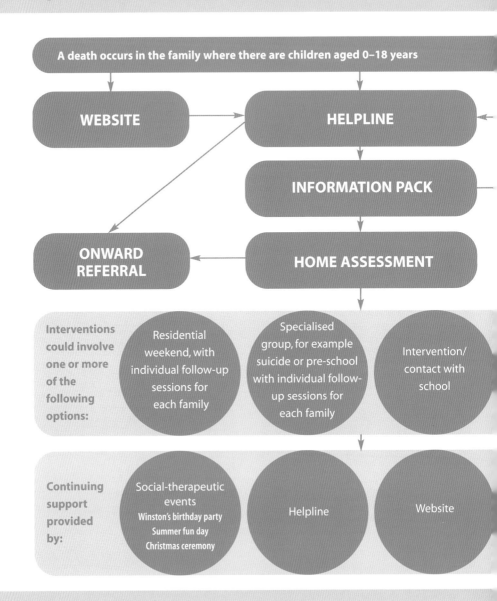

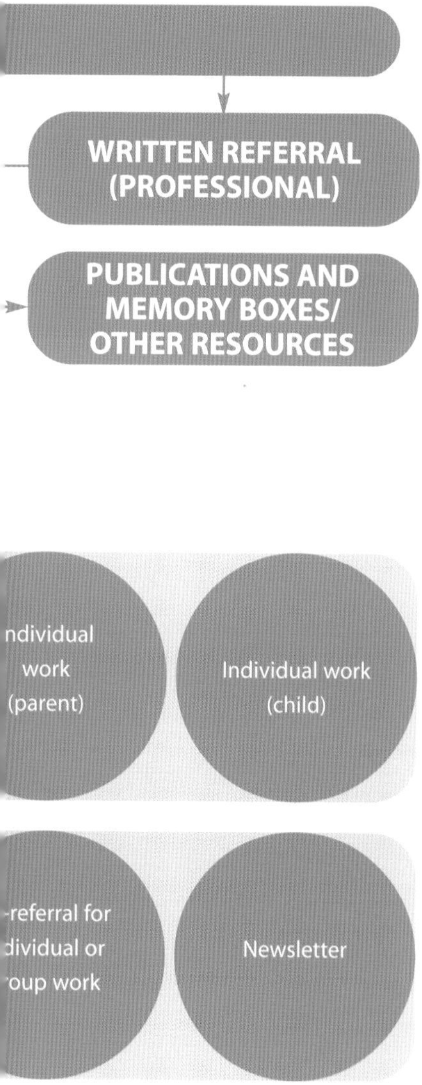

WRITTEN REFERRAL (PROFESSIONAL)

PUBLICATIONS AND MEMORY BOXES/ OTHER RESOURCES

ndividual work (parent)

Individual work (child)

-referral for dividual or roup work

Newsletter

a) Our programme of direct support for families in Gloucestershire includes:
- individual assessments to accurately gauge the needs of each bereaved family, carried out in the family home
- individual work when grief is complicated
- residential weekends for children and young people aged 5 to 18
- simultaneous weekends for parents and carers of bereaved children
- support for children when a close member of the family is dying
- specialised group work for those affected by suicide and for parents with pre-school aged children
- a support programme for schools
- social-therapeutic events to help maintain friendships.

b) Our nationwide programme of support for families includes:
- telephone helpline, supported by books, leaflets and memory boxes
- interactive website primarily aimed at 12 to 18-year-olds
- statutory or privately funded referrals for families who live outside Gloucestershire: services as listed in a) above. (In 2001–02 this accounted for 17% of children who received a service.)

Winston
enters it's
10th year!

Many families choose to stay in touch remotely by receiving our quarterly newsletter *Pawprint*.

In this cohort the percentage of deaths described as sudden is 62% whereas deaths that involve palliative care (expected deaths) is 38%.

Figure 7 shows that in the vast majority of families the death is clearly unexpected (for example, suicide, murder, RTAs, heart conditions and so on). Even though 38% of deaths have been classified as 'expected' from a medical perspective (such as cancer, motor neurone disease), for many children they would also have experienced the death as unanticipated.

Eventually the hospital acknowledged

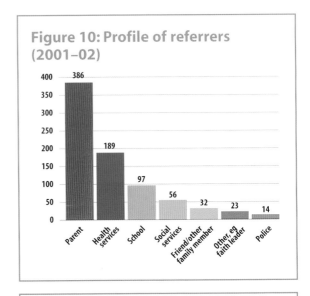

Figure 10: Profile of referrers (2001–02)

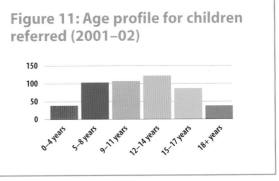

Figure 11: Age profile for children referred (2001–02)

that it was unable to fund a service for families who were bereaved by sudden deaths. This presented us with a challenging choice: we could either remain in the NHS, confining our services to referrals from palliative care, or try to establish Winston's Wish as a voluntary organisation, capable of generating its own funds on a charitable basis. To say to a bereaved parent: 'Your child is not eligible for our service because your partner died of a heart attack and not cancer' seemed inappropriate. So we decided that we would at least try to set up a community-based service which did not discriminate on the basis of cause of death. There is an

Families should be able to access support easily and for as long as they need. Parents remain the main referrers of children.

increasing trend for hospice services to persuade their boards to extend their criteria to include sudden deaths. This is really encouraging as a recent mapping exercise of child bereavement services indicated that 44% of host organisations are hospices (Rolls and Payne 2003).

After 10 years we are now able to offer a range of services (see Figure 9) to children over a wide age range (see Figure 11). Some of these are available to families nationwide, while the programme of direct support is largely available to families who live in Gloucestershire. Gloucestershire has a population of about half a million: this results in approximately 200–250 new referrals each year. Services are tailored to individual needs but are also capable of accommodating large numbers of referrals.

'I don't remember seeing dad cry – he wasn't a man who showed his feelings. And we quickly realised that mum had become a taboo subject. Dad never mentioned her – perhaps that was his way of coping – but for us it was very hard.'

Janie, now aged 41, reflecting on her mother's sudden death when she was 14

Parents/carers should be encouraged to refer directly.

The privacy and speed of an 'open access' system minimises any judgment or perception that the family is 'not coping'. The service is available routinely to any family following the death of a mother, father, brother or sister. The service is for 'ordinary' children, coping with an 'extraordinary' life event.

Figure 10 gives a profile of people who first contact Winston's Wish to refer a child and/or parent(s).

The service should be responsive to factors which can complicate the mourning process.

We have invested in a comprehensive home assessment process (see Chapter 3) and also made available an individual service for those whose mourning is complicated (see Chapter 6). In addition, some causes of death (for example, suicide – see Chapter 7) or ages (for example, pre-school aged children) benefit from a specifically tailored group programme.

Families should be able to access support for as long as they need.

Most families choose to remain in touch with the service for over two years (see Chapter 11); many more choose to stay in touch remotely by receiving our quarterly newsletter *Pawprint* and by knowing that they can call the Family Line, 9.30am to 5pm, Monday to Friday (see Chapter 9). Re-referrals are not uncommon (see page 237). As children develop, they often need additional help to progress on their personal grief journey.

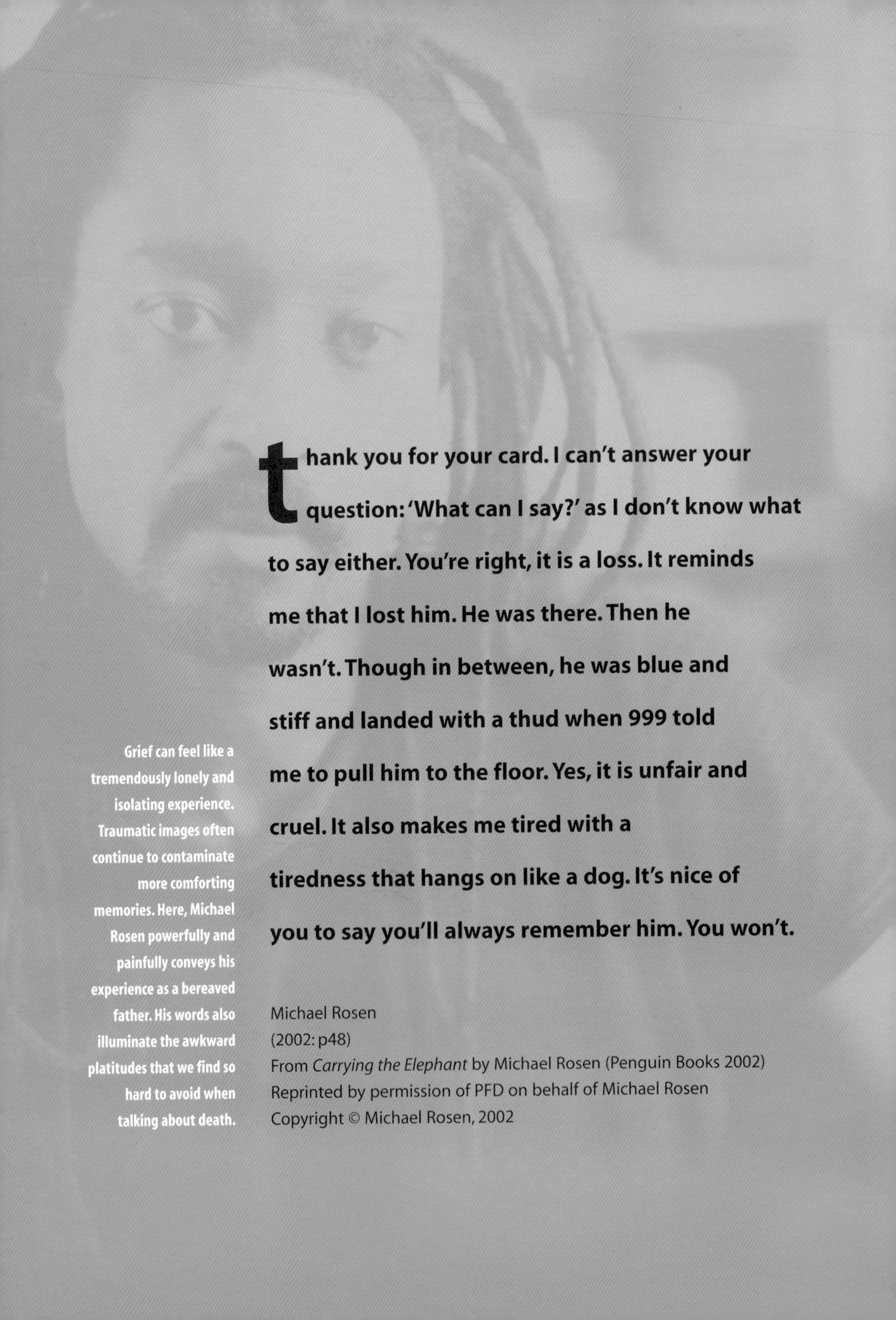

thank you for your card. I can't answer your question: 'What can I say?' as I don't know what to say either. You're right, it is a loss. It reminds me that I lost him. He was there. Then he wasn't. Though in between, he was blue and stiff and landed with a thud when 999 told me to pull him to the floor. Yes, it is unfair and cruel. It also makes me tired with a tiredness that hangs on like a dog. It's nice of you to say you'll always remember him. You won't.

Grief can feel like a tremendously lonely and isolating experience. Traumatic images often continue to contaminate more comforting memories. Here, Michael Rosen powerfully and painfully conveys his experience as a bereaved father. His words also illuminate the awkward platitudes that we find so hard to avoid when talking about death.

Michael Rosen
(2002: p48)
From *Carrying the Elephant* by Michael Rosen (Penguin Books 2002)
Reprinted by permission of PFD on behalf of Michael Rosen
Copyright © Michael Rosen, 2002

Primary clinical objectives

Winston's Wish has identified five primary clinical objectives for its work. Our services are designed to help bereaved children and families by providing increased opportunities for:

- **support, information and education** – supporting children and families to understand death and what it means to them

- **understanding and expressing grief** – encouraging children and families to share and understand the feelings, thoughts and individual ways of coping with loss

- **remembering** – helping families to find ways of remembering the person who has died

- **communication** – encouraging family members to talk openly with each other

- **meeting others** – providing opportunities to meet other families with similar experiences.

Most families need support, not therapy. Although supporting a family fragmented by an untimely death can seem daunting, we have found that for most families there are simple, straightforward and practical ways which can make a real and lasting difference to a grieving child. With support and information, children and young people can be helped to understand what has happened and can slowly learn to live with their loss.

This chapter has identified some of the issues which need to be considered when developing a community-based child bereavement service. It outlines the services developed by Winston's Wish which aim to support not only the child, but also others who play a key role in the child's life. Each of these service interventions is described in greater detail in chapters 3 to 11 of the book. The next chapter briefly reviews the literature which has informed this service development to date.

Children need to be given hope for their future so they feel resilient in the present and can take comfort from the past.

Chapter Two

Scientist and practitioner

Linking theory and practice

'A person is a person
no matter how small.'
Dr Suess

**It is irresponsible and potentially damaging to offer services to
bereaved children which are not planted, rooted and carefully
nourished by an accurate assessment of their individual needs.**
In questioning the value of 'bereavement counselling', Professor Harrington
(Harrington and Harrison 1999; Harrison and Harrington 2001) sparked off a
healthy debate which has encouraged both practitioners and researchers to
think carefully about the theoretical models and research evidence which
underpin bereavement services for children (Cross 2002; Winton 2002). This
chapter provides a brief overview of the literature which has led to a growing
network of child bereavement services and discusses the viability of making
community-based services available to all bereaved children.

'I am scared that
someone else will
die in my family. I
drew a picture of my
mum going to work,
and I am sad because
I am not with her
and I don't know if
she will die or not.'
Greg, aged 6, whose
brother died

Different ways to develop services for bereaved children

The Harvard Child Bereavement Study (Silverman and Worden 1992; 1993) is one of the few studies of a normative population of bereaved children. The two-year study followed a non-clinical community sample of 125 children after a parental bereavement, compared with a control group of non-bereaved children. Researchers interviewed both the surviving parent and the children. Although it is acknowledged that more longitudinal studies are needed, the findings of this study continue to have important implications for service development. Worden (1996) later incorporates these findings to identify three key models for children's services (see Figure 12).

Figure 12: Models of intervention for bereaved children

(Adapted from Worden 1996: pp150–151)

Model A

To offer intervention *only* where children display levels of emotional and behavioural problems or psychological distress. Worden recognises that such an approach requires *observable* levels of distress and we need to be satisfied in two areas: firstly, that children not displaying certain behaviour *do not* require intervention and, secondly, that emotional and behavioural difficulties do not have to reach exaggerated levels before intervention is offered.

Model B

To offer intervention to those children identified *at risk* by using a screening measure. The preventive mental health model of early screening aims to target potential 'at risk' groups for early intervention in order to reduce the likelihood of long-term negative outcomes. If the development of an effective screening measure is possible, more longitudinal studies are needed to develop a valid tool that is reliable over time and across differing populations.

Model C

To offer intervention routinely to all bereaved children and their families, recognising that 'the death of a parent is one of the most fundamental losses a child can face'. However, Worden reports that one-third of the children observed were considered 'at risk' during the two-year study. He therefore questions both the need and cost-effectiveness of a preventive approach.

Organising services so they can accommodate all children bereaved of a parent or sibling (model C) is often considered too costly because of the general lack of mental health resources available to children's services (Harrington and Harrison 1999). In the development of community-based bereavement services, targeting those children with the greatest need aims to maximise the resources available. When services are stretched to their limits, or potential referrers do not have the skills to identify those who require support, priority is often given to the children who are *seen* to be experiencing 'problems' (model A). While this approach ensures that some children receive support, it gives a clear message that certain behaviours require intervention. However, while some children 'act out', others do not. Studies concerned with children's pain behaviour suggest that a quiet or playing child is not necessarily a pain-free child (Collier 1997). Attention to behavioural criteria alone may result in some children not getting the support they need.

Adopting model B in the development of community-based bereavement services provides a response to some of the above concerns. With limited resources, a screening measure is preferable to relying solely on the presence of behaviours described in model A. Screening measures developed from longitudinal studies with bereaved children, for example Worden 1996, may be used to target those needing help. However, reliance on such a rigid tool to identify risk also raises a number of potential problems. Managers will of course be keen to target resources at those who are most in need. At the same time, clinicians need to feel comfortable that such a screening tool is totally reliable. A survey of risk assessment tools used with adult populations revealed that this is not always the case (Payne and Relf 1994).

Two general concerns about the development of a screening measure are validity and efficacy across populations and over time. The assumption that a distinct and observable 'at risk' or 'potentially at risk' group can be identified has implications for the administration of a screening measure. Can such a measure be sensitive, yet robust enough to account for the changing needs of bereaved children and their parents? Could a screening tool, used at a single point in time, produce an accurate picture of a family's needs? Would the family measured to be 'coping just fine' not be offered any support? If so, this may not necessarily be a view that accurately reflects the experience of the family. Furthermore, is there sufficient evidence to indicate *when* such a tool should be used: at one week after a death, one month, six months, a year? When?

'After our son Ben died, our 4-year-old daughter kept asking if she could go to visit him and God. Her older brother got angry and said "no 'God' would have let this happen!" and he kept shouting at his sister for asking such stupid questions. I didn't know what to say.'

Caller to the Family Line

'The girls got so much from the weekend – realising they weren't the only ones and that it was OK to feel all sorts of emotions. We still talk about the weekend and I find it a great way to open up a conversation about their dad which used to be such a hard thing to do. For me, I felt their lives were ruined and as a mum I found that devastating. The weekend taught me that life is *different* but *not ruined* and knowing that has had the biggest impact on me. Just knowing we are under your "umbrella" is such a help.'

Feedback from parent, Service Evaluation 2003

A community-based support service for all bereaved children?

In taking account of the limitations of models A and B described above, a growing number of child bereavement services advocate the use of model C. As such services emerge, it is important to develop an effective umbrella network: for communication, for agreement on standards and to provide up-to-date information for the general public and professionals. The much-needed Childhood Bereavement Network is giving this important structure to UK-based services.

Most services acknowledge the importance of both involving the whole family and providing the opportunity to meet others with similar experiences. This is underpinned by the belief that parental support is an integral part of supporting bereaved children. Services provided routinely may also have a health promotion function to *prevent problems from escalating to a more serious level*. Indeed, it is possible that community-based services may serve to relieve the burden on specialist services, such as child and adolescent mental health teams (CAMHS). Working in partnership, community-based interventions could act as a screening measure in themselves, a filter for referrals onto specialist mental health services where necessary.

Interestingly, while the Harvard Child Bereavement Study reports that self-esteem is not significantly affected initially, at *two years following the death of a parent, self-esteem is significantly lower among bereaved children* in comparison to non-bereaved peers (Silverman and Worden 1992). This provides a compelling case for preventive early intervention.

One-third of children in the Harvard Child Bereavement Study were considered 'at risk' during the two-year period. However, did that imply that two-thirds of the sample required no intervention at all? It is perhaps interesting to consider the effect of the research interviews for children who were involved in the study. Bereaved children who are offered a simple intervention are reported to be more able to talk about their dead parent (Black 1991). The opportunity to 'tell their story', to be heard and to ask questions, even as part of a research process, could be considered an intervention in itself.

A continuing bond for children?

After a bereavement, adults often express a need for opportunities to talk about their experience of the illness, the death and their relationship with the deceased to try

2

At two years following the death of a parent, self-esteem is significantly lower among bereaved children in comparison to non-bereaved peers. Silverman and Worden 1992

to discover what it all means. Evidence from studies on parental grief suggests that parents continue to have a relationship with the deceased child, that bonds continue in some form rather than being completely severed, and that this is adaptive (Klass 1988). In a similar way, other studies suggest that bereaved children also maintain a connection to their deceased parent, reporting the importance of objects belonging to the deceased, dreams and a sense of presence (Silverman et al 1992; Worden 1996).

Bereaved children also need to find an appropriate place for the dead person in the context of their on-going lives. They need to engage into a meaning-making process which enables them to work out 'why' their parent died and also 'what role' this parent would now have in their lives. These are part of a concept described as 'continuing bonds' (Klass et al 1996), one which fits well with the development of the dual process model (Stroebe and Schut 1995; 1999) and current interests in biography and narrative models (Walter 1996). Clinical observations of over 2,000 children referred to the Winston's Wish programme suggest that being given permission to talk about, and remember, their dead family member in a way that is meaningful for them is very comforting for most children and their families (Stokes et al 1997).

Silverman and Worden (1993) also refer to 'a dynamic interactive process to which time must be an added factor'. Indeed, it has been suggested that it is more appropriate to use the developmental term 'accommodation' rather than words that imply a finite process, such as 'recovery' (Klass et al 1996). Feelings, behaviour and understanding can change over time, and depend on factors such as the previous relationship with the deceased, the context of the bereavement, and access to support and resources. Certain 'risk' factors may not be sustained over time or may be precipitated by significant life events. For example, children may appear to cope well at school and seemingly adjust to their bereavement but may later experience difficulty, perhaps when changing school, starting a family or experiencing another bereavement.

Model C (see page 36) – a community-based service (available to all children experiencing parental or sibling death) – aims to facilitate coping strategies that can be used throughout life. Even for a family that might well be considered 'resilient', the process of meeting others can significantly enhance coping.

The bereavement literature has provided practitioners with useful criteria to understand the impact of a parental death, on a particular family, at a particular time.

As shown in Figure 13, Parkes and Weiss (1983) outlined what they termed 'determinants of grief' which influence an individual's grief response.

'Last night I dreamed that my mum came to meet me from school: she hugged me and gave me the softest blanket ever to wrap round because she thought I was cold. I kept some of that softness and warmth when I woke up.'

Georgia, aged 7, whose mum died

Figure 13: Determinants of grief

1. Who the person was in relation to them	To know about a person's grief response we need to know who the deceased was. This is a very simple, but powerful determinant of grief. Was the person who died a spouse or a child? A friend or a neighbour? For example, grief after the death of a child is likely to be expressed differently to grief following the death of a grandparent.
2. The nature of the attachment	The nature of the attachment between the person who died and the griever is also important to the grief reaction displayed and this is influenced by aspects outlined below.
a) Strength of the attachment	The strength of the attachment between the griever and the deceased underlines the grief response. An increased intensity of attachment tends to be associated with greater intensity of grief.
b) Security of the attachment	The sense of security provided from the attachment also contributes to the grief response. Did the existence of the deceased provide security in the griever's life? If so, this may exacerbate their grief response. Did the deceased boost the griever's self-esteem? If so, following the death of this important person, their self-esteem may be adversely affected and increase the intensity of their grief response.
c) Ambivalence of the relationship	The extent of ambivalence within a relationship is a very important grief determinant. What was the proportion of positive and negative feelings involved in the relationship? If the relationship was highly ambivalent and negative feelings were almost experienced in equal amounts to positive feelings, the grief may be expressed extremely intensely and in a difficult manner often involving anger and guilt.
d) Conflicts with the deceased	Conflicts with the deceased throughout life can influence the grief reaction and guilt involved. This can range from the normal, everyday relationship conflicts through to physical and sexual abuse (Krupp et al 1986).
3. Mode of death	How the person died also contributes to the grief response. Modes of death can be categorised in terms of the NASH categories: natural, accidental, suicidal and homicidal. Grief responses will manifest differently according to the mode of death. Other factors important to the grief response are the location of the death, whether the death was sudden or to some extent expected, and the situation in which the death occurred. For example, did the griever have any involvement in the accident in which the person died? This would have a profound effect on the grief response, possibly involving feelings of guilt.

'When separation occurs, we will grieve, we will suffer. No one is immune. It is the price we pay for commitment.' Catherine Saunders

4. Historical antecedents	Any losses the griever has had prior to the death (for example, illness, divorce, other deaths, redundancy), how these were dealt with and the outcome of these losses are important to the grief reaction displayed. More specifically, how the individual cognitively views these losses and adversities within their life is important. For example, a history of mental illness or even the death of another loved one would play a central role in the grief response.
5. Personality variables	Personality variables of the griever play a significant role in the grief response. Bowlby's (1980) instrumental work on attachment and loss has been the main advocate for taking personality variables into account in the case of grief reactions. These factors include age, sex, openness with feelings, how they cope with anxiety, how they cope with stress in general, dependence on others and ease/difficulty of forming relationships. The grief reaction may be exacerbated in those who suffer from any 'personality disorder'.
6. Social variables	Social variables can be very important determinants of how an individual displays their grief reaction: social, ethnic and religious factors will all play a role in forming this background for an individual. Religious and cultural backgrounds determine practice of rituals following a death and influence the mode and extent that grief is expressed. The level of perceived social support from others can also influence the intensity of the grief reaction.
7. Rituals	Participation in death-related rituals and activities: was there a ritual or not? If so, how did the grieving person participate and how was such participation experienced, what kind of involvement did the person have in decisions regarding the commemoration of the deceased, the handling of his or her belongings and so on?
8. Concurrent stressors	Additional life stressors following the death can make the grief even more intense. For example, the development of financial worries as a result of a decline in household income since a partner's death may increase the intensity of grief.

(Adapted from Parkes and Weiss 1983 in Worden 1996: pp31–34)

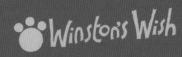

Charter for bereaved children

Winston's Wish has supported many thousands of bereaved children in the last 10 years. This 'charter' is based on our conversations with them. If we live in a society that genuinely wants to enable children and young people to rebuild their lives after a death, then we need to respect their rights to:

B   Bereavement support
Bereaved children are entitled to receive the support they need.

E   Express feelings and thoughts
Bereaved children should feel comfortable expressing all feelings and thoughts associated with grief, such as anger, sadness, guilt and anxiety and to be helped to find appropriate ways to do this.

R   Remember the person who has died
Bereaved children have a right to remember the person who has died for the rest of their lives if they wish to do so. This may involve re-living memories (both the good and the difficult) so that the person becomes a comfortable part of the child's continuing life story.

E   Education and information
Bereaved children are entitled to receive answers to their questions and information that clearly explains what has happened, why it has happened and what will happen next.

A   Appropriate and positive response from schools or colleges
Bereaved children can benefit from receiving help and understanding from their teachers and fellow students.

V   Voice in important decisions
Bereaved children should be asked if they wish to be involved in important decisions that have an impact on their lives (such as planning the funeral and remembering anniversaries).

E   Everyone involved
Bereaved children should receive support which includes their parent(s) or carers and siblings.

M   Meeting others
Bereaved children can benefit from the opportunity to meet other children who have had similar experiences.

E   Established routines
Bereaved children should be able to choose to continue previously enjoyed activities and interests.

N   Not to blame
Bereaved children should be helped to understand they are not responsible and not to blame for the death.

T   Tell their story
Bereaved children have a right to tell their story in a variety of ways and for those stories to be heard, read or seen by those important to them.

'I helped to choose mum's favourite music, which they played at her funeral.'
Kim, aged 12, whose mother died of a heart attack

'My teacher remembers the days which are difficult, like Father's Day and dad's birthday.'
Alex, aged 9, whose father died of motor neurone disease

'I now understand it wasn't anyone's fault.'
Chris, aged 12, whose dad died by suicide

'It's alright to cry and OK to be happy as well.'
James, aged 9, whose mum died from breast cancer

Dear mum

How are you geting

on? What is it like in heaven? I think it is scary. Because I'm scared of heights. I've now got a bedroom of my own. I miss you and wish you was alive so I could move back home. I don't want to move school.

I've got a Play Station and I will be getting a Play Station2 for my birthday. I wish I could hug you again.

From
Ryan

RS2

Reproduced with permission from Ryan, aged 9

This letter was written to place on Ryan's mother's grave. His mother had died suddenly seven months previously. Her death signalled a series of secondary losses for a young lad already struggling to make sense of his mother's sudden death. He now lives in short-term foster care many miles away from familiar community networks. It is always hard to move school, make new friends, get used to a new home and new carers … how much harder must this be when you are 9 years old and your mother died less than 12 months ago? Community child bereavement programmes need to work in partnership with statutory agencies to ensure children like Ryan are linked up with families who can offer secure long-term foster care (preferably adoption) and, ideally, close to the community networks which they value.

We live in a health culture that is able to react positively for all at the beginning of life, while advocating the rationing of services following the end of a life.

Financial implications

People have valid concerns about the availability of funding sources to develop and sustain child bereavement services. However, the evidence from a growing number of community-based programmes demonstrates that there is both the demand and need to provide such services. Over time, local communities are often willing – and capable – of generating financial support for services (see Chapter 12). The funding of existing services also illustrates the potential for healthy partnerships with statutory agencies, local communities and corporate fundraising. A core structure of paid staff supported by a larger group of trained volunteers can further emphasise a service philosophy that is truly 'community-based'. For instance, there are currently 60 people in the Family Services team at Winston's Wish: 12 staff members and 48 volunteers.

Education, social and health services have an important role and can provide much-needed support, stability and credibility for developing services. However, statutory services are unlikely to be solely responsible for service development and service provision. The development of community-based bereavement services must be built on detailed financial planning, encouragement of sponsorship and the development of sustainable income, such as developing resources, and training and consultancy programmes (Papadatou 1997).

Life *and* death … a final thought

Expectant mothers, most of whom will have perfectly healthy pregnancies, are rightly offered many hours of *routine* check-ups with GPs, hospital gynaecologists, midwives and antenatal teachers. There are repeated opportunities for *education*, *support* and *meeting others in a similar situation*. Such support is recognised as important in helping prospective parents to cope with an important life event. Although government programmes (such as SureStart) will aim to target those identified to be 'at risk', antenatal services funded largely by the National Health Service will continue to be provided routinely for every pregnant woman – whether deemed at risk or not. It could be argued that antenatal health promotion services have become an accepted and expected part of the 'birth experience'. Indeed, it would be bizarre to imagine a midwife informing a couple that they had 'scored' too highly on a measure of adjustment and therefore would not receive an invitation to join an antenatal group.

People have valid concerns about the availability of funding sources to develop and sustain child bereavement services.

This raises interesting questions about a health culture that is able to react positively for all at the beginning of life, while advocating the rationing of services following the end of a life. This is of particular concern if we accept Worden's (1996) proposal that: *'The death of a parent is one of the most fundamental losses a child can face'.* We must ask ourselves whether basic education about death and grief, and the opportunity for peer support, are too much to expect when a child is bereaved of a mother, father, sister or brother (Stokes et al 1999[1]).

This chapter has recognised that service developments for bereaved children need to be based on clearly articulated service aims against which outcomes can be described and measured. (Service evaluation is discussed separately in Chapter 13.) It has considered how interventions are developed based on an understanding of the determinants of grief and related research findings. It remains a controversial issue to suggest that bereavement services are provided routinely. While the need to refer every person for bereavement 'counselling' is undoubtedly ill-advised (Parkes 1998), our experience indicates that community-based services which meet the five primary clinical objectives (see page 33) appear to be valued and seem to make sense to the vast majority of families referred.

---

[1] This chapter contains excerpts from Stokes J, Pennington J, Monroe B, Papadatou D and Relf, M. 1999. Developing Services for Bereaved Children: A Discussion of the Theoretical and Practical Issues Involved. *Mortality*, 4 (3): 291–307.

'In every conceivable manner,
the family is our link to our past
and bridge to our future.'

Alex Hayley

Chapter Three

Preparing for the journey

How assessment can guide the most appropriate route for each family

This chapter discusses some of the issues which we consider when conducting an assessment in order to ensure the services offered address factors which will promote resilience and coping for the bereaved child and their family.

The assessment can be viewed as an intricate dance, where the assessor may well know the 'steps' but has the confidence to allow the 'rhythm' to be determined by the family.

How families experience bereavement

For children who grow up within a family, that family is a key context for determining their development and their well-being. As such, it is a crucial component of any assessment of a bereaved child or young person who may be in need of a bereavement service. The assessment also needs to extend to other key relationships and contexts, for example school, peers and so on. Each family is different. Everyone will experience their grief differently: this will be shaped by their individual, family, cultural, social and religious beliefs, and means that no two deaths are ever mourned in exactly the same way.

During the early weeks and months after a death, the family unit is inevitably fragile, vulnerable and seemingly frozen in time. Shapiro (1994) describes grief as a crisis which becomes interwoven with family history, and has a dramatic effect on how the family develops as a new unit – 'a family in developmental crisis'. Each family will struggle to stabilise after a death, and its first priority in managing the crisis is to work towards a stable equilibrium within which the family can try to move forward. 'With a developmental approach that considers the family as a unit of distinct yet inextricably interconnected members, we can help families survive and grow while bearing the burden of death and loss.' (Shapiro 1994: p18)

Assessing the family as a whole provides insight into the way a child is related to as part of a family group. This information is central to understanding the ways in which a family is able to safeguard and promote the well-being of the child, and whether there are aspects of family life and relationships which compromise its capacity to do so.

A family assessment provides a vehicle for observing and describing what the practitioner can learn from talking with families and from their interaction together. The technique used can be a positive intervention in itself: promoting clarity and understanding of how individuals within a family are experiencing the bereavement. It is a way of learning about families in a detailed, relatively objective, evidence-based profile of family competence, considering family strengths alongside difficulties (Glaser et al 1984).

Starting out – initial contact

Many families will start their contact with Winston's Wish by calling our Family Line. The helpline will be answered by a practitioner who has experience of working directly with parents, young people and children. As most calls take at least 30 minutes, the 'assessment process' effectively begins at this point. At the end of the call, if appropriate and feasible, the practitioner will explore with the parent or carer the possibility of arranging an initial meeting at home. An information pack will be sent after this helpline call, together with confirmation of a suggested date and time for the home assessment.

The service has been established for over 10 years, which now means that many families in Gloucestershire may have heard of the organisation. However, the initial meeting at home is often the first time that the family actually comes face to face with the service. It is therefore vital that the assessment is perceived as a positive, engaging and relevant experience by *all* members of the family.

55% of families are assessed within six months of being bereaved.

Aims of the assessment

During the assessment we aim to establish:

- the impact of this particular death
- for this particular family
- at this particular time
- living in this particular community.

The purpose of the home assessment is to:

- build trust so that the family feels 'safe' working with the organisation
- give information about our services so that the family can make an informed decision about future involvement
- collect information about the person who has died and attempt to understand how the death has affected the child(ren), other members of the family and the wider community
- find out about the child's knowledge and understanding of death
- demonstrate how we can safely talk to children about death and grief
- allow the family to talk about the death in as much detail as they want to: this can be the first opportunity they have had to do this, and is often a therapeutic intervention for the family
- evaluate the degree of resilience/vulnerability observed in the family
- assess whether the services on offer could enhance resilience/reduce vulnerability
- assess whether referral onto another agency is also appropriate
- draw up an action plan: this may include some time to think and reflect before deciding to participate in the suggested intervention.

Who is involved in the assessment?

It is our usual practice for two practitioners to make this initial visit: this helps to ensure that each family member has a chance to share their story individually. It also enables the practitioners to be confident that they themselves have reached a shared understanding of the key issues relevant for this particular family.

Skills needed by assessors

The expert practitioner has an intuitive grasp of situations based on deep, tacit understanding of family dynamics.

The ability to understand the influence of a variety of interconnecting factors is an essential skill in carrying out a systemic assessment. Grief is a deeply shared family developmental transition, involving a crisis of attachment and a crisis of identity for family members, both of which have to be incorporated into the on-going flow of family development. The assessment process needs to take stock of all facets of the family system both before and after the development has been interrupted by death and grief. Our assessors use a set of question prompts which allow factual information to be collected about the family. We have a structured assessment pack to ensure a systemic framework is adopted for all assessments. However, experienced practitioners will inevitably use their 'clinical intuition' to decide the order of questions rather than rigidly following the order of questions in the pack. Such clinical intuition makes sure they engage with family members and allows individuals to work in their own time and to their own priorities.

What do we mean by clinical intuition?

Greenhalgh (2002) describes intuition as a crucial and valid component of *expert decision-making*. Features of intuition are described as follows:

- it is a rapid, unconscious process
- it is context-sensitive
- it comes with practice
- it involves selective attention to small details
- it cannot be reduced to cause-and-effect logic (for example, B happened because of A)
- it addresses, integrates and makes sense of multiple and complex pieces of data.

Experienced practitioners will inevitably use their 'clinical intuition' in navigating a family assessment.

The *novice* practitioner is characterised as someone who:
- adheres rigidly to taught rules or plans
- possesses little situational perception
- has no discretionary judgment.

The *competent* practitioner:
- is able to cope with 'crowdedness' and pressure
- sees actions partly in terms of long-term goals or a wider conceptual framework
- follows standardised and routinised procedures.

The *expert* practitioner:
- no longer relies explicitly on rules, guidelines and maxims
- has an intuitive grasp of situations based on deep, tacit understanding
- uses analytic (deductive) approaches only in novel situations or when problems occur.

This means that an expert assessor intuitively tends to demonstrate a high level of listening skills and a relaxed ability to explore relevant issues. They need to be sensitive to the verbal and non-verbal cues from all family members. They also need to have the confidence to explain carefully why it is relevant to explore so many issues. Although confidence will come from having listened to the experiences of many bereaved families, practitioners will need to develop a set of skills informed by a theoretical framework (Bentovim and Bingley Miller 2001).

The assessment requires the ability to stay with a difficult subject for some time and not be diverted into talking about something more comfortable for the assessor or the family. If the family appears uncomfortable with a certain line of questioning then the assessor needs to draw on his or her skills to gently reframe their questions. It is crucial that the parent or child does not feel 'judged' and feels sufficiently secure at least to reflect on the issues being raised.

An excellent training manual supported by the Department of Health – *The Family Assessment: Assessment of Family Competence, Strengths and Difficulties* – is an excellent resource for practitioners seeking further guidance on how to complete a systemic assessment (Bentovim and Bingley Miller 2001).

Figure 14: Factors associated with resilience in childhood

- Strong social support networks.
- The presence of at least one unconditionally supportive parent or parent substitute.
- Positive school experiences.
- A sense of mastery and a belief that one's own efforts can make a difference.
- Participation in events outside school and the home.
- The capacity to reframe adversities so that the beneficial effects are recognised.
- The ability – or the opportunity – to make a difference by helping others or through part-time work (for teenagers).
- Not to be excessively sheltered from challenging situations which provide opportunities to develop coping skills.

(Newman 2003: p8)

Method of assessment

The assessment model we use recognises, firstly, the need to consider the child within his or her *family system*. Secondly, it aims to consider the impact of the death on the wider *community system* – for example, school, friends, religious institution, sports clubs and so on – and thirdly it assesses the *situational factors* arising from the death itself: for example, if the death was by suicide. The determinants of grief (see page 40) also provide a clear framework to understand the unique grief response of individuals within the family system. The complexity and scope of a general family assessment framework is summarised in Figure 16. Much of the information-gathering begins through drawing up a genogram.

Genograms have several functions in a bereavement assessment:
- On a purely practical level genograms provide a written account of *who is who* in the family. It improves communication and trust significantly when the assessor can refer to family members using their family names and other details.
- Genograms help to identify *previous losses* – for example, deaths, divorce, chronic illness, disability and unemployment – and to gauge their severity based on the perceptions of family members.

- Genograms also allow the assessor to identify how the family has *coped with such previous losses*. They can explore which coping strategies were positive and helpful, and identify potential trends that proved unhelpful. For example, a parent might say: 'When I lost my job I suppose I turned to drinking quite heavily' and, in response, the assessor may legitimately explore questions such as: 'Have you found yourself drinking more since Marion's death?'
- Finally, the genogram can be used to determine the impact of the death on the *current family system*. In particular, are there any *key transitions* for this family, such as moving schools, marital separations, emigrations, weddings, retirements, serious illness in another family member, conflict relationships, dependency issues or other current or imminent issues? It is a reasonable hypothesis to assume that a family coping with the death of a parent or sibling will find such transitions an additional burden.

As well as the genogram itself we aim to assess self-esteem, knowledge of issues relating to death and bereavement, a child's capacity or willingness to remember, and their relationships with peers, teachers and others. Throughout the general assessment process we are mindful of the factors which may have promoted *resilience* throughout childhood (Newman 2002, 2003) (see Figure 14 opposite).

Figure 15: A comparison of characteristics of bereaved children and resilient children

The significant seven characteristics of bereaved children

- External locus of control
- Lower self-esteem
- Higher levels of anxiety/fearfulness
- Higher evidence of depression
- More accidents and health problems
- Pessimism about the future
- Underperforming

Five personality traits or predispositions of resilient children

- Internal locus of control
- Healthy self-esteem
- Easy-going temperament
- Affectionate
- Good reasoning skills

(Schuurman 2003: pp130–131)

Figure 16: The family assessment model of family functioning and methods for systematically describing, rating and assessing family life and relationships

Emotional and behavioural development

Health

Education

Family and social relationships

Identity

Social presentation

Self-care skills

CHILD'S DEVELOPMENTAL NEEDS

Family identity

Family adaptability

Family alliances

Family functioning

ENVIRONM

Community resources

Family's social integration

Income

(Adapted from Bentovim and Bingley Miller 2001: p60)

PARENTING CAPACITY

Basic care

Ensuring safety

Emotional warmth

Stimulation

Guidance and boundaries

Stability

Family history

Family communication

Family organisation

AL FACTORS

Employment

Housing

Wider family

Schuurman (2003) developed a comparison of bereaved children and resilient children (see Figure 15).

Schuurman believes: 'the key at-risk factor bereaved children demonstrate in greater proportion than their nonbereaved peers, is an external locus of control. Resilient children have a strong belief that they can control their fates by their own actions; bereaved children show a higher evidence of externalizing control, believing that their fate is in someone else's hands. No wonder they display higher levels of anxiety, depression, pessimism, health problems, underperformance, and lower self-esteem' (Schuurman 2003: pp130–131).

Before the assessment

Research consistently shows that it is not easy for parents to connect emotionally to their children's grief (Dyregrov 1991). However, research also shows that parents often have the greatest influence on their child's adjustment (Silverman 2000). It is therefore absolutely crucial to fully engage the parent or carer, and for them to feel confident with the assessment process. This is one reason why we often telephone a parent before the home visit to check if there are any issues they are concerned about discussing in front of the children. This can liberate a parent reluctant to access services because they feel paralysed by a 'secret', for example: 'I can't face telling the children that their brother killed himself … not yet anyway'. In time, we would usually hope to work towards a family understanding of the suicide – however, it is very important that the parent feels in control of the information-sharing process. It is not the role of a child bereavement service to 'take over' and enforce principles of open, honest discussion before the time feels right for the parent.

Allocating sufficient time

Family assessment can be a key intervention in itself and ideally should not feel rushed. It takes time to build rapport, in order to share emotional information and get a realistic sense of how the family relates. Time is also needed for the practitioners to tell the family about the range of services. We find it helpful to see each member of the family individually as well as assessing how the family functions together. Up to half a day is usually allocated for an assessment. This includes a practitioner's travelling time, and time to write up the notes.

'Resilient children have a strong belief that they can control their fates by their own actions; bereaved children show a higher evidence of externalizing control, believing that their fate is in someone else's hands.' Schuurman 2003

The importance of engaging the whole family

We suggest to parents that they keep their children home from school so that the whole family gets the most out of the assessment. As the school will need an explanation for absence this can provide an opportunity to reinforce the school's awareness that a child in its care is coping with a significant bereavement.

In family discussions when the children are present, assessors take care to use words that they can understand so that they do not feel excluded.

The home setting

Assessments in the family's home follow policy guidelines on the health and safety issues involved in home visiting. When it is time for the children to be interviewed, the practitioners ask them where they would like to talk. This is often their bedroom, or a separate room downstairs. Parental consent must be given for any room used. Doors should be left open and other safety precautions followed.

Absent family members

Practitioners need to plan how they will respond if key family members are missing. There is always a balance between affirming and working with those who attend and letting those who are not there know how difficult it is to get to know the family as a whole without their presence and perspective. Asking the family's views about how the absent member(s) might respond to a further invitation to attend can be a good way of exploring family realities (Bentovim and Bingley Miller 2001).

Family members who are reluctant to join in

Sometimes a parent will say: 'Simon is home, but he is in his room and doesn't want to come down'. Here it is useful to ask who in the family would be best at persuading the child to come in, and perhaps sending them to see the child with a message from you. Your approach could go something like this: 'Am I right in thinking Simon is upstairs and not sure about joining us? Could someone in the family go and say from me that it would be great if he could join us, even for a short while? Who would be best to do that?'

Research consistently shows that it is not easy for parents to connect emotionally to their children's grief.

Framework for a home assessment

Although each home assessment is tailored to meet each family's needs, the visit is likely to take place flexibly within the following framework.

Understanding the reason for the visit

With all the family together, we check that the child(ren) knew about the visit; in other words, we ask if they know why someone from Winston's Wish has come to see them.

Background and history

We explain a little about the history of Winston's Wish – why it was started, where it is based, how many children we meet each year and so on.

Rationale for assessment

We make sure that the child(ren) understand that the visit is not because they have been naughty or are 'sick' but that it is quite natural and usual for Winston's Wish to help when an important person in someone's life has died.

Referrer

If the parent was not the referrer then it may be appropriate to talk about the person who contacted Winston's Wish, and their connections with the family.

Explaining the assessment format

Starting on time, and continuing to keep to the agreed time boundaries, is one indication to the family that we will work professionally and respectfully with them. It tells the family that they can rely on us to keep the agreements we make with them. The practitioner needs to find a balance between formality and informality which recognises that the assessor and the family have some important work to do together. The assessor needs to reinforce the approach that their focus will be on eliciting responses from the family and their life together, rather than expressing their own views.

In explaining the format for the visit the assessor could suggest for a family with a mother and two children (called John and Vicky): 'What we would like to do now is suggest that perhaps I have a chance to talk with mum on her own. John, perhaps

The practitioner needs to find a balance between formality and informality which recognises that the assessor and the family have some important work to do together to fully understand the impact of the death on the family unit.

you could meet with my colleague Jim? That means that Vicky can have a break for half an hour until John and Jim have finished. Does that sound OK? When we've finished we will all catch up together as a family and we can talk about the ways Winston's Wish may be able to help'.

Establishing rapport

When making an assessment of the emotional, cognitive and behavioural issues arising from the death, an experienced practitioner will confidently and carefully explain *why* it is necessary to explore these avenues. The parent or child needs to feel *in control* of what information they choose to share. A skilled assessor will make sure that their questioning is objective and non-judgmental. For example, asking about 'your partner' rather than 'your husband' might make it easier to explain that a couple were not married or that their partner was the same sex. Similarly, an assessor gently exploring the meaning a wife is giving to her husband's fatal drink-driving road traffic accident might say: 'If I am hearing you correctly – it seems that most people were very surprised that John's post-mortem suggested he had been drinking quite heavily. Did it come as a surprise to you?'

Using a family tree to gather information

As mentioned on page 52, a useful way to begin the assessment is to construct a family tree or *genogram* (Dobson 1989). If the children appear reluctant to leave their parent then it can be informative to do the family tree with the children present. Children often enjoy doing this, and it can give the assessor valuable insights into how the family functions. For example, it becomes clear how much the children know about their family, how the parent(s) and children communicate with each other, and the level of respect each shows for the other in the way they give and share information. Some parents speak for their children while others encourage them to work out the family relationships and everyone's ages for themselves, only helping out when necessary.

It is usually helpful to have different colours or symbols for male and female, for people who are alive and those who have died and so on. It is also useful to put dates on for deaths and separations, including divorces. The assessor may want to invite the family to show, again through symbols or colours, who is especially close or has particularly distant or ambivalent relationships. The discussion can focus on a range of aspects using these techniques. Finding out what influences the family

The picture of family life is rarely as neat as others see it ... in reality family life consists of a complex network of interwoven relationships which are embedded in the family's history and hopes for the future. A careful, non-judgmental assessment process enables the reverse side of the tapestry to be appreciated and understood.

perceives other members from past generations have had on them can provide useful and interesting information. Asking who takes after whom can help to identify ways in which the family members are bringing forward their understanding of the past. Asking children how much they know about past generations or their extended family can give a sense of how much the immediate family identifies and feels part of the rest of the family, past and present. This may also present an insight into how motivated parents are at helping to preserve memories. 'Mum says that I am just like grandad, always grumpy and picky with my food.'

However, it is likely that the parent will, at times, decide to protect the children from certain information. If the genogram is completed with the children present, the assessor will need to check out later if there was anything that the parent had chosen not to mention in front of the children. A parent might then say, for example: 'I didn't like to mention this in front of Becky, but my husband was actually married before and so Becky has a half sister' or 'The children don't know but I had just petitioned for divorce. He had been unfaithful but now he's died I don't want it to affect the kids' memory of their dad'.

In constructing a genogram the assessor will also try to establish family members' own perspective of themselves and to see how far they recognise their strengths and difficulties. This can provide a useful insight into the resilience demonstrated by the family as a whole. A great deal can be gleaned by the way family members talk about their perception of their strengths and difficulties. It also gives an indication of the degree to which the relationships in the family are supportive and appreciative, or otherwise, and how the family attributes strengths and difficulties. 'Even though dad has died we are still a family.'

The following case study provides an overview of the process outlined in constructing a genogram. In particular, it is intended to show careful cross-referencing, establishing the 'meaning' which each family member gives to the 'facts' as they emerge.

Case study The Malloy family tree

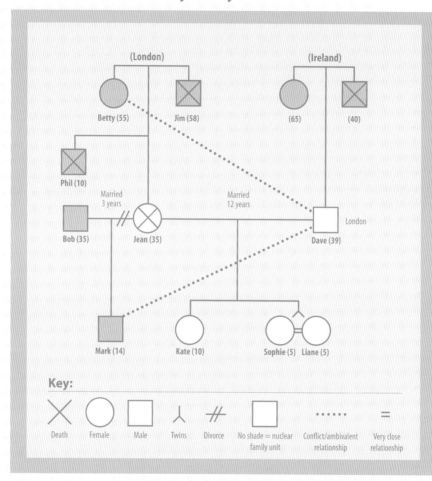

Key:

×	◯	☐	人	#	☐	••••••	=
Death	Female	Male	Twins	Divorce	No shade = nuclear family unit	Conflict/ambivalent relationship	Very close relationship

By constructing a genogram, the assessor would quickly identify a number of key facts and issues, a few of which are listed on the next pages. Taken in isolation these facts tell us very little: the richness comes when *the meaning and relevance of these issues to various family members* have been discussed in order to complete the picture of interwoven threads.

The following information was obtained when drawing the genogram with the children's father (Dave):

- Dave and Jean had been married for 12 years and they had three daughters. Jean had been married before: the marriage lasted three years and she had a son (Mark) from the marriage who is now 14.
- Jean died in a road traffic accident. She was not driving; the driver survived. Jean was not wearing a seatbelt. She was 35 years old.
- Kate was a passenger and witnessed her mother's death. She is showing symptoms of post-traumatic stress.
- Kate is in her last year at primary school. She will change to a secondary school in September.
- Dave is currently thinking that this might be a good time to make a fresh start by moving closer to his mother who lives in Ireland.
- Dave's father died suddenly aged 40. Dave was 8 at the time, and he will be 40 next year.
- Mark, a step-brother, has a volatile relationship with his step-dad (Dave) which worsened significantly when his mother died.
- After Jean's death Mark decided to move back to live with his father. He is still local and hasn't changed school.
- Sophie and Liane are together in the reception year at school. Jean had decided with the school that the twins would go into separate classes after completion of their reception year.
- Dave has a complicated relationship with Jean's mother, who has expressed her belief that he is 'too busy' with his job to care properly for the children. She helps with household chores and insists that all Jean's things remain in place.
- Betty is devastated by her daughter's death but seems hard to reach and needs to blame others.
- Betty is in close contact with Mark.
- Betty's husband (Jean's father) died last year. The cause of death was confirmed as suicide, from carbon monoxide poisoning in a car. Jim had struggled with depression since his son's death from leukaemia 20 years earlier. He died on his son's birthday.
- The children were told that their grandad had had an accident in the car. Dave said he felt uncomfortable with this explanation as it was misleading.

- Bob (Jean's first husband) enjoyed a good relationship with both Jean and Dave. 'They married young, had Mark, but split up when he was a baby.' Bob lives close by and tries to build bridges between Mark and Dave.

These are just *some* of the many issues which emerged, helping the assessor to build a picture of the impact of Jean's death, at this particular time, for this particular family, living in this particular community.

a) The smaller picture

Understanding different viewpoints – illustrated by taking one specific issue arising from this assessment

The assessor's role is to establish *facts* and then try to understand their *meaning* for different family members. *It is not just the actual facts themselves which determine risk – it is the meaning that different family members give to them* (Nadeau 1998). Using an example from this genogram we could reflect on the meaning different people might have for the seemingly inconsequential plan to separate the twins when they return for their second year at school. While Jean had been aware of the school's policy and had agreed to the separation, the plan took on a different meaning for different people after her death.

Dave's view

Since Jean's death Dave is desperate to make sure that the family feels safe and secure. He says Jean was really good at this and he sometimes feels he doesn't know where to start. He is anxious that nothing unnecessary should upset the balance of family life. Dave remembers a long period of refusing to go to school when his father died. His mother was happy for him to stay at home and responded protectively to even fairly minor physical symptoms. Dave is worried that the girls are starting to complain of stomach pains, and he knows this will be difficult with his work. 'I just want to do my best for the girls. At times I feel like running away because it's all too much. The twins being put into separate classes is the final straw!' Dave says that he feels furious with the school and strongly believes that regular stomach aches experienced by the twins are connected to their worries about being separated from him and each other.

Sophie's view

Since mum's death Sophie seems to have become more dependent on Liane; she is also unusually aggressive. Sophie says she is scared that boys at school will make jokes about the fact that her mum has died. 'I want to be with my sister, always.'

Liane's view

The quieter twin, she frequently wets herself at school and is rarely vocal, allowing her sister to speak on her behalf. Liane whispered to the practitioner: 'I wish my dad could give up work so I can stay at home, or perhaps mum can come back from heaven'.

The school's view

With Dave's permission, the practitioner telephoned the school after the home assessment. The head teacher explained that he has not yet personally spoken to Dave about the twins. 'Dave has got so much on his plate that I don't want to burden him further at the moment. I'd be happy to talk about next year when he is ready.' The girls' class teacher believes that Liane would benefit from greater independence from Sophie, but is reluctant to say this to Dave as she senses his vulnerability and quick temper. So, it would appear that a breakdown in communication has meant that Dave now perceives the school as being cold and inflexible, and gives him further evidence for his belief that he is isolated and vulnerable.

So, it is only after the assessor has gleaned an understanding from various perspectives that they can then try to generate a hypothesis about what is going on and how a seemingly small issue, such as the twins' school attendance, needs to be moved forward or resolved in a positive way while the family is in crisis following the mother's death.

b) The bigger picture

Assessing risk and resilience

The overall assessment revealed a variety of issues which informed the practitioners how past family history affects how different family members are coping with Jean's death. In addition, it identified the impact of her death having occurred at this particular time: for example, Kate will soon be changing to secondary school, Dave is considering moving to Ireland, the twins had just started school and it is only a year since the maternal grandfather died by suicide. Additionally, family members appear to hold differing views on the factors which led to both the grandfather's and Jean's deaths.

The assessment process aims to unravel how different family members reacted to previous losses and, again, to relate this to the current situation. For example, while Dave was understanding about Betty's devastation following the deaths of her children and husband, he felt frustrated by her emotional outbursts and angry that she couldn't offer more practical help with child care. He also felt that Betty intensified the difficulties he had in relating to Mark.

While the assessment is about collecting information, it can also become an intervention in itself especially if the assessor uses techniques (such as circular questioning) to 'loosen' family assumptions. For example, the assessor could ask:

- Who do you think is most upset about mum's death?
- If I asked dad if he was thinking of moving to Ireland what do you think he would say?
- If granny Betty could have three wishes what do you think they would be?
- If you could have three wishes what would you ask for?
- If I had met your family before mum died, what would an average week have been like?

At the end of 2–3 hours the assessment was completed. The family reported feeling both exhausted but relieved to have spoken so openly and honestly.

Sharing information with the rest of the family

The family regroups once all the individual interviews have taken place. It is important for everyone to check out what information they are willing to have shared when the family unit 'regroups'. Sometimes the assessors will need to reframe ideas for the children: this may enable the children to share something in a way that they believe will be more acceptable to their parent. For example, the assessor might say: 'You know you said that your mum is always shouting and angry since your dad died … when we meet back up with mum would it be OK to say something like: "The children have noticed that you sometimes seem to be more irritable and tired since their dad died, and they were wondering if they or Winston's Wish could help in any way?"'

The family regroups once all the individual interviews have taken place.

Closing the assessment and leaving the family with a task

If appropriate, families are introduced to the possibility of choosing or developing their own 'memory box' (see Chapter 4). The rationale is explained, and children and parents are invited to share ideas on how they might build up the contents of their own individual box. This exercise provides a stimulating closing activity for the assessment and, in addition, leaves a tangible attachment and reminder of the purpose of meeting with the family.

Planning appropriate interventions

Before leaving, the assessor will give a broad outline of what they think might be the best way forward. This could be a combination of some of the following:

    a) family invited to attend a residential weekend (see Chapter 5)

    b) discussion with a child's teacher or any other significant agency (see Chapter 8)

    c) individual work with the parent (see Chapter 6)

    d) individual work with a child (see Chapter 6)

    e) invitation for the family to attend a group: our current group programmes particularly focus on families affected by suicide (see Chapter 7) or a group for families with pre-school aged children

    f) referral to another agency

    g) no further contact.

If appropriate, families are introduced to the possibility of choosing or developing their own 'memory box'.

The next steps

We encourage families to think about, and reflect together, on the options over the next few days and then we call to agree an action plan. Plans are only progressed after parental agreement. In families perceived to be reasonably resilient the most usual interventions are a) a residential weekend and b) liaising with the school.

This chapter has explored the ways in which a detailed assessment can guide the most appropriate route for each family through a child bereavement service. Assessment of family functioning, and of the wider context in which a child exists, is one of the hardest yet most important skills a practitioner has to develop. The well-being of bereaved children depends on our being able to identify those strengths within a family on which we can build, and to define those difficulties we are aiming to help alleviate. There are many effective ways to bring up children, so any approach must be non-judgmental and flexible to respect that variety.

Three key points are raised:

- A comprehensive assessment involves the bereaved child, their parent(s) and the community in which the child lives.
- The assessment is used to establish the needs of this particular family and plan appropriate interventions.
- Assessors will need a range of skills which enable them to hold assessment criteria in their head while being intuitively responsive to subtle signals from the child and/or parent. The assessment can be viewed as an intricate dance, where the assessor may well know the 'steps' but has the confidence to allow the 'rhythm' to be determined by the family.

'A friend is someone who knows the song in your heart and can softly sing it back to you when you have forgotten the words.'

Unknown

Chapter Four

Looking forward
while looking back

Memory work with bereaved children

This chapter reflects on the role a child bereavement service could have in developing interventions which facilitate a healthy 'continuing bond'. We consider the questions that might be clarified by bringing together expertise from childhood memory development with the findings arising from bereavement research, for example:

- How do developmental and cognitive factors affect memory work with bereaved children?
- What type of memories are more easily retrieved?
- Conversely, how soon do certain memories fade?
- Which memories have the most positive and significant impact on a child's self-esteem?
- Is it *always* helpful to have a strong continuing bond?
- Who are the best people to help a child engage in memory 'work'?

Although it is not yet possible to answer these questions fully, we consider our current approach to memory work while recognising the need to better understand the cognitive and developmental issues involved in understanding childhood memory (Pressley and Schneider 1997).

Memories don't sit there like a stone: they have to be worked at like the best bread, kneaded and gently warmed so memories can slowly rise to the surface.

Maintaining connections

A major finding from the Harvard Child Bereavement Study concluded that children who are highly connected to their deceased parent seem better able to show their emotional pain, to talk with others about death, and to accept support from family and friends. Although they experience emotional pain, this does not mean they are experiencing difficulty in the mourning process (Worden 1996).

Children who are highly connected to their deceased parent seem better able to show their emotional pain, to talk with others about death, and to accept support from family and friends.

This means that if we are to accept the central tenet of the continuing bond model, there is an important role for a children's grief programme to ensure it offers children practical ways to maintain connections (Silverman and Nickman 1996). Precisely how this can be carried out requires a careful assessment of a variety of cognitive and developmental factors. For example, consider a child looking at a photo of his father in his fire fighter's uniform:

He might be thinking:
   a) 'I hate dad's job – the fire killed him. I hate it. I can't bear to think about it!'

Or he may organise his thoughts in a different way:
   b) 'My dad was so strong and fit, he loved being a fire fighter. I am proud that he was my dad. I remember the day mum took that photo, it was on the morning of the summer fun day at my school. Dad and his mate Phil brought the fire engine to school. We had great fun – he even turned the hose on at the end.'

In this example, the same memory prompt – the photograph – has the potential to create two totally different thought (cognitive) processes in the child. In b), where the thought processes are more comforting, the retrieval of memories appears more free flowing. Similarly, developmental issues would also be relevant to memory retrieval, such as how old the child was when his father died, the time that has since elapsed, how memories were encoded at this time and what has happened since to affect the original memories.

Case study Chris (aged 9)

Chris was 4 when his grandfather died of lung cancer. Five years on, Chris' mother asked him to think of things he remembered about his grandfather.

Children like to review photos which remind them of the relationship they had with the person who has died.

Without prompts, he recalled the following memories, in this order:
- grandad smoked
- he was a good builder
- he didn't eat enough vegetables
- he lived near the beach where his white hair blew in the wind
- we played character stories together.

The range of memories recalled is interesting and provides us with some insights into how memories develop and are recalled in children. At the age of 4 the possibility that someone he was attached to could actually die was not within Chris' sphere of understanding, so he needed to establish whether this death thing happens to others. If so, most importantly, would it happen to his mum or dad? Initially, he craved reassurance. At the time Chris' mum gave him a simple explanation which centred on the importance of staying healthy. Smoking was highlighted as 'unhealthy' and could have been linked to grandad's death. He readily grasped the explanation, as he didn't want to think that death could 'just happen' without reason. Grandad having smoked was the first memory recalled.

The range of memories recalled is interesting and provides us with some insights into how memories develop and are recalled in children.

Chris had been a regular visitor to his grandparents and could still visualise in his mind's eye a picture of his grandad's house. He remembered the importance of the house because his grandad had built it. Perhaps this emerged early in his recollections as he had recently spoken with his grandma about her sadness at selling the house. His grandma needed to talk about her loss often, emphasising the 'greatness' and skills of her husband. The third memory about vegetables was curious. Chris' mum explained that he was not a great lover of vegetables and much family effort goes into persuading him of their health benefits. His mother thought that he may have deduced that if he didn't eat vegetables he would not be healthy … concluding to himself that if you are not healthy you get cancer and die.

The fourth memory described by Chris was a visual image, memories of the beach and his grandfather's white hair being buffeted by the wind. As he described the memory he appeared to be connecting to a range of sensory prompts – gusts of wind, smells of the seashore, softness of his grandad's hair and the smell of his hair cream. The final memory was the only one which involved Chris directly. 'We played character stories together.' This memory would not exist without Chris having established a clear sense of his identity in

'I remember
collecting crabs in
the rock pools with
grandad.'

Chris

playing story-telling games with his grandad. This process of seeing a separate self takes time to develop in young children. When asked which of the five memories he would say was the most important he said 'playing with grandad'. This supports the observation that children are most powerfully impacted by memories in which they were actively involved. Equally, they are more likely to retain memories that were repetitive and predictable. 'Every time I went to grandad's house he would get out my bag of characters so we could make up stories.' Seemingly insignificant but regularly repeated encounters, which convey to the child that they are valued, are more likely to have a lasting impact on self-esteem than, say, the memory of a one-off expensive day trip.

It was interesting to hear Chris continue to access other memories which were then triggered by his thoughts, and the responses of his mother. For example, she said: 'Do you remember that you left two of your characters in the coffin with grandad?' Chris replied: 'I'd forgotten about that, but now I think about it, yes I can – it was a black knight and a turtle'.

This conversation between a 9-year-old and his mother demonstrates our need to have a good understanding of memory development, family and cultural beliefs, and the meaning the child has given to these beliefs, before embarking on memory work with a bereaved child (Young and Papadatou 1997). It also shows the tremendous influence adults have on the child's capacity to establish a long-term memory bank.

To highlight the developmental issues further, consider the response from Chris' younger brother Ben, aged 6. Ben looked blank when asked to think about memories of his grandad. It was only when he was shown a photo that he simply recalled: 'I was 2 when grandad died'. He became slightly tearful and somewhat irritated. 'Why did he die before I was grown up? Did he not want to know me? Why did he know Chris, and not me?' He then went on to ask questions: 'What was he good at?' Ben was interested in the answers and particularly fascinated by stories which involved his grandfather talking about him or when similarities were drawn. His mother said: 'Grandad was a fast runner, just like you'. The agenda for Ben's memory work would therefore have a different focus from his brother's, based on developmental and cognitive issues.

Regularly repeated encounters, which convey to the child that they are valued, are more likely to have a lasting impact on self-esteem than, say, the memory of a one-off expensive day trip.

Is it always helpful to have a strong continuing bond?

In recent years there has been a great enthusiasm for the adaptive effect on the grieving process of a 'continuing bond', thereby encouraging an on-going, internal attachment between the mourner and the person who has died. Without doubt, memories can be a source of comfort and inspiration. However, as practitioners, we need to be able to distinguish between a continuing bond which is an attempt to deny reality, as evidenced by Beth in the next case study, and one which is a healthy expression of the proactive impact of the deceased, carried forward into the new life of the bereaved (Gal-Oz and Field 2002).

'There were no photos of me with mum, so it was hard to find a connection, any proof of our bond. For a long time, I secretly harboured fears that I'd been adopted.'
Sarah, aged 33, reflecting on her mother's death when she was 3

Case study Stuart (aged 10) and Beth

Stuart was 8 when his father, Tony, died suddenly of a brain haemorrhage. His dad's death occurred when his parents had separated for a trial period. Beth (Stuart's mother) was devastated and she appeared to compensate for her feelings of regret by seeking every opportunity to express her attachment to Tony. She talked and reminisced with 'everyone and anyone' who would listen: she told them how much they missed him and how her life was unbearable without him. Her reminiscing consisted of carefully collected examples of how completely wonderful he had been both as a father and husband. Beth kept reminders on show and regularly found new objects which could be publicly displayed. In private she 'talked' to her husband and regularly expressed to others the feeling that he was close by. Beth took up watercolour painting (her husband's hobby) and tended to absorb his habits and values into her everyday life, including things that had previously caused ill feeling in the marriage, such as his untidiness and interest in political issues. She joined a group which campaigned actively to build wind turbines. Her husband had been a member of the group. She now felt it 'would be Tony's wish to make sure this was sorted'.

When important decisions needed to be made involving Stuart, Beth would tell him: 'This is what your dad would have wanted'. At the time of referral, two years after Tony's death, Beth was still insisting that Stuart visit the grave every Saturday. Stuart started to develop a range of somatic symptoms (stomach pains, headaches, ear infections, asthma attacks) which we thought might be connected to the somewhat complicated and potentially unhealthy 'continuing bond' being expressed by his mother. On this occasion a series of individual sessions was offered to Beth – specifically to loosen a bond which appeared to be repressing issues that needed to be expressed before they could move forward as a family.

'Winston's Wish
helped us grieve as a
family and we still
know we can phone
them if we ever have
a bad day. They
managed to focus
our thoughts
towards positive
things and their
little coping
strategies were
crucial to me.'
Dawn Cattanach
(full article reproduced
on pages 76–77)

After several sessions Beth felt more able to acknowledge the existence of their marital difficulties and, in doing so, present a more balanced and realistic picture of family life. The fourth session involved both Stuart and Beth gently revisiting their beliefs about dad and how family life had been before and after his death. Stuart showed that he was relieved they could now be more open and managed to tell his mum that he no longer needed to visit dad's grave. However, he asked if he could put some of dad's things away in a memory box which he would keep under his bed and get out when he felt he wanted to. Beth agreed that it was time to move on and, over time, gradually took steps to establish a more adaptive continuing bond. In particular, she could tolerate 'regrets' (rather than guilt) while recognising that the intense strength of their love had sometimes been overwhelming, and led them to believe they would be better apart.

Memory making in families

The press cutting on pages 76–77 demonstrates how the Cattanach family is finding ways of 'looking forward while looking back'.

Shortly after this feature appeared in the newspaper we received the e-mail reproduced in part below. It is from a 56-year-old woman who was prompted to reflect on a much less secure continuing bond after her father's death when she was 3 years old. The article and the e-mail response bring alive the many challenges for practitioners involved in offering appropriate memory interventions.

Sent: 6 January 2003 20:25
To: info@winstonswish.org.uk

When I bought my *Herald* this morning, the reference on the front page, headed 'Losing Dad', caused me to turn to the relevant page before anything else. (That, in itself, was significant.)

I read the article about the Cattanach family with intense interest and emotion.

I am 56 years old, happily married to a Merchant Navy officer (soon to retire) and we have four grown-up sons. My father died suddenly when I was 3 years old. His death was sudden, in his sleep, in 1950, leaving my mother and me.

A small object can symbolise and evoke powerful meaning, accompanied by challenging conversations.

I am writing to say that I am so glad your charity exists. If there is one thing that has unfailingly irritated me over the past 53 years, it is people saying that children are resilient and 'get over' losses such as mine. Only if they are helped.

I read that Mrs Cattanach had been shocked to find out how angry she felt inside. Only on reading that did I fully appreciate that that was what had been my mother's problem. She once accused me of not allowing her to talk about my father. She needed someone to talk it through with, someone who understood, but I was not the one as I, too, needed an understanding ear. I found it embarrassing to tell people that my father was dead, because they were embarrassed by it and I then felt obliged to help them deal with their embarrassment.

For years, I had a vague picture of going to visit my father in an office and his giving me money to buy an ice-cream. I always wondered if it was a figment of my imagination. Then, about 20 years ago, my cousin learnt that our maiden aunt, my father's sister, had kept letters he wrote to her during the war. My cousin arranged for her to give them to me. I wondered if that was being morbid, perhaps I 'should not' value them. Now I know it was alright to treasure them and the link they provided. Among them was a short note he had written to her the night before he died. She was away on holiday and he told of my mother taking me to enrol in a dancing class but because the class was over-subscribed, we were asked to return on another day. I was, apparently, bitterly disappointed, so my mother had taken me to see him, in the building where he did a small voluntary job – and my memory fell into place! I also worked out the explanation for another incident. When I started school, a friend and I were taken to an elocution class, held in a house further along the terrace from where that office was. I remember crying my heart out, being removed from the class and plied with chocolate biscuits to try to calm me down. I was not popular for this outburst and was made to feel that I had let myself down. In addition, I could not understand why I had reacted in this way. I was in my 40s when it clicked. I think that being in another building in that terrace caused me to remember the earlier incident, which was followed by the disappearance of my father and my young mind was terrified that this was going to herald another catastrophe, perhaps the loss of my mother, who, of course, had left the building for the duration of the class. Subsequently, I had great difficulty in reconciling my eagerness to do things with a need to be in contact with my mother.

I honestly have to say that my father's death left a huge void in my life and did blight it. I have always wondered who I am, which may sound dramatic, but people

'The memory box is so important and there if you need it. If I feel that one of the girls is feeling sad I get my memory box out and open up a conversation. Talking and remembering, but focusing on the objects in the box, somehow makes things easier.'
Feedback from parent, Service Evaluation 2003

A SINGLE silver cuff link twinkles beside an old photograph and some crumpled cinema tickets from an outing years ago. All are meaningless when regarded in isolation. But, to one young girl, together they weave a powerful picture of a much-missed parent.

The odds and ends that fill the treasured cardboard box allow Saskia Cattanach to best remember her father, Steve. Over Christmas, the nine-year-old and her sisters, Steffi, 16, and Alix, 11, sorted through the precious items they have kept for the past six years and talked at length to their mum, Dawn, about what dad would have done had he been with them.

"It's a bit of a tradition for us now," said Dawn, 41, at the family home in Inverkeithing, Fife. "The girls like me to describe what Steve enjoyed about the holidays. It makes them feel closer to him."

When Steve Cattanach died from a massive asthma attack, his youngest daughter Saskia was three years old. It would have been easy for her childish mental picture of him to fade, but, thanks to help from bereavement charity Winston's Wish, she and the rest of the family have found comfort in being able to keep his memory alive.

The organisation was created when clinical psychologist Julie Stokes visited the US and Canada in 1992 on a Winston Churchill travelling fellowship. Inspired by the child bereavement services there, she returned to the UK and set up Winston's Wish. A teddy bear called Winston became their mascot and organisers tell those coming to them for help that it is his wish that every child should receive the help they need to cope with the death of someone important in their lives.

Being unable to picture a parent's face, recognise their smell, hear the sound of a voice, or clearly recall the games you played together can leave a huge void in a youngster's life and may even go on to blight their future.

How to encourage a child to speak openly about this loss is a difficult task, especially when bereavement involves such intense and sometimes frightening emotions. This was the challenge for Dawn, whose youngest daughter was practically a toddler when her father died. As the surviving parent she was already struggling to cope with the crushing blow of facing life alone and seeing her hopes for the future end so brutally.

Dawn, somehow, had to cope with her own emotions and

Article written by Lorna MacLaren. Reproduced with permission. *The Herald*, Mark Douglas Home, Editor

provide support for her three children. It was a painful transition, and it wasn't until contacting Winston's Wish, three years after Steve's death, that she fully realised how much she, too, needed help. "I saw a programme on television about the organisation and got in touch with them," she recalls. "They are based in Gloucester so we had to travel down to see the counsellors there and took part in one of the charity's weekend camps.

"It was mainly for the children's benefit, but after talking about my own feelings I was shocked to find out how angry I felt inside.

"I felt cheated that this had happened to my husband and had been bottling up a lot of emotional pain. I was suffering from bad dreams and sleeplessness."

The family's turmoil was no surprise to anyone who knew what they had been through. Dawn was a nurse and Steve a fit and strapping petty officer and radar operator in the Navy when the couple had met in 1984.

"There was no sign of asthma before we were married," Dawn says. "He would go out, play football like anyone else. He first became ill when Saskia was about six months old and he had to leave the Navy."

Steve's respiratory condition worsened and he developed a severe and unpredictable form of asthma called brittle asthma.

For six months before his death, aged 38, he was very ill. His days became disrupted by hospital visits and the children grew used to seeing their dad with breathing apparatus over his face.

Then, one night, Dawn called the ambulance team once again as Steve suffered a violent asthma attack, but this time he died in her arms. Still in shock she knew she would have to wake her girls and tell them their beloved dad was dead. It was the most painful few hours she could contemplate.

"Although I knew how ill he was I had never really faced the likelihood of him passing away. Usually if the children got out of bed in the morning and he wasn't there they knew he was in hospital, but this time I had terrible news for them. My mum and dad came over to the house and just sat with me while I tried to sort out my thoughts and face waking the girls."

She adds: "Saskia was really too young to understand, but her elder sisters did. Your first instinct is to protect them, but I decided I would not lie or fudge the truth as it could upset them even more in the long run.

"The girls went to the funeral and placed flowers on their dad's coffin. I was so proud of how they got through that day. Alix had some problems accepting things for a while, she thought Steve would be coming home on birthdays, or for special occasions. We just had very gently to tell her that was not the case."

The year before the tragedy the couple had taken their daughters on a dream holiday to Australia. It was difficult for Steve, who had to use breathing apparatus, but they all had fun and tried to capture every aspect of the trip in video and photographic images.

Dawn says: "There was nothing said, but I think deep down Steve and I were collecting happy times for the girls."

Years later it was the counsellors at Winston's Wish who suggested the children make memory boxes and keep safe all their treasured bits and pieces to do with their dad. They could take them out when they felt sad, or wanted to be close to him. It is thought this habit is particularly helpful to younger children who may have fuzzy memories – or none at all – of the bereaved parent. Keeping little trinkets, notes, and photos helps keep the feelings associated with the mum or dad alive.

"The memory boxes have grown over the years as the girls add their own bits and pieces to each one. At difficult times they are still brought out and we will go through the contents together and talk about Steve," Dawn says.

"Winston's Wish helped us grieve as a family and we still know we can phone them if we ever have a bad day. They managed to focus our thoughts towards positive things and their little coping strategies were crucial to me."

Saskia and her sisters follow a family tradition in taking Christmas cards to their dad's grave, and, as another new year begins for them, they are still able to hold close the essence of their father.

Dawn says: "It's been difficult for us. There has been so much heartache and tears shed, but the girls and I are lucky to have wonderful memories of Steve.

"He will never seem far away and will be part of this new year, as always."

Making a Jar of Memories

You may like to make a coloured "Salt Sculpture" to help you remember important things about the person who has died.

You will need:

- A small jar with a lid and wide neck (e.g. baby food jar)
- Salt
- 5 coloured chalks
- 6 pieces of paper

What to do:

1. Fill your jar to the brim with salt. On one of the pieces of paper write down 5 things you remember about the person who has died. These could be things you know they liked, something they enjoyed doing, perhaps somewhere you went together or what you remember about them as a person. Then choose a different colour to represent each memory and put a dot of that colour next to each memory.

2. Spread out 5 sheets of paper and divide the salt from the jar between them.

3. Then colour each pile of salt using one of the 5 chalks. Rub each chalk backwards and forwards into the salt. The salt will begin to take on the colour of the chalk. The harder you rub the brighter the coloured salt will become.

4. Carefully pick up each piece of paper and pour the coloured salts into your jar one at a time. (If you tilt your jar you can make waves of colour appear)

5. When all the colours have been added, hold the jar and tap it down on a work surface to settle the salt. Do not shake the jar unless you want to mix up all the colours. Then fill any remaining space with plain salt (right up to the very top!) This is important and will prevent the colours mixing.

6. Secure the lid firmly and use some sellotape to hold it in place. Try to keep your list of what the colours mean to you close by your jar. You may like to show other people in your family your 'jar of memories'. Can you think of a special place where you can put your jar?

my dad
his smiles and his funny jokes
Fishing
Camping
Man.United
Sometimes he would get cross with me

Winston's Wish

who knew him say I am like him. I inherited his sense of humour, but I am sure it would have been more in evidence if I had been able to hone it against his and if I had grown up more self-confident. (People have always told me to be sure of myself, more self-confident, but no-one could answer my question as to HOW. I think I am starting to crack that now, though, and might manage to find my niche by the time I reach 60!)

I look back on the difficulties (with deep regret sometimes), but I can rejoice that we live in more enlightened times, at least with regard to some of the problems I faced. In recent years, although I have met some health professionals who do not understand, I have met other people who lost parents in childhood and at last I have been able to open up to them and have found they see things as I do. And the joy of finding such kindred spirits is immense. Thank you for 'listening'.

E-mail reproduced with permission

Who are the best people to help a child engage in memory work?

In her thoughtful response, the writer communicates a wonderful insight into the lifelong journey encountered by a bereaved child. It demonstrates the yearning a child has to recapture memories which build their own sense of self. She recognised that her own mother's grief (and her reaction to it) often meant that her mother was not always the most effective mentor to help retain and build her memory bank. This is perhaps particularly the case in the first year of bereavement.

In a small study we asked teachers of pupils who were coming to a residential weekend if they had talked with their pupils about their bereavement. A staggering 90% of teachers said they 'didn't like to bring it up' but indicated that they would be happy to talk *if the child started the conversation*. Interestingly, 85% of teachers questioned after the child had attended the weekend said the child had spontaneously talked openly and easily about the weekend and consequently about the person who had died. In particular the teachers described rewarding

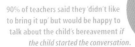

90% of teachers said they 'didn't like to bring it up' but would be happy to talk about the child's bereavement *if the child started the conversation.*

conversations stimulated by 'props' in their memory box and from a 'memory jar' activity (see Chapter 5, page 114).

We know that adults often struggle to engage in conversations with a bereaved child. We know that prompts are important triggers for memory recall. Some adults may inadvertently hide away sensory prompts such as photos, videos, perfume, music and clothes to 'protect' both themselves and their children from 'painful' reminders. This is understandable. A small object can symbolise and evoke powerful meaning, accompanied by challenging conversations. 'Mum said she loved me when I gave her this ornament – we didn't say those kind of things to each other after I went to my secondary school. If only I'd known she was going to die.' Equally, for some families their religious or cultural beliefs may encourage the removal of reminders (Young and Papadatou 1997).

'It's not remembering mum that hurts, it's forgetting that makes me feel like I'm letting her down.'
Katie

Case study Katie (aged 22)

Katie was 13 years old when her mother died after a short illness. Katie lived in a loving family and went to a school which was equally protective. The drive for 'protection' meant that the adults in Katie's life rarely mentioned her mother's death. Dad 'tidied' the house and was encouraged by family and friends to remove his wife's clothes and belongings. Special mementos were carefully put away 'safely' to be brought out some day. In reality, this never happened. Photos were carefully stored in shoeboxes – they never quite made it to the album or out of the cupboard under the stairs. The teachers at school never quite found the right moment to bring 'it' up. Katie therefore had limited chances to rehearse the stories involving her mother, which were fading fast as she grew older, and which became further distanced as she moved up to secondary school. Three years later, her father remarried and it became even more difficult to find an appropriate way of remembering mum without feeling she might upset her new step-mother.

Nine years on we had the opportunity to talk with Katie's father. Katie had been bereaved at a time when there was no access to any child bereavement service. At the time, none existed in her area and the needs of bereaved children were to some extent masked by adults' fears of 'making matters worse'. However, an enlightened hospice worker had helped her mum construct a simple letter which has become an invaluable link to her mother. We asked her father how she was now; he felt that, as a 22-year-old, her greatest sadness was that she could not remember her 'real' mum properly. We talked about some practical ideas which he could put in place to re-ignite and legitimise fading memories. Katie later reassured her dad: 'It's not remembering mum that hurts, it's forgetting that makes me feel like I'm letting her down'.

So, there appears to be a compelling case to try and identify an adult who the child trusts but who is perhaps less emotionally connected than either a parent or even a busy teacher. Memory work, especially for younger children, needs to begin soon after the death. Their experience of time is obviously very different from the older members of the family, as is their capacity to remember. A younger child will have a strong impulse to reduce their sense of 'separation anxiety'. Within hours, let alone weeks and months of a parental or sibling death, they can derive comfort from holding a piece of clothing which carries the smell of the person, or a photo of them *with* the person who has died to reinforce the fact that they had a meaningful relationship that does not simply disappear with the death. It therefore seems that a child bereavement service has a key role in trying to identify who may be an appropriate adult to support a child in the immediate aftermath of a death, and give guidance and reassurance on the rationale for this early intervention memory work.

When is a box so much more than simply a box?

A 'memory box' is essentially a metaphor to communicate to the child that it is perfectly natural to need some assistance in holding on to and retrieving memories. It is perfectly natural to feel that there are times when they will want to remember and to have times when it does not feel OK. Their memory box reminds them that they are in control of and can choose to share their stories (memories) with people they trust. The box can symbolise a way for a parent and child to have safe conversations and say things that may otherwise go unsaid for fear of upsetting each other.

Smell is one of the most powerful triggers for autobiographical memories.

A memory box can be a real comfort, and can be used to collect and treasure things that help people connect with someone who has died. Such cherished objects might include birthday cards, photos, jewellery, music or anything that holds or triggers important memories. Looking through the memory box can help with the process of grieving for all the different aspects of the person who died – who they were, what they liked or did not like, what they were good at and not so good at, as well as the things that were important to them.

A memory box can be a real comfort, and can be used to collect and treasure things that help people connect with someone who has died.

An activity sheet offers practical and creative ideas on how they can develop their own very personal memory box.

Children need to feel that their box is really special. Any box or container can be made special. We have developed a range of memory boxes and currently offer families a choice of five designs. Two of the boxes are plain for children who prefer to customise their box in whatever way they want. All the boxes have a slot for a photo in the lid of the box. Ideally, the photo should show the person who has died pictured together with the child who is making the memory box. As discussed earlier, this helps to reinforce the importance of their relationship with each other.

In essence, the memory box provides physical reassurance that memories can be contained – precious and intimate – full of priceless triggers to stories that can have a profound effect on a child's sense of 'self'.

One important skill for memory retention involves 'rehearsal': in other words, repeating memories over and over again. The memory box offers a safe vehicle for such story-telling adventures. For stories to be a truly positive experience they need to be shared spontaneously and listened to avidly. If the adult knows the child is comfortable in their reminiscences – whether they cry, laugh or express regret – then they can be alongside the child, and even contribute to the richness of the recollections.

'You know you decided to put dad's passport in your memory box – I'm not sure if I ever told you about the time when you were a baby and you, me and dad decided to go on holiday for the first time? Well, it was all going well until we got to the airport and we found that dad had left the passports at home!' And so, as the child matures, their memory bank is further embellished, accompanied by an expansion of the meaning and significance they give to their memories.

Collecting memories can help children evolve a realistic sense of the person who has died, and in doing so also helps them to develop a more mature self-identity (Silverman 2000).

Traumatic memories

So far, we have focused primarily on those memories which a child will access which remind them of a positive relationship. As service providers we also need to be clear about how 'memory work' may differ when the events being retained and retrieved are particularly stressful or traumatic. Although research on this topic remains in its infancy, it has long been believed that trauma is particularly well remembered – if not consciously, then at least unconsciously (O'Connor and Russell 2003). There is also evidence to suggest that traumatic memory is encoded in a different way from non-traumatic memory (Siegel 1997). 'The more disturbing memories are likely to be inaccessible to verbal recall because they reside in a part of the brain that is not readily accessed by language. They are primarily sensory: sound, touch, taste, smell and vivid visual imagery. Later they might be experienced as "flashbacks" or intrusive thoughts.' (O'Connor and Russell 2003: p22)

There is, therefore, a belief that traumatic events remain with people for most of their lives and that, even if they cannot recall them, people's memories continue to affect them unconsciously (Howe 2000). An overview by Kagan (1996) suggests that this may be particularly true for traumatic events experienced early in life, as it is during this formative time that experiences are thought to be crucial. Our capacity to remember traumatic events seems to make great intuitive sense. For example, although forgetting what you had for school dinner might not seem that unusual, forgetting the experience of seeing your dad collapse and witnessing unsuccessful attempts at resuscitation does seem less likely. However, in a careful analysis of the literature, Howe (2000) concludes that memory retention of traumatic events is not straightforward. The review explores what it is about traumatic events that children remember, and whether these remembrances differ in any way from their memory of other non-traumatic experiences.

The evidence is unanimous in its assertion that children can and do recall traumatic experiences such as the murder of a parent (Terr 1988; 1991). Indeed these same children not only recall those events but they also experience *intrusive* memories of the episode (Malmquist 1986; Pynoos and Eth 1984). However, recent reviews on recovered memory have tended to concentrate on the *reliability* of the child to provide evidence against those accused of child abuse. Coming from the bereavement world we are of course interested in a somewhat different perspective; namely, how does a child retain memories which are positive/adaptive and, in cases where there are more difficult experiences or trauma, how dominant

We need to be clear about how 'memory work' may differ when the events being retained and retrieved are particularly stressful or traumatic.

are these over other memories? When grief and trauma co-exist, is grieving impaired by the emotional consequences of the trauma? In practice there seems to be a range of responses. For example, some children can think of nothing else other than a dominant, frightening image: 'I see his head on the pavement covered in blood. That's all I can remember about Jack, so I try not to think about him'. Others appear to have adopted a different strategy. Although the child may retain traumatic memories he or she may be able to counter such memories by accentuating far more pleasant information that is not associated with the trauma. For example, a child who witnessed his brother's death in a road traffic accident, but doesn't tend to talk about the accident, might say: 'Jack was a great brother. We went to the match each week and always had fish and chips on the way home with dad'.

Practitioners then have the task of trying to evaluate whether the child's process of distracting themselves from the trauma is adaptive or if the symptoms being shown are indicative of a more deep-seated distress (for example, a child who is showing aggressive behaviour may need help to articulate the impact of a traumatic event).

Case study — Fiona (aged 8)

This case study is summarised from O'Connor and Russell (2003: p23). It briefly explains the treatment provided for an 8-year-old child who had been involved in a major disaster in which many of her friends had been killed or injured. The treatment was provided by a clinical psychologist one year and 10 months after the disaster. Treatment consisted of eight sessions, lasting about one hour each, during which Fiona told her story in words and drawings. Each time she was better able to tolerate her scared feelings and, with them, sensory detail to what she was remembering. She described the smells of blood and smoke, saying: 'I am just hearing things', 'I can hear the screams', 'I can hear the quiet'. She talked about movements and gradually added colour to her descriptions. She spoke of her belief that she was going to die and that her mother was already dead, of feeling scared, creepy, sad and sick. Each week she would go back over the same

'In keeping the memory of my children's dad alive, it is important for them to know that he will never be forgotten. My children worry that they will forget what he sounded like and how it felt to hold his hand. Ian is with us every day, at all times. It is always OK to talk about him. As long as we live, so will he. As my youngest said the other day: "Dad will not die until the last person who knew him dies".'

Feedback from parent, Service Evaluation 2003

memories, adding in more and more detail as she did so. She began to ask questions to fill in part of the story she did not have, building up a more logical coherent narrative each time. Whereas she had begun by recalling only peripheral detail of what had taken place, now she gradually talked about her friends, and then about what she herself had experienced. By the eighth session Fiona was able to put together the whole sequence of events and voice her guilt that she had survived when others had died. She said she felt 'calm now and not scared', though she continued to feel sadness. She spontaneously voiced her belief 'I can be safe'. Her mother reported that Fiona was now able to sleep alone and that her nightmares and flashbacks had stopped. She had begun to talk to her family about some memories of her friends who had died. Our sessions were finished. Fiona's sense of safety had been shattered by the tragedy and she continued to present with separation anxiety, remaining in therapy for some time to develop strategies to deal with this. During this period she was able to begin to grieve for her friends who had died in the tragedy. At follow-up four years later she continued to make good progress.

In another case study, we can see how a bereaved daughter has been able to consolidate and positively focus on the memories she has of her father long before he became seriously depressed. Although Jenny remains acutely aware of the traumatic weeks which led up to her father's death by suicide, in the five years since his death she has tried hard to maintain a relationship with the father who she respects and naturally wants to be part of her current and future life. We see that the 'resources' she draws on to build her memory bank become her bridge to the past, present and future. In the afterword of *Never Too Young to Know* (Silverman 2000: p246) a child says: 'Learn to remember and learn how to carry on with your life'. While this is undoubtedly true, perhaps Jenny's story takes this sentiment a step further in our understanding of her efforts to resolve traumatic memories while actively working to maximise her positive memories of her father. This has had a profound effect on her mourning process.

Case study Jenny (aged 23)

'It has been a little over five years since my dad died. Throughout these past five years I have experienced a wide range of emotions. I have felt a tremendous

Cherished objects might include letters, birthday cards, photos, jewellery, music or anything that holds or triggers important memories.

amount of sadness and guilt. I have experienced anger towards my dad and the difficult situation I have been faced with. While all of these emotions have been strong, and at times left me feeling lost and alone, the emotion that would leave me feeling most unsettled and panicked was fear. I was scared of what my dad had endured and I feared that I would not be able to remember all of the positive qualities my dad had to share with his family and friends. I feared that I would always have memories of him during the last couple of weeks in which he suffered severely from depression and ultimately ended his life.

'For weeks I felt haunted by my dad's illness and death. I worked hard in counselling, confronting all of the emotions I was experiencing surrounding my dad's death. While I was able to steadily and successfully work through my sadness, guilt and anger, I became increasingly scared. I remember waking up one morning in a panic. I could not clearly remember my dad's voice. I was terrified that I could not recall his soft-spoken words and his wonderful laugh. I was dealing with the loss of my dad as best as I could, but I was scared that as time went by I would lose even more memories of him. I needed to remember his laugh, his smile and his humour. I went through my house collecting pictures of my family on various "family adventures" and during celebrations. While I was able to use these pictures as a resource to remember my dad, I was feeling uneasy with the fact that I couldn't hear his voice. I decided to make a tape compiled of all our family videos we had collected over the years. I felt a sense of relief watching the videos and being able to hear my dad's voice, and his laugh, and be able to see his personality, all of which were difficult for me to remember only through pictures and memories.

'Not only have I found comfort in knowing that I can see and hear my dad whenever I need to, but this video has served as a resource in another way as well. My dad died when I was in sixth form. I was surrounded by family and close friends who knew my dad and could reminisce about shared experiences. Since then, I have gone to college, moved away from home and have met many individuals who have become a very important part of my life. I have enjoyed bringing close friends home to meet my family, but felt sad that none of these new friends would be able to know my dad. It has been important to me that I have been able to, in a small way, introduce my dad to some of these very special people in my life who were not able to meet him in person. It means a great deal

'I remember waking up one morning in a panic. I could not clearly remember my dad's voice. I was terrified that I could not recall his soft-spoken words and his wonderful laugh. I was dealing with the loss of my dad as best as I could, but I was scared that as time went by I would lose even more memories of him.'
Jenny

'I don't remember my mother at all. My aunt recently told me that after mum died I lay curled up on the front doormat sobbing and calling out for her, but I have no memory of that either ... even though I never really knew my mother I still miss her.'
Sarah, aged 33, reflecting on her mother's death when she was 3

to me that my friends have been able to catch a glimpse of my dad's wonderful humour and spirited nature, which I truly value and hope to carry with me forever.

'While I still think about the last couple of weeks my dad was with us, I am able to enjoy and find comfort in all of the happy memories I have experienced throughout my life with my dad. I am able to share these wonderful memories with special people in my life (new friends and old), and keep my dad's spirit alive. Through pictures, words, writing and video, I feel that I have a strong collection of resources that have been – and will continue to be – helpful throughout my healing process.'

Jenny's account shows her success in adapting her thinking processes to establish adaptive memories of her father. The Sloan Kettering Study (Christ 2000) also found that children (whose parents had died from cancer) really concentrate on the positive aspects of the parent and not the distressing, painful stages of the illness. The researchers reported children's efforts to construct an image of the parent that they could take with them into their later lives. Both Jenny and the children and young people in the Sloan Kettering Study (Christ 2000: p157) had support to facilitate this process. There is also research that shows that children with abusive histories seem to be better at accentuating and building on positive memories than dwelling on the pain of abuse (Cloitre et al 1996). For example, a child who was regularly kicked by his mother may instead focus on the memories he has of his mother reading stories and comforting him when he was ill. For some children this process of remembering good and reassuring situations may somehow be intensified during the grieving process. In relation to abused children it has been suggested that some may 'unconsciously' focus on remembering positive events not associated with the abuse. By doing this, the child reduces the cognitive dissonance associated with remembering events that are personally threatening.

'The abused child may not forget instances of abuse, but rather may elaborate in his or her own mind instances of care and loving by the caretaker as a way of preserving the attachment to the caretaker. This interpretation is consistent with the perplexing phenomenon anecdotally reported by clinicians and potentially exploited in courtrooms, that some abused individuals have heightened memories of positive experiences with their caretakers even though they have acknowledged them as abusive.' (Cloitre et al 1996: p209)

Children really concentrate on the positive aspects of the parent and not the distressing, painful stages of the illness. Christ 2000

These findings are crucially important for child bereavement practitioners who will need to pay careful attention to assessing the individuality of each child's experience of trauma. Early referral and intervention are often encouraged but rarely achieved in practice (Black and Kaplan 1988; Dyregrov and Mitchell 1992). This means that by the time a family is assessed, individuals within the family will already have developed their own ways of responding. Therefore, memory work and debriefing for post-traumatic stress disorder (PTSD) need to *complement* each other. The intervention needs to strike a balance between addressing the trauma while also giving space for non-traumatic recollections. Above all, the child needs to feel in control of the journey, with a guide who is equipped with a good theoretical understanding of memory development, grief and trauma (Schneider and Pressley 1997; Pynoos et al 1995).

'Often, as my daughter grows older, I see a lot of her dad in her mannerisms and expressions and I always tell her this. She beams with delight and this helps her to recall what her dad looked like.'
Feedback from parent, Service Evaluation 2003

In his book *The Fate of Early Memories* Howe (2000) has carefully reviewed the literature and suggests: 'Memory is conceptualised as being fundamentally adaptive in the sense that it seeks to store meanings or the gist of experiences so that the world people live in becomes as knowledgeable and predictable as possible. In essence, memory serves as *a record of the meaning of experiences*, so that people can not only understand the world but also anticipate and plan for future actions and behaviors' (Howe 2000: p139).

However, someone (parent or child) who has experienced a significant trauma or loss often finds that they cannot wholly embrace their old assumptions but at the same time may not be entirely ready to accept new ones. In the depths of grief people often perceive the world as unjust and *meaningless* (Janoff-Bulman and Berg 1988). In 'memory work' the practitioner therefore has a vital role in supporting the parent and child to develop *a new perspective that fosters the re-establishment of a meaningful life*. In this next case study, one father talks about his personal journey since his wife's death from a hit-and-run drink-driver.

 **Case study** Bill

'When Sally died I questioned whether there was any good in the world. I believed her death was painful, barbaric and totally avoidable. We were a happy family, going about our business and suddenly *this* happens. There seemed no point in going on; how could I bring up children in a world which was so unsafe? As time moved on and we talked it through with Jane [practitioner] I began to see that this was not what Sally would have wanted for our family. What happened didn't have to mean that we were no longer a family. It took some time but slowly I accepted that we could have a future together. Of course, the kids have learnt a very hard lesson, far too early in their young lives. We enjoy looking through and adding to their memory boxes – it helps me to focus on what is important and will always be important. The guy who killed Sally will have that on his conscience for the rest of his life. Somehow he will have to learn to live with that just as we have managed to face the future supported by a mum and wife who can't physically be here. She certainly lives on in her four wonderful children. As Emily said the other day: "Without mum there would be no me, daddy".

Developing a memory bank over time – how do children at different developmental phases recall a parent who has died?

To endure, memories must be refreshed (consciously or not) and during the process of refreshing these memory 'traces' they gradually become modified to fit the child's new stage of development (Howe 2000). In 1987, Buchsbaum identified the need for a developmental perspective when remembering a parent who has died.

Figure 17: Memory: a developmental perspective

- From infancy to about 2 years old, remembering can be demonstrated through recognition. A baby, for example, reveals familiarity by becoming animated when he sees his mother's face.
- After the age of 2, overt behaviour, such as imitation of experiences, reflects the child's ability to reconstruct a memory. Eventually, recall is available without the aid of external cues, props or actions.
- By the age of 3, the child can verbalise or fantasise about past events. At this age play, integrating both words and fantasy, still remains a prominent form of recall.
- After about the age of 5, children tend to use auditory or visual precepts in order to remember, so imagery is typically associated with verbal reports of past events.

(Buchsbaum 1987: p117, in *Continuing Bonds*, Klass et al)

Although Buchsbaum (1987) raised these developmental issues over 15 years ago we have perhaps been slower to integrate the implications of her findings into memory work with bereaved children.

Recently, we categorised the memories put forward by children when compiling their memory books from Camp Winston (see page 115). In a sample of 100 children:

- 21% remembered a *physical description* – for example: 'I liked her very curly hair'. Remembering a smile was also a frequent memory for children, perhaps reminding them that they were cherished and had a parent who was 'happy'.
- 26% recalled a memory indicating an *emotional relationship* – for example: 'He hugged me a lot' and 'She was funny, smart, caring and loving'.
- Only 11% recalled something which *the person liked* – for example: 'He liked motor bikes'.
- The majority (42%) recalled something that *the child and parent did together* – for example: 'My dad took me to see Southampton v Bradford and Southampton won 3–0 at home!'

Generally speaking, younger children were more likely to immediately recall a physical attribute. The older groups were more able to infer subtle personality traits in their memories. 'My mum was kind and really good at organising everything.'

Buchsbaum argues that it is only when a child reaches adolescence that they have the intellectual capacity to produce stable, coherent memories. 'My dad often seemed angry or irritable in that last year. I knew he was worried about work: he had to work long hours and had a difficult boss. Our last holiday together in Spain was very special – we all relaxed and had time for each other. It meant a lot to mum and dad and me. I was the Scrabble champion on that holiday – even dad couldn't beat me!'

Stable, coherent memories are believed to be essential for the mourning process to be concluded, and it has been suggested that younger children will mourn in an incomplete manner, by virtue of the fact that their personality development is not yet complete. Wolfenstein (1966) described the final phase of mourning as the achievement of a 'separate and autonomous self'.

'The resolution of mourning would also be characterised by a view of the parent as a self-contained, independent person whose unique identity is preserved in the mind of a bereaved son or daughter.' (Buchsbaum 1987: p123) This sentiment is clearly encapsulated in the poem Natasha (aged 14) wrote for her father following his death in a road traffic accident.

'When I need inspiration, I watch a video my dad made of me running at an athletics event – he was cheering me on, encouraging me, telling me: "You can do it Jo!" in his lovely Yorkshire voice. He is and always will be my mentor, keeping me on the right track.'

Jo

Fathers and Daughters

*You may be gone from this life, but
in my mind you still live as you always did.
No one, nothing and nobody can take me away
from you. You, my father, and me, your daughter
had and still do have a very special relationship in
which I can tell you anything. And you always
listen, without anger, ignorance or irritation.*

*I want you to know that although you were taken
away from this world too early, I can feel
you with me all the time in spirit. You'll
never leave me or our family. Some people die
and leave for good. Not you. You remain alive
as you always were, forever with me. You made
me, and I live for you. We can't be separated
ever, not in any way.*

*I ask for your help when I'm in danger; I
ask for your joy in my happiness and
I ask for your peacefulness in my
rage. I want you to know that you taught me
everything I'll ever need to know just by
being you.*

*I appreciate you and your kindness
as being the best in this curious world.
I absolutely adore you for being
the remarkable person you are.*

*You'll never be forgotten by me or
anyone else in our family. The best people
live on for eternity, as you do. So live with me.
Live with me every second of every day of
every year.*

*I'm so young yet I know and knew you
better than anyone else. I would do anything
for you.
Call out to me – I'll be listening for you.
Whenever you need me, I'll be there, without fail.*

*I'll never say you're dead and not coming back, because it's not true at all. You'll forever be in
my mind. The best father I could have hoped for. I miss you so much,
but my love for you is stronger than
my grief, and that keeps me alive
in the peace that love binds us together.*

Natasha Prest-Smith (aged 14)

Understanding memory development in children is clearly a key challenge for bereavement practitioners. Memory work runs through all the interventions described in this book. In other chapters we describe the way we use activities such as 'rocky rocks' (see page 107) to enable children to hold onto and handle the scope of different memories in their memory bank – the process of making memory jars, developing memory boxes and exploring the meaning of the memories in photographs are core to our individual and group work. Helping children and parents to understand and control traumatic flashbacks, nightmares and persistent negative thoughts all have a central focus in memory work. There is however much to learn about the complex relationship between memory, child development and mourning. Importantly, we need to create partnerships with colleagues involved in childhood memory research so we can continue to offer memory work which has a sound theoretical basis.

This chapter has highlighted a range of issues and questions, many of which require further research. However, as service providers there are perhaps two key factors to embrace:

- Firstly, because childhood bereavement occurs within a changing developmental framework, an open door policy able to take re-referrals for on-going memory work is likely to be necessary (see Chapter 11).
- Secondly, younger, pre-adolescent children will need concrete 'memory work' to assist in the retention, refreshment and retrieval of memories in order to maximise their chance of developing a healthy continuing bond. This memory work will involve both cognitive interventions, such as beliefs and the meaning of memories, as well as behavioural interventions such as making memory boxes, anniversary rituals, visiting the grave and so on.

'Good company on the road is the
shortest cut.'

Italian saying

Chapter Five

A weekend with Winston

Bringing people together on a residential group

In this chapter, we describe a residential group intervention which has become known as 'Camp Winston'. The weekend is a key component of the overall service and facilitates a therapeutic process that is highly valued by both parents and children.

'Camp Winston' can be both challenging and great fun. Above all, it is an experience which builds a child's self-esteem and reduces their sense of isolation and feeling 'different'.

What is Camp Winston?

'Camp Winston' offers a residential weekend for 5 to 18-year-olds, and can be both challenging and great fun. A simultaneous (but non-residential) weekend for parents and carers runs parallel to the children's residential.

Practical and creative activities encourage teamwork, building confidence and self-esteem. This sets the scene for participants to begin sharing their own stories, to untangle and express a range of feelings, increase their knowledge about death and to continue their individual journeys towards understanding their grief.

Everyone learns that it is a valid part of grieving to feel sad or angry, and to cry or laugh while they are reminiscing.

The importance of meeting others

Camp Winston enables us to bring together large numbers of families and ensures that we can potentially provide services for every child bereaved of a parent or sibling in Gloucestershire. We are also able to offer this intervention to a small number of families outside the county, subject to funding.

The advantage of a group intervention is not only measured by the effective use of resources, of course. A prime motivation is to reduce the isolation frequently felt by bereaved children and young people and to enable them to meet others who have also been bereaved.

Aims and objectives of Camp Winston

The programme has been designed to make sure that children and their parents can participate in a variety of appropriate activities relating to our primary clinical objectives (see page 33).

The main aim of the residential group is:
- to assist bereaved children and their parents and carers in taking the next steps on their bereavement journey.

The intervention creatively engages participants to:
- explore and express a wide range of feelings, including difficult ones
- remember the person who has died
- gain understanding and explanations about the death

Everyone learns that it is a valid part of grieving to feel sad or angry, and to cry or laugh while they are reminiscing.

- tell the story of the past, consider the present and look to the future
- increase family communication
- meet others who have been bereaved.

Who attends?

Following the assessment of the family, the most appropriate intervention is agreed. If this is to attend a residential group, the family will usually be invited to attend at least six months or so after the death. However, families are not only referred to us in the immediate period after a death – some families attend years after the death.

Children come to remember either a parent or a sibling. On occasions, they may be remembering another relative where the relationship was especially strong (for example, a grandparent who collected a child from school every day). Parents and carers are, therefore, usually remembering a partner or a child.

Although available to 5 to 18-year-olds, children are normally aged between 6 and 16 when they attend the residential weekend. Children attending at age 5 tend to be those who either have an older sibling attending, or who are sufficiently confident to leave their parent(s) for a night and are deemed able to benefit from the group. Young people over the age of 16 are welcomed to the group, but fewer in this age group choose to attend.

The parents' and children's groups run separately for the main part of the weekend and meet up on the Sunday afternoon. Wherever feasible, the whole family (subject to the children's ages) are encouraged to attend at the same time.

The team

There are a number of areas that need to be considered when choosing the team:
- the roles and responsibilities of individuals
- the range of skills needed to make up an effective team
- recruitment and training of volunteers
- ratio of staff, volunteers and participants
- briefing and de-briefing
- confidentiality.

The staffing mix for a residential weekend

For a children's group which will accommodate 20–25 children, we plan for two staff co-ordinators supported by 15 volunteer group leaders and two practical helpers.

Children are sub-divided into four or five age-related groups. Each group is supported by three group leaders.

Camp Winston is a therapeutic process which evolves from a carefully planned sequence of activities.

Additional functions, such as catering and sports challenges, are provided for us by the staff at the venue we use.

There are two staff co-ordinators on the parents' weekend, usually supported by two volunteers and a practical helper.

Whenever possible, we aim to staff both the children's and parents' weekends with a good gender mix. Unfortunately a 50:50 split is rarely achievable, so we aim for at least one male in each bear group (see page 106). The gender mix is an important variable – particularly as the majority of children will have experienced the death of their father.

Co-ordinators for Camp Winston

The staff co-ordinators for Camp Winston need a broad set of skills and knowledge, covering:

- expertise in child development, both physical and psychological
- theoretical and practical knowledge of bereavement issues and how they affect children and adults
- awareness of agreed policies within the organisation: for example, child protection
- the ability to assess situations as they arise and to make sound clinical judgments
- awareness of the emotional responses of participants: this will include awareness of any who are perceived to be at risk.

In addition, the following group management skills are essential:

- demonstrably excellent leadership and effective communication with participants and other team members
- efficient planning skills to ensure good organisation and delegation
- time management expertise to plan, prepare and run the residential weekend: when the full group is divided into smaller groups, the co-ordinator needs to help group leaders to support different age groups, who will sometimes take different amounts of time to complete activities
- skills in handling a large group of children: these include effective voice projection, and confidence in handling challenging behaviour and setting clear boundaries.

Staff need time management expertise to plan, prepare and run the residential weekend.

The volunteers

Without volunteers, our residential weekends could not take place. Each group involves around 20 volunteers (about 15 at the children's group, two or three at the parents' group, plus two practical helpers with the children and one with the parents' group).

Recruitment and selection process

Volunteers are carefully selected from a wide range of backgrounds and from a wide age range. It has proved quite challenging to ensure we have sufficient male applicants. This variety helps to give the team balance and ensures that the individual needs of children and their families can be met.

The following steps outline the recruitment, selection and training process:

- To date we have done virtually no advertising for volunteers. We have been in the highly fortunate position of having sufficient people seek us out to offer their services.
- Once a year, we write to anyone who has expressed an interest, enclosing an application form, a role description, a person specification for the role of volunteer and information about Winston's Wish. We make it clear that there is a *selection* process and we also carefully detail the level of commitment expected.
- We shortlist around 20 prospective volunteers from their written application forms and invite them to attend a selection day. The unsuccessful candidates are given positive feedback, are encouraged to support Winston's Wish in other ways (for example by fundraising), are encouraged to consider other voluntary opportunities and, where appropriate, invited to apply another time.
- The 20 prospective volunteers attend a selection day. This day includes some activities that reflect what happens during the children's and parents' groups. The candidates all have an interview with one of the practitioners. We also assess how each candidate works within the team and their intuitive understanding of how children may respond in certain circumstances.
- We select 12–15 people from the group of candidates. The unsuccessful candidates are given detailed feedback and, where appropriate, are encouraged to find an alternative way to support Winston's Wish, to seek other voluntary opportunities or perhaps to re-apply in the future.

Without experienced and trained volunteer group leaders, our residential weekends could not take place.

On average, volunteers stay in the programme for five years. This may reflect the fact that volunteers are deeply motivated and rewarded by the positive changes they witness in families over the course of the group.

- Police checks are conducted in accordance with legislation (and re-conducted every two years).
- The successful 'cohort' of prospective volunteers attends a residential training weekend. This training closely echoes the programme at the children's group. They are assessed throughout the weekend as part of the selection process.
- All prospective volunteers must complete the weekend successfully. However, supervision is a continuous process throughout the volunteer's period of service with the organisation, not only during training sessions.
- Four further mandatory training sessions are held to cover issues in depth.
- We integrate up to five new volunteers at a time in the children's group, initially to observe the process.
- New volunteers will normally take on the practical helper role at a children's group before working in a small group with children.
- Regular in-service training takes place throughout the year and an annual update day is held for all volunteers (including those who assist with fundraising or with administrative tasks). Volunteers are *expected* to attend all in-service training sessions and are *required* to attend at least two a year.
- Depending on skills, experience and aptitude, volunteers will normally have attended at least three children's groups before they attend a parents' group.
- An annual review is conducted with each volunteer to provide feedback on their progress and development, to address any issues of concern and to highlight any specific training requirements.

We have developed a 'charter' outlining what we expect to receive from our volunteers and what they can expect to receive from us.

A regular newsletter is produced for volunteers and, on average, volunteers stay in the programme for five years. This is perhaps surprising given the level of commitment required, and may reflect the fact that volunteers are deeply motivated and rewarded by the positive changes they witness in families over the course of the group.

The role of the team in facilitating effective group work
Group work tends to work best when the participants:
- **feel safe and secure within the group** – members of the staff team need to reassure and encourage, and also be aware of those who show insecurity so

A regular newsletter is produced for volunteers.

that they can get alongside those participants in a way that avoids drawing attention to them.

- **share a common situation or condition** – the team's role is to help group members share common thoughts, feelings and experiences while, at the same time, acknowledging that everyone is unique.

- **are helped to express their feelings, thoughts and diverse points of view** – because everyone's experience is unique, each group member needs to feel that they can choose to show or withhold their feelings. The team should try to find a number of ways to encourage expression of feelings to try and meet as many individual needs as possible.

- **experience a positive self-image** – if activities are about building self-esteem, every opportunity to encourage a positive self-image needs to be taken and the role of the team is to identify and capitalise on these on behalf of group members.

- **support and encourage each other in trying new activities and ways of thinking** – by being encouraging and supportive, the team enables group members to support and encourage each other. The team should also make it feel possible and acceptable to try something new.

- **participate in group tasks of graded difficulty** – the team needs to build each activity from a familiar, safe start to more challenging tasks that require group members to take more risks. For example, the team can start the session by asking group members to share factual, non-emotional information, such as their name and where they come from, before moving on to information about who has died and then moving on to how they feel about the death.

- **experience safe risk-taking with success** – when group members do start to take risks, they should feel that the team is managing the situation and they should feel supported by the team.

- **receive and offer help to each other** – as the group develops, members should be able to look to each other for support as well as to the team. However, the lead and model for doing this will often come from the behaviour and the group management skills of the staff and volunteers.

- **apply what they have learnt to new situations** – the real test of the success of the group activity will be after the residential weekend. Time will be needed to consider how group members can apply what they have learnt in 'the cold light of day'.

The team's role is to help group members share common thoughts, feelings and experiences while, at the same time, acknowledging that everyone is unique.

Group leaders will
know the children in
their group, and will
know who died,
and how and when
they died.

Describing the groups

The children's and parents' groups run separately for the main part of the weekend and meet up on the Sunday afternoon. While the programmes for the children's and parents' groups are closely linked, we describe the two separately to highlight key points about each group.

Preparation for Camp Winston

Staff preparation for the children's residential group

Practical preparations for a children's camp begin well in advance of the weekend. As the families confirm their attendance, the staff co-ordinators begin to discuss the children they will be working with throughout the weekend. They plan how they might facilitate the small group work, and consider how they can maximise each child's experience. The staff members who did the home assessments are available to answer any queries about the children and their families (see Chapter 3).

Preparation for volunteers

It is important to note that Camp Winston, while therapeutic, is not seen as 'therapy' in the traditional sense, so the volunteer group leaders only need information relevant to the therapeutic process and activities planned for the weekend.

Volunteer group leaders will therefore know the children in their group, and will know who died, and how and when they died. They will also have access to a profile of each child on the evening before the children arrive at the weekend.

Checklists – attending to small details

We have produced very detailed manuals for both the children's and parents' programmes to ensure that small details are attended to. It is crucial that co-ordinators do not overlook their role in facilitating a therapeutic process because they are distracted by practical issues such as: 'Where are the pens?' 'Is the hot chocolate still at the office?' 'Is Ben allergic to plasters?' 'Is Sally arriving by taxi?'

The children's residential needs a great deal of practical organisation to enable the weekend to run smoothly. Practical helpers prepare snacks, check that rooms and art materials are ready, and support venue staff if necessary. They also ensure that the camp venue is tidied and cleaned as we go along to avoid delays when the weekend closes on Sunday evening.

We have produced very detailed manuals for both
the children's and parents' camp programmes to
ensure that small details are
attended to.

Practical helpers are briefed by the co-ordinators the evening before the residential begins when they are given a 'task sheet'.

Preparation for families before the group
Before attending a weekend, families will need to know what to expect and what sort of activities will be involved. We send each family an information pack which outlines the following information:

- a brief description of the purpose of the weekend
- what participants can expect to get from the experience
- who the staff team members are and what they will be doing
- an overview of the programme
- a 'kit list' for the children
- a summary of their right to choose to participate or decline involvement at any point
- confidentiality agreement.

In addition, wherever possible, one of the co-ordinators or another practitioner will visit in the period immediately before camp; this visit is an important part of the preparation for the residential weekend. An encouraging phone call in the week before camp is also appreciated by the families attending.

'I felt a bit worried before I went, not sure if it would be my sort of thing – but it was so good to meet others my age who knew exactly what I was going through.'
Jack, aged 17,
Adolescent Service
Evaluation 2003

Staffing Camp Winston
As stated before, each children's camp needs two staff co-ordinators, around 15 volunteers who will work with the children, two practical helpers and one person (but preferably two people) on the night shift who takes responsibility for the children during the night. (This last role is filled by a local social worker.) It is also possible that there may be an observer present (for example, a new member of staff or a researcher) whose role is clearly defined before camp.

The 20–25 children attending each camp are divided into four or five age-related 'bear' groups. Each group is usually supported by three volunteer group leaders.

Volunteer group leaders
The group leaders accompany the children as they progress through the weekend. They join in the whole group sessions supporting their own group and take on a facilitating role in the small group sessions. They also eat with the children, play

'Steve was great fun.
Our group played lots
of football and
we were there for
each other during
the candlelight
ceremony. I liked
him – even if he
doesn't support
Man U he's OK.'
Child on camp

with the children and make themselves available for relaxed informal conversations. Their whole focus throughout the weekend is on the needs of the particular group they have been assigned to. For the younger children this will inevitably also involve practical caring, such as finding coats, tying shoelaces, putting them to bed, reading stories and so on.

Volunteers are also required to provide children with clear expectations and boundaries within which they need to operate. As a result, discipline is rarely a problem on the weekends.

The venue for children's camp

For 10 years, we have used the same venue. The Wilderness Centre – a youth and community centre in the Forest of Dean – is situated in glorious countryside and can sleep up to 50 people which allows us to accommodate up to 25 children, plus staff and volunteers.

The venue fulfils the following expectations:

- The children feel comfortable in the environment. The venue used is run by Gloucestershire County Council Education Department, Youth and Community Service, so it is specifically geared up for children. Generally the venue needs to be considered an 'OK' place to be, and not have unhelpful associations. When we previously used a hospital venue, for example, we found it had difficult associations for some participants.
- Sleeping arrangements allow for everyone to be accommodated comfortably and take account of different age groups and gender.
- Sole use of the centre during the weekend is essential.
- Space is available for artwork, drama and/or music activities.
- There are sufficient group rooms for individual groups to work in.
- A central room is used for the whole group to meet.
- Outside space is needed for some of the activities and in which the children can run around and relax between organised activities.
- An indoor area for the children to run around in is useful, especially if the event is in the winter months. (Our venue does not have this facility, but we manage by preparing group leaders for this eventuality and having plenty of raincoats!)

Sleeping arrangements allow for everyone
to be accommodated comfortably and take
account of different age
groups and gender.

- Staff at the venue are aware of the purpose of the residential group and supportive of the work.
- The catering is suitable and provides nourishing food that children and adults want to eat.
- Times of meals fit in with the weekend's programme and have a reasonable degree of flexibility in case sessions over-run.
- It is useful to 'decorate' the venue in an appropriate way: for example, names on doors where groups will meet and sleeping areas. The Wilderness Centre allows us to cover the place with banners and colourful signs to make it welcoming when the children arrive.
- Physical access to the facilities at the venue is checked, especially if any of the children or adults are wheelchair users or have other specific access needs.

The Wilderness Centre provides a stimulating and safe venue where children can be together and also have time to reflect thoughtfully on the changes in their lives.

Planning the programme content

Planning an effective programme takes time and creativity. Having decided the programme's aims and objectives, the next stage is to select activities that meet these objectives while, at the same time, being mindful of the therapeutic process. Activities need to build on each other so that there is a paced flow throughout the programme. Planning opportunities for relaxation, 'time out' and physical activity to intersperse with the emotionally demanding content of other activities should be part of the overall design.

Consideration should be given to the needs of different age groups and the time they may take to complete the same activities. No-one should feel rushed, so additional interim activities may need to be available to allow for these developmental considerations. Plans should include the needs of any children with learning difficulties, disabilities or varying faith traditions.

Summary of programme

First of all, the children are helped to get to know others in the group and gain their trust before 'telling their story' about how the person in their family died. Throughout the programme the children and young people are then encouraged to find ways to remember the person who has died and to develop strategies to cope both now and in the future. Games and fun activities are carefully planned into the programme to achieve a balance for the children and young people – laughter, tears and frustration are equally encouraged and contained.

Programme for children's residential weekend

Saturday

9.00	Families arrive, children meet group leaders, say goodbye to parents/carers
	Memory table
	Team-building activities in small groups
10.00	Welcome and introductions
	Rocky rocks
	Lighting the candle
	Introductions to the group
10.30	Snack
10.45	Outdoor activities – Winston's wilderness challenge
12.30	Lunch
13.30	Challenge completed with stories
14.00	Small group work – telling the story of what happened
15.30	Snack
16.00	Questions for the doctor
17.15	Supper
18.00	Indoor activity
19.00	Candlelight ceremony
20.00	Campfire and night walk
21.00	Bedtime for younger children, craft activities for older children
22.00	Bedtime for older children

Sunday

7.00	Wake-up time
8.00	Breakfast
8.30	Welcome to day two – energising ice-breaker
9.00	Small group work – exploring difficult feelings
10.00	Small group work – a jar of memories
11.00	Snack
11.30	Small group work – focusing on the future
12.45	Lunch and packing
13.45	Goodbyes to small group Memory sheets and balloon messages Wool web
15.00	Friendship bracelets
15.15	Parents arrive
15.30	Bearduation
16.00	Closing ceremony – balloon release
16.15	Families leave Tidy up Staff debrief
18.00	Home for everyone

Children are given colour-coded Winston name badges. The colour indicates the person they have come to remember.

The programme may change depending on the mix of children, their ages and needs, the weather and other factors, but the purpose of the activities in each time slot is fixed. The correct balance of the programme is essential to achieve the maximum impact for the children. The juxtaposition of the activities is carefully considered and it is important to look at the programme as a whole process and not simply as a series of discrete activities.

The programme

For the full timetable, see pages 104–105, Programme for children's residential weekend. The main activities are described in this section.

Day one

Registration and introduction

An hour is allocated to welcome the children and their parent(s) or carers. When they arrive, children are told which 'bear' group they have been allocated to: Pooh, Paddington, Yogi, Honey or Huggy. Where possible, siblings are allocated to different groups. Being in separate groups allows them to say as much as they like in the small group sessions, yet share the common experience of attending the residential weekend, which can bring them closer together. Children are then given their colour-coded Winston name badge. We explain that the colour indicates the person they have come to remember. For example, blue indicates the death of a father. All adult team members involved on the weekend also wear a badge, so the children can readily identify that most of the group leaders have also experienced the death of someone important in their lives and they can recognise those who have experienced a similar death.

Care is taken to involve the parents in the registration process, as they are often anxious at the prospect of leaving their children. Attention is also given to checking specific dietary or medication requirements.

The volunteer group leaders are on hand, ready to make contact with the children when appropriate. The group leaders are introduced and they then take the children to collect their Winston sweatshirt and choose which bed they would like in their allocated dormitory. At this point, parents are gently encouraged to say goodbye and leave for their own group, which is located a mile away. Children seem to settle very quickly, excited by the prospect of what is in store at Camp Winston. This sometimes leads them to be quite unaware of the 'separation anxiety' shown

A blue badge indicates the death of a father.

by some parents. Care is therefore taken to make sure that each child takes responsibility for saying goodbye properly before a parent leaves, and children and parents are reminded at what time they will meet up again the next day.

Welcome to camp

The children's group formally convenes at 10am and everyone is welcomed by one of the co-ordinators. We explain that Camp Winston is a very special place for children and young people who have experienced the death of someone *important* in their lives. (We use the word 'important' deliberately, as not everyone who dies is 'special'.)

The 'friendship tree'; any of the weekend's participants, child or adult, can add 'leaves' to this tree.

We then introduce the concept that we call 'rocky rocks'. Each child chooses a smooth pebble, a rough-edged rock and a polished gemstone. The co-ordinator explains that the smooth pebble represents the ordinary, everyday memories of the person who has died – for example that they had cornflakes for breakfast every single morning. The rough-edged rock represents the difficult memories about the person – for example an argument or the way in which they died. And the gemstone stands for the precious, bright-shining memories – for example of a special day on the beach. The message that the weekend will make space for all types of memories can help children who have more complicated or difficult stories to share. This particular concept is returned to and referred to throughout the weekend.

All children will already have placed a photo on the 'memory table' in the central room. They gather round the table and a large candle is lit that will burn on the table throughout camp (we blow it out at night!) The aims of the weekend are identified and some of the activities are briefly described. In addition to the statement that 'it is alright to have fun', we explain clearly that there are some expectations and boundaries about behaviour. We also introduce the 'friendship tree'; any of the weekend's participants, child or adult, can add 'leaves' to this tree. The leaves are made of paper 'post-its' which people write messages on reflecting their appreciation of someone else. For example: 'Jamie was very kind to me when I felt sad' or 'Dave is funny and really good at archery'.

Group leaders then break the ice by singing Winston's welcoming song. After this we show a cartoon video about a child's reaction to the death of his pet or, alternatively, read a story which highlights similar issues. After the video or story, each child and group leader is invited in turn to say their name and who they have

The Winston's wilderness challenge includes archery, wall climbing, flag painting and puzzle solving.

come to remember. For the first time, the 45 people sitting in a large circle hear that they all have a shared experience of bereavement. This is the start of a powerful therapeutic process.

Winston's wilderness challenge

This begins after a snack. Winston challenges the bear groups to complete a series of activities. The activities – including archery, wall climbing, flag painting and puzzle solving – are designed to promote a sense of team-building, trust and self-esteem for both children and group leaders. It is, at times, both physically challenging and great fun. Care is taken to select activities which can be completed by 5-year-olds, as well as by teenagers: these activities are usually rated as one of the high points of the weekend by children of all ages.

When each challenge has been completed, the group is given a small object (such as a car, dragon or hospital) and at the end of the wilderness challenge the groups are invited to construct a story using these objects. This allows them an opportunity to begin to present a story using safe metaphors. Although the children have the choice to construct a story that does not relate to death, they often do incorporate their experience of death. This may well be a reflection of the preparation process which openly communicates that Camp Winston is a place where children go to understand more about death.

Small group work – telling the story of what happened

After lunch (during which there is intentionally scheduled free time for team games and informal chats) the groups reconvene for the first of two small group sessions. How these groups operate is very much determined by the children's needs and their stage of development. The aim for the first session is to create an environment which enables the child to tell *their* story of what happened as *they* understand it. The older children often choose simply to explain verbally what happened; however, the younger children will usually use a variety of creative media, for example paint, collage, puppets or clay to tell their story.

We often use 'filmstrips' in this session. Five or more sheets of A4 paper are joined at the shorter sides to make a long strip. Sprocket holes are inked in along the top and bottom of the strip. Children are encouraged to think about what life was like before the person died, what happened the day before the death, to describe the death, what happened during the next day or days, and what life is like

Each child is given a smooth pebble, a rough-edged rock and a polished gemstone to represent the different types of memories we may have in connection to a person who has died.

now. Children may either draw pictures or write down words to tell their story. As children create their artwork they are encouraged to explain how and why their relative died. During this process group leaders will try to identify any issues which may benefit from clarification. These issues are then crafted into questions which are written down and posted in Winston's post box to be answered in the 'Questions for the doctor' session which takes place later that afternoon.

Questions for the doctor

One of the key aims of the weekend is to provide *education* on all aspects surrounding a child's experience of death. Children have important questions which often go unanswered. In addition, in the absence of reliable information, they formulate their own (often incorrect) conclusions about medical and spiritual issues. Many children are confused about what happened, why it happened and what happens next. The absence of such information can complicate their grieving process.

In this session, each of the small groups joins together with another group or groups to have their anonymous questions answered by the Winston's doctor. The session is made comfortably informal, taking its tone from the doctor concerned.

There are a number of personal qualities which are important in selecting a doctor for this session. Experience has shown that ideally the doctor needs to be someone who:

- has an ability to describe medical terminology in plain English, using child-friendly and, when appropriate, humorous metaphors
- will abandon their white coat and other medical 'armoury'
- is comfortable talking about death
- can explain medical issues in a child-centred way, acknowledging a variety of influences (for example, social, psychological, spiritual) as well as the physical and biological components
- is able to say 'I'm not sure' and is comfortable in engaging in an open discussion with one of the co-ordinators who joins the doctor in facilitating the session
- can respond to additional, impromptu questions from the floor and is at ease talking to a large group of children.

Many questions have been asked during residential weekends which can broadly be divided into five categories.

Younger children will usually use a variety of creative media, for example paint, collage, puppets or clay to tell their story. Here, a child represents the very difficult story surrounding his father's death by hanging and later asks the doctor: 'Why do some people choose to die?'

'Why did the doctor give mummy too much medicine?' Such questions need to be handled with respect, honesty and sensitivity by the doctor.

Factual medical information

By far the greatest number of questions (70%) that children ask the doctor are about medical issues – treatment, medication, hereditary conditions and pain, for example:

- What is cancer – is it catching?
- What is a heart attack – will I die from one too?
- If I have the HIV virus, and I pass it on, does that mean I don't have it any more?

Many questions also seek to demystify treatments:

- Why does morphine make you see things?
- What is radiotherapy?
- Why do they have computers in intensive care?

Some questions seek to understand the complexities of medical practice – how doctors work. There are often unresolved dilemmas about blame behind such questions:

- Why can't doctors make all people with chest problems better?
- Why didn't the operation work on her heart tubes?
- If the doctors had known earlier that my dad had cancer, would they have been able to save him?

Such questions are obviously challenging and need to be handled with respect, honesty and sensitivity by the doctor.

Emotional issues

Another group of questions relates to emotions and fears rather than specific medical issues, for example:

- Why are some people nasty to us when someone special has died?
- Why do some people cry and some not, even when they both knew the dead person?

One of the basic principles behind Winston's Wish is that children should be able to understand the variety of feelings that people have when someone important has died as well as the reactions of other people around them. They learn that it is OK to feel sad, to be angry, to cry, to laugh, to have regrets and that all these feelings are a valid part of their grieving.

Children have important questions which often go unanswered. On camp, they can have their anonymous questions answered by the Winston's doctor.

Searching for an explanation
The third category of questions focuses on the child's search for an explanation. The questions are varied and are often related to a child's level of cognitive development and how this relates to their knowledge and understanding of death, for example:

- Why do people die?
- My brother died in a car crash. Some of the other people in the car didn't die, so why did my brother have to die?
- Why do doctors get it wrong and why did they let my dad die?

'My brother died in a car crash. Some of the other people in the car didn't die, so why did my brother have to die?'
Child on camp

Issues relating to suicide
The fourth group of questions can be categorised into issues generated from someone 'choosing' to die:

- Why do some people choose to die?
- If people are depressed, why can't they ask for help from their family and friends, instead of killing themselves?
- How do car fumes kill someone?

Spirituality
The final category identified is about spiritual questions. In such situations it is obviously important for the doctor (and indeed co-ordinators and volunteers) not to adopt any particular spiritual or religious stance. It is more helpful to generate a selection of alternative answers. The child will then usually choose the answer that best fits their cultural and family beliefs, while recognising that other explanations exist.

Spiritual questions include the following:

- Where do people go when they die?
- If people go to heaven, can they see you all the time? (In other words: Can mum see me even when I am misbehaving?)
- Will people ever come back?
- What do you eat in heaven?
- Why do people have to be buried or burnt?

For whatever reason – whether it is the child's own knowledge of death, the desire to protect the child or the child spontaneously jumping to their own conclusions – it has become increasingly clear that children (like adults) need to understand and make sense of significant events in their lives. 'Questions for the doctor' opens the door to this process. A full analysis of the questions posed to doctors on Camp Winston is presented in Thompson and Payne (2000).

Candlelight ceremony

After supper, we hold a candlelight ceremony. It is a simple ritual which allows participants the opportunity to remember the person who has died and to connect with some of the feelings of deep sadness that may have rarely surfaced outside the group environment. Each child and group leader is given their own Winston candle and they bring their photograph of the person who died to the ceremony. We explain that it sometimes helps to light a candle on special occasions to remember people who have died. Sometimes we can remember funny events, sometimes more difficult memories, sometimes happy times and also sad times. A reference is made to the 'rocky rocks'. We explain that in thinking about how much we miss someone it can sometimes make us upset. Some instrumental music is played initially to set a reflective tone. Then, one by one, everyone is invited to light their candle and given the option to say: 'I'm lighting my candle for … and the thing(s) I would like to remember about them is …'

Most children do choose to say something. However, occasionally, the younger children may whisper their message to a group leader who will then repeat it to the larger group. It is very important (as with all the activities on the residential weekend) to provide a sense of safety and choice so children do not feel pressurised to speak. Eventually, when all the candles have been lit, some more music is played which gives time to reflect on the feelings that have been aroused. The second track is usually a ballad with appropriate lyrics. Plenty of tissues and physical comfort are available throughout the ceremony. The fact that group leaders participate fully in the ceremony can provide a useful role model for children who may believe that crying is somehow a sign of weakness.

One by one, each candle is blown out and the ceremony reaches its conclusion. The children are encouraged to keep their candles, and we invite suggestions about when they may decide to light the candle on important future occasions such as birthdays, religious holidays and anniversaries. Children also choose to light their

'At the end of camp we have a candlelight ceremony which is when all of us form a circle and one by one we say who has died in our lives. This is a special moment.'
Lois, aged 11, whose mother died in a road traffic accident

'I'm lighting my candle for … and the thing I would like to remember about them is …'

candles to mark important personal events. For example, one boy decided he would light his candle each year to mark the beginning of the fishing season as this was an activity he had always shared with his dad.

Although the candlelight ceremony is emotionally draining for all who participate, it often facilitates an emotional release for many children. It has also been observed that within half an hour of the ceremony ending, children seem to have the capacity to distance themselves from their sadness and engage in the rest of the evening's activities. It has consistently been observed that the candlelight ceremony marks a transition point on the weekend and that the children appear more relaxed and calm afterwards.

In the evening we have a campfire with songs and hot chocolate followed by a suitably exciting night walk in the forest for the older children (although we can usually arrange to take the youngest ones on a short walk if they are feeling sufficiently confident).

Bedtimes are enforced, usually with little difficulty. Group leaders and their night staff help to settle the children in their group. Safety is always a priority, and all staff and volunteers follow appropriate child care practices and health and safety policies. The staff on the night shift ensure a safe environment overnight (and allow co-ordinators and volunteers to have some restorative sleep).

Before that sleep, however, the whole team will meet to discuss how the day has been, talk about particular concerns for any of the children and to confirm the programme for the following day.

Day two

The morning begins with an energising ice-breaker to get everyone moving. The first session focuses on difficult feelings. There are many emotions and feelings following the death of someone close, but some are more easily expressed than others. Children frequently mention feeling angry; others will talk of feeling confused or guilty or even relieved.

Exploring difficult feelings

Perhaps one of the most difficult feelings is anger. On the camp weekend this feeling is acknowledged in an 'anger wall' activity. Children are invited to think about what it feels like to be angry – or indeed any other difficult feeling – and to think about events, behaviour or actions in connection with the person who died

The children are encouraged to keep their candles, and we invite suggestions about when they may decide to light the candle on important future occasions such as birthdays, religious holidays and anniversaries.

that have made them feel that way. They create targets on which their anger or other feeling is focused. Pictures or words can be used to depict the target of this emotion. These are then attached to the wall and wet clay 'bombs' are made to throw at the targets. Children are encouraged to throw the clay bombs repeatedly, sometimes releasing energy by shouting at the same time.

At the end of the session children are encouraged to take some clay and to make it into a model of something constructive which they connect with the dead person. For example, a 10-year-old who felt angry with her father's violence and heavy drinking created a model of her father watching his favourite television programme. She modelled herself on a separate chair also watching the programme, and recalled that it was one of the few times she felt safe in her father's presence. During the model building, positive and non-harmful ways of coping with angry feelings are also explored. For example, when people feel angry they can help express that feeling by drawing a picture or writing about the thing they are angry at, which they can then tear up. Finally, the children choose what to do with their clay models – to keep them, to return the clay for recycling or to throw the model away.

Creating a jar of memories

In the next group activity, each child identifies five memories which they associate with the person who has died. Different colours are used to represent each memory. Five piles of salt are then coloured by rubbing with chalks. The different colours are then poured into a small jar in various combinations of the child's choice. Spectacular salt sculptures are easily created and the exercise can be completed simply and meaningfully by all age groups. Memory jars form three-dimensional representations of recollections about a person who has died. The sculptures look different from different angles, just like people, who at certain times might display certain characteristics more than others. This can be particularly helpful when children have difficult memories about their relatives and they can see that some things were worse or better than others.

The children are invited to share their jar of memories with the larger group and say where they might put them when they go home. This is one of several activities which is also repeated on the parents' weekend, creating the opportunities for family members to talk about and share each other's jars. Group leaders may assist children in accessing memories or, for some, help them to construct connections

Memory jars form three-dimensional
representations of recollections about a
person who has died.

which are meaningful. For example, help would be offered to a child whose sibling was stillborn or a child who was very young when a parent died.

Small group work – focusing on the future

After a mid-morning break, the children assemble into their groups for the second small group session. The focus for the small group session on the first day was 'telling the story of what happened'; on the second day the focus is on 'the future' and how life can continue after a family death of someone important. The two small groups essentially mirror the two facets of the dual process model (Stroebe and Schut 1995; 1999). The model identifies the need to focus both on the past (loss orientation) and on the future (restoration orientation).

This teenager used clay from the anger wall activity to construct a box with a lid. Inside, a question mark symbolises the pain of the seemingly unanswerable: 'Why my dad?'

There are likely to be some children attending the group who may have been bereaved recently. Although a child is unlikely to attend camp until six months after a death, some may come many years after the bereavement. Consideration must therefore be given to children who do not feel ready to consider a future without the dead person. A variety of methods is available to facilitate this session including bulb-planting, making a first aid kit (see Chapter 7, page 168), creating a diary of significant dates, decorating a Christmas bauble and others.

Acknowledging attachments

Although Camp Winston is only a two-day residential event, the children and volunteers form strong attachments via the therapeutic process. For this reason, and the desire to provide a positive experience of saying goodbye, the greater part of Sunday afternoon concentrates on memories of camp and preparing to say goodbye. Throughout the afternoon, parallels are drawn between saying goodbye at the end of the residential and saying goodbye to someone important who has died. Children complete memory sheets which, together with their photograph and autobiographical information, explain who they came to Camp Winston to remember, their favourite memories of the weekend and their wishes for the future. These are collected, copied and collated as a memory book which will be sent to the family a few weeks after camp.

Since this session is the last time the children and volunteers will be together as a group without the parents, this is acknowledged and the group takes time to say its own goodbyes. Each small group will weave a 'wool web'. A ball of wool is given to a group member. They are asked to hold onto the end of the wool and then

throw it to someone while saying that person's name out loud. They then say something positive they have noticed about that person. This person then holds onto their end of the wool and throws it to someone else. This is repeated until everyone is holding part of the ball of wool. The result is a web of links people have made with each other over the two days. Finally, the wool is cut so that each person has a few strands of the wool to take home with them as a reminder of the wool web.

Then the whole camp joins together around a tree in the courtyard that is festooned with friendship bracelets. Everyone takes one to wear as a symbol of the friendships that have been made at camp.

These goodbyes are a vitally important part of the process. Originally, when the goodbyes were left to the very end (as happened on early residential groups) some children acted up, and were angry and dismissive when they met up with their parents. Since changing the programme we have not observed this process and children and parents seem enthusiastic about reforming as a family unit.

The 'bearduation' ceremony

This is a very important point in the process. It marks the reuniting of parents with their children, and formally acknowledges the achievements of families taking part in the weekend. The ceremony starts with the children and group leaders performing Winston's welcome song for the parents. Parents are very proud to see their children looking confident, having coped with a clearly emotional experience. A parents' co-ordinator and a children's co-ordinator give a short talk to link the events which have taken place on both the children's and parents' weekends. They reinforce the importance of families working together.

The bearduation itself is essentially a simple graduation ritual. It is based on identifying achievements, 'moving on' and marking the occasion by giving the children their own Winston bear to provide a tangible connection with their experience at Camp Winston. After some vigorous calling, 'Winston' appears – this time as a life-size bear who is available for hugs, paw shakes and friendly waves. The

After camp, each child is sent a memory book which is a lasting record of all the friendships they have made during the weekend.

actual appearance of 'their bear' has proved enormously important for younger children. Winston only appears at this time and further underlines the importance of the family's achievements symbolised by the ceremony. Each family is introduced one by one and the children are invited to receive their Winston bear.

Most parents will have attended the parents' weekend. However, for those who decided it was not for them, we strongly recommend (almost to the point of insisting!) that the child's parent or carer is present for the bearduation ceremony.

The balloon release
Immediately after the bearduation, families are given a helium-filled balloon. Earlier in the afternoon children and parents will have written two messages on a balloon label – one message to the person who died and the other a wish for the future. The family then attach their labels to the balloons. (We are careful to purchase balloons and string which are biodegradable to minimise any threat to wildlife.)

Outside, all the families and group leaders assemble for the balloon release. Any child or adult on their own is supported by a volunteer. The co-ordinator thanks everyone for taking part in the weekend and asks the families to take a few moments in silence to think about the person who has died. A large red balloon (symbolically belonging to Winston) is released and this leads the way for the other balloons. Slowly, when each family feels ready, they release their balloon with its attached labels and watch it float out of sight. The ceremony seems to work on a number of different levels. Children often attach tremendous significance to the prospect of their message actually reaching the dead person, while some parents often comment on the need to 'let go' of their grief metaphorically and begin to construct a different life for their family. This marks the end of the residential weekend and all families leave the centre by 4.15pm.

The balloon release. Children often attach tremendous significance to the prospect of their message actually reaching the dead person, while some parents often comment on the need to 'let go' of their grief metaphorically and begin to construct a different life for their family.

Debriefing volunteers and staff
Participating in a residential weekend is a physically and emotionally draining experience and setting aside time to debrief volunteers and staff is paramount. This is completed in three ways.

Firstly, group leaders meet in their groups to record any concerns they may have about particular children. This information is then processed carefully after the residential weekend by the staff co-ordinators. Volunteers are therefore reassured that any appropriate action will be taken, and that they no longer need to feel responsible.

Thank you card from William, aged 5, who
came to camp to remember his dad.

Friday 14th March 2003

Dear Camp Winston,

Thank you ever so much for letting me come on the camp. At candle lighting ceremony, when the candles were all lit and the lights were all off, the room was full of light and memories.

When we did all the activities, I really enjoyed them, there was something about them that always had a bit of dad in them. I hope you enjoyed camp Winston as much as I did. Love from Susie

Secondly, after a brief period of clearing up, members of the whole group assemble and are invited to share a memory from the weekend or to contribute 'one thing I will leave and one thing I will take away with me'.

Finally, the volunteers are sent an evaluation form after the weekend, with a thank you note from the co-ordinators. They are encouraged to write in with their reflections on the weekend and any proposals for change.

Issues that may arise

Of course, not every group runs perfectly smoothly, however carefully planned and carried out. These are some of the issues that need to be considered in order to be prepared:

- Disruptive and/or disturbed children – most difficulties will have been apparent at assessment but occasionally are only appreciated in a residential setting. With planning, it may be possible to have one volunteer dedicated to the support and care of the child over the weekend enabling the child concerned to derive the most benefit possible from the process and minimising the effect on the rest of their small group.
- Illness – if a child or group leader is taken ill at camp, care is needed to communicate this honestly to the rest of the group while also striving to avoid increased anxiety.
- Bedwetting, soiling and other personal difficulties – these can be accommodated with preparation and with discretion.
- Weather – if it *can* rain, it *will* rain. We think of ways to ensure the children still have space to run off their emotional energy. Raincoats come in handy, as do wellies, and group leaders who do not make a fuss if they get a bit wet!

Be prepared ... Raincoats come in handy, as do wellies, and group leaders who do not make a fuss if they get a bit wet!

Parents' programme

The parents' programme is designed in conjunction with the children's programme. It mirrors much of what happens at Camp Winston and, in doing so, provides families with a separate but shared experience.

The first day of the programme provides parents with the time and space to meet with others in a safe and welcoming environment. It offers them the opportunity to explore their own personal experience of grief while not having to care for or concentrate on their children. The second day has a more educational focus and is designed to help parents explore and understand any concerns or worries they may have about their children.

Developing ideas and strategies to support both themselves and their children after the weekend is also an important element. Although the parents' weekend can feel intense, there is also much humour and general camaraderie.

The parents' programme offers parents the opportunity to explore their own bereavement experience and to gain a greater understanding of their child's grief.

Who attends?

Parents and carers are actively encouraged to attend the parents' group when their children are attending the children's camp. Numbers average around 12–15 depending on a number of factors including, for example, the number of children per family.

Venue for the parents

The parents' weekend is held at a local secondary school. Unfortunately, the weekend is currently non-residential. Some parents stay together at local bed and breakfast accommodation, while others travel home. If resources allowed, and we could find a suitable venue close to the children's camp, we would run the parents' weekend as a residential too.

Preparation

For staff and volunteers on the parents' weekend

The preparation for the parents' weekend involves two staff co-ordinators and up to four volunteers who meet on two separate evenings. At the first briefing, they decide on the content of the programme and who will lead on various activities. Small changes may be made depending on the experiences of the parents attending. One co-ordinator will lead, taking overall responsibility as a 'master of ceremonies'.

Programme for parents' weekend

Saturday – 'A day about you'

9.00	Parents leave children at the Wilderness Centre and continue to their venue
9.30	Welcome and introductions Lighting the candle Memory table
9.50	How am I feeling right now? Individual introductions
10.30	Brief break
10.40	Small group work – telling the story of what happened
11.50	Brief break
12.00	A jar of memories – activity
13.00	Lunch
14.00	Exploring difficult feelings – activity
15.10	Break
15.30	Candlelight ceremony
16.00	Break
16.15	Visit from children's camp volunteer
16.30	How's it been for you today? How will you look after yourself tonight?
17.00	Goodbye for now – parents leave

Sunday – 'A day about you and your children'

9.15	Parents arrive
9.30	Welcome back and introduction to the day How was last night? How am I feeling today?
10.00	Helping children cope with grief (part 1) – stepping stones: childhood memories
10.45	Brief break
11.00	Helping children cope with grief (part 2) – talk and general discussion
12.00	Group leaders from children's camp visit to provide feedback on each child
12.45	Lunch
13.30	First aid kits
13.45	Preparing to say goodbye Balloon messages
14.30	Keeping in touch Books and hand-outs to take home
14.45	Goodbye to this group – 'one thing I want to leave here and one thing I want to take with me'
15.00	Parents and team leave for the Wilderness Centre
15.30	Bearduation
16.00	Closing ceremony – balloon release
16.15	Families leave Tidy up Staff debrief
18.00	Home for everyone

In an ideal world, it is helpful to have one female and one male co-ordinator leading the parents' weekend.

The second preparatory meeting will focus on the profiles and particular needs of parents attending.

Planning the programme

When planning the programme for adults, group co-ordinators tackle the following issues and questions to make sure the programme will be truly relevant and beneficial:

- The gender mix – one man on his own may not feel comfortable in the group.
- The size of the group – neither too large nor too small.
- The range of causes of death.
- The range of relationships to the person who died – parent/spouse/ex-partner.
- The importance – or otherwise – of both parents attending when a child has died.
- Time since death.
- The nature of the relationships with the person who died – estranged, ambivalent, impassioned, loving.
- The social range of the group.
- The use of similar creative activities to those on the children's camp – how to make these appropriate and therapeutic for adults.

The programme for the parents' weekend

For the full timetable, see pages 120–121, Programme for parents' weekend.

Day one: 'A day about you'

Welcome and introductions

After registering their children at the children's camp, parents and carers are invited to convene at the venue one mile away.

The programme begins by welcoming everybody to the group, introducing the team, acknowledging the parents' achievement in getting themselves and their children to camp, and outlining the programme and practical details for the next two days. An agreement for working respectfully and safely together over the two days is also discussed and agreed.

The gender mix is important – one man on his own may not feel comfortable in the group.

A candle is lit to mark the beginning of the weekend and parents, like their children, are invited to place a photo or memento on a memory table. This provides an important place of focus and informal sharing for many parents over the weekend.

How I'm feeling right now

An air of anxiety among the parents at this stage is fairly typical and one we begin addressing with a simple paper and pen activity that enables each person to state anonymously 'How I am feeling right now'. Each person is encouraged to simply draw a 'feelings face' or write down one or two words on a post-it note about how they are feeling at that moment. Once collected and displayed on a flipchart the words and drawings are summarised by one of the co-ordinators. While feelings may range from 'scared', 'tearful' and 'anxious' to 'relieved' and 'happy to be here', there is always some overlap or duplication which tends to provide a real sense of relief to group members. This activity also provides a useful point of reflection over the two days, often helping individuals and the group to recognise the shift and change that takes place.

Individual introductions

Parents often feel daunted when asked to introduce themselves in a group setting, particularly when they are asked to include who has died and how that person died. We therefore invite parents firstly to introduce themselves to one other person in the group, usually the person they are sitting next to. Spending five minutes with one other person to tell them a little about who you are and to talk out loud about the person who has died often provides parents with the courage to introduce themselves in the larger group. Reminding people that the weekend is essentially about meeting others and 'telling their story' of what brought them to camp helps this process. In essence their introduction becomes 'the title of my story' for that weekend.

Each person's name, the name(s) and age(s) of their child(ren), the name of and their relationship to the person who died and the way in which that person died are all written up on a flipchart. This provides a useful reminder of names and family circumstances to everybody in the group. It also helps parents identify and begin the formation of connections to others.

'It helped enormously when the children went to Camp Winston and were able to talk and be with children in the same position. I also found the adult camp good to meet other adults in the same position as myself. It was good to realise that you were not the only one with the fears, worries and anxieties of being a bereaved parent.'
Feedback from parent, Service Evaluation 2003

Telling the story of what happened

Following a short break, time is planned for parents to begin telling their story. A brief but sensitive introduction to the session takes place before moving into small groups, each with up to four parents and a member of the team. Within each small group, parents are encouraged to talk and listen to each other's stories. For many this is the first opportunity to talk openly with others who have experienced similar circumstances and a time for further connections and relationships to be built.

Small group membership for this session is planned carefully. For example, depending on the make-up of the whole group, smaller groups may be influenced by gender, type of death or the type of relationship with the person who died. The participants may choose to tell their story by describing what life was like before the person died, what happened immediately before they died, how they died, what happened afterwards and what life is like now. Approximately one and a half hours are allocated for this session. This usually provides sufficient time for each person to introduce his or her story and time for small group discussion.

A jar of memories

This activity closely mirrors the children's session to create a memory jar (see page 114) and has proved to be an important and tangible communication tool for many families after the weekend. In addition to memories, parents will often include feelings associated with the person who has died or the events surrounding their death.

Exploring difficult feelings

This session is introduced by the exercise we call 'rocky rocks' (see page 107). The parents are encouraged to share a 'pebble' memory of an ordinary, everyday thing. Then they are asked to look within to the feelings that are linked to the rough, jagged rock. All write the words for these feelings onto a large sheet of paper. The paper rapidly gets covered with scrawled words such as 'rage', 'fear', 'guilt', 'if only', 'relief', 'bitterness'. To see the confusion of difficult feelings is in itself a powerful moment.

The second part of the session uses one of a range of creative ideas to work with one of these feelings – the one that each parent relates to their own 'rough rock'. This may be to work with clay (see page 114), to write a letter to the person who has died or a similar activity.

Each parent is helped to share memories or feelings which may be uncomfortable and difficult.

The final part of the session leads the participants back to reflect on their 'gemstone' memories, a special and good time involving the precious, shining times with the person who died.

Candlelight ceremony

The candlelight ceremony at the parents' weekend essentially reflects the ceremony that takes place at the children's camp where children are invited to light a candle and to say something about the person who has died (see page 112). Music and poems are used to enhance this simple but powerful ritual which provides a time of quiet reflection in a shared and safe setting.

The ceremony provides important time and space for parents to get in touch with their sadness and is therefore often very emotional, with many tears being shared. The release of deep emotions leaves some parents feeling emotionally drained but calmer than they may have felt for some time.

The ceremony provides important time and space for parents to get in touch with their sadness and is therefore often very emotional, with many tears being shared.

Visit from children's camp

Towards the end of the first day, a volunteer from the children's camp joins the parents' group to provide a brief update on how their day has been and to reassure parents that their children have settled in and are doing well. This is an important part of the programme that enables most parents to leave the parents' group feeling secure in the knowledge that their children are safe and being well looked after. Parents are also reminded that a further visit will take place on the second day when they will have an opportunity to speak individually to one of the volunteers who has been working directly with their child(ren).

How's it been for you today? How will you look after yourself tonight?

Day one ends with time spent reflecting on how the day has been for everyone in the group and preparing parents to leave. This allows the team to assess any vulnerability in the group, especially as for some parents this will be the first night they have spent away from their child(ren) since the death. The importance of parents finding ways of looking after themselves during the evening and overnight is strongly encouraged.

Team debrief

After the parents have left and the venue made ready for the next day, members of the parents' group team spend approximately an hour and a half debriefing from the day. This includes peer support, self-care and discussions about each participant in the group. This helps identify any individual or group concerns, and provides opportunities to discuss and plan small changes to the programme for the next day. It also provides an opportunity to acknowledge individual, group and programme achievements.

Day two: 'A day about you and your children'

Welcome back

Parents are invited to arrive at 9.15am for a 9.30am start. Despite an emotionally draining day on the Saturday, many parents actually arrive earlier than this, surprisingly eager to be back to continue the group experience.

The welcome back includes time for the group to reflect on how the previous day had gone and for each individual to share how their evening had been. Parents are also asked to say how they are feeling and their feedback typically includes comments such as 'tired but pleased to be back' or 'feeling much lighter, knowing I'm not the only one in this situation'.

Parents are generally keen to know how their children have coped overnight and are looking forward to seeing them although, for some, eager anticipation is counterbalanced by a nervousness or anxiety about meeting up with their children or about how their children will be after the camp experience.

Helping children cope with grief

Supporting children becomes the main focus of day two. The first session is aimed at increasing parents' understanding about how children grieve. The format, content and method of running this session vary according to who is leading it but typically includes some information about children's levels of understanding and expression of grief and the factors that may help or hinder them. This information proves invaluable in normalising children's experiences of grief and helping parents to understand their children's behaviour and responses.

The session also provides an opportunity for parents to ask lots of questions and raise concerns. It always generates a good discussion especially when the

Charter for Bereaved Children (see page 42) is used which provides both prompts and a focus for the group in relation to a wide range of issues.

Feedback from children's camp

After a short break, parents are introduced to some of the volunteers who have been working with the children. This involves one group leader from each 'bear' group who provides individual feedback to each parent about their particular child. This feedback is thought through in terms of content, any issues about confidentiality, careful phrasing about any concerns and the importance of ensuring that parents hear positive, constructive feedback. (More detailed written feedback is provided after camp.)

    The session is run a bit like a school parents' evening and needs careful planning and managing to ensure that every parent receives feedback about every child – quite a challenge for those with three or more children at camp.

Looking after yourself – first aid kits

This session involves a paper and pen activity based on the activity of the same name that takes place at children's camp. As well as helping parents understand first hand one of the activities the children will have completed, it also provides an important metaphor for the importance of self-care and personal support.

    Once the metaphor has been explained, parents are encouraged to think about the resources that help keep them strong. This can prove really difficult for some people, and this in itself can be an indication of how low they are. With help, however, everybody is able to share at least one or two things that they know help them get through and something they might do differently in the future. For some, this session provides a simple but important reminder of the things that helped in times of stress before the death.

    Parents are encouraged to take their first aid kit home with them and to stick it on the fridge as an important reminder. See Chapter 7, page 168, for more information about this activity.

Balloon messages

In preparation for the balloon release that marks the end of the whole camp, parents are invited to spend time writing a label with a message to the person who has died and a wish for the future. It is something that the children will also have

'Pete: I know it wasn't always easy for us but I miss you so much – it's so hard to face life without you being here. I hope that I can stay strong for the girls and help them to understand properly how much their dad loved them.'
Parent's balloon message

Emotional first aid kit: parents are encouraged to take it home with them and to stick it on the fridge as an important reminder that they need to look after themselves too.

completed. This can be a really tough thing for parents to do and often generates tears. Building in enough time to reflect on the task is important, typically about 10 minutes with some gentle music playing in the background. Parents are asked to hold on to their balloon labels and to keep them safe until they are needed.

Keeping in touch and preparing to say goodbye

Marking the end of the time spent together as a group is really important and sufficient time is allowed for goodbyes. We prepare the group for the likely reactions of their children on being reunited and for their own reactions in the following days and weeks. We remind the parents that we will contact them in the next few days by phone and in the next four weeks by letter.

We frequently end with a simple sharing around the group of 'one thing I want to leave here and one thing I want to take with me'. The participants may choose symbolic items from a bowl or write a word on paper. For example, one parent recently chose to leave behind a shrivelled leaf to symbolise how she had seen herself becoming and chose to take with her a chocolate wrapper as a reminder of 'all the sweetness of the past and for the future with my son'.

Bearduation and balloon release

On arrival at the children's camp, parents are invited into the large group room which has been specially prepared for the bearduation. Once seated, parents wait in anticipation for their children to arrive. They are usually amazed and overwhelmed to hear the sound of happy singing voices as the children line up to enter the room.

The reuniting of families can be tense but a balance of fun and serious acknowledgement of everybody's achievements and a staged approach help this process immensely.

Finishing camp and team debrief

As camp closes, the parents' group team returns to the school to clear up and tidy away. The team also spends about an hour and a half debriefing from the event, celebrating its achievements and reviewing and assessing each parent's experience of the group. This provides important feedback about what further support may be needed or any issues which need to be followed up with the families.

A further debriefing session for those working on the parents' weekend is held one evening, about 10 days later, to review the programme. (Even after running over

50 weekends, we still make small changes or developments every time!) It also offers an opportunity to feed back constructively to the team that worked on the parents' group. In an ideal world we would also include children's camp volunteers in this debriefing session. However, the number of people involved often makes this impractical, especially because many travel from outside Gloucestershire. Those working on the parents' weekend tend to live locally.

Issues that may arise

As mentioned in the children's camp section, however carefully we plan and run the programme, it would be impossible to expect every group to run perfectly smoothly. These are some of the issues that need to be considered in order to be prepared:

- couples expressing marital or relationship tension within the group
- one member of the group dominating
- unexpected revelations – such as drugs, suicidal thoughts, alcohol dependence
- child protection issues
- people not returning for the second day.

What happens after Camp Winston: follow-up for families

A follow-up procedure is carried out using information recorded at the debrief session. This includes information for each child about how they coped with camp, friends they made, things they learnt, enjoyed or found difficult, and concerns that may need further individual work. In the week after the residential weekend the co-ordinators contact each family by phone. Follow-up letters are sent within four weeks to provide further feedback to both the families and those who referred the family to Winston's Wish. Memory books are also sent out to children within four weeks. All families will have the opportunity to attend further social-therapeutic events so they can remain in touch for as long as they need to (see Chapter 11). At the time of writing we are piloting the possibility of arranging follow-up appointments for each family within eight weeks of attending camp. While we believe this face-to-face follow-up is beneficial, current workloads can make it difficult to achieve. Key performance indicators have been developed to monitor our progress against set targets (an example is presented in Chapter 13).

'The camp was fantastic, a genuine help in dealing with it all and one which I and my children will never forget.'
Feedback from parent, Service Evaluation 2003

'One thing I want to leave here is my guilt and bitterness.'

15th March 2003

Dear Team Winston,

Many thanks to you all for your efforts and support at last week-ends Camp. Susie and Charlie have been telling me snippets of what they got up to and we have compared "notes" about our activities. They love their bears and the red tops were worn at school for Red Nose Day.

We look forward to receiving the list of phone numbers of the other families so we can keep in touch.

With best wishes,

Rosemary

What do families say about Camp Winston?

It appears from the letters we receive from children and parents that the weekends provide a highly valued and quality service that is deemed to be meeting their needs. However, anecdotes and opinion can only be used as short-term expedients and reliable knowledge from methodologically sound surveys and studies is necessary. In 1994 an independent researcher evaluated two weekends. Parents and children were visited at home and a semi-structured interview completed. The results of the evaluation (Wyer 1994) showed that:

- children benefit from the programme
- children's behaviour changed in a positive way as a result of the residential
- children were more open and more settled
- children's understanding of death increased
- communication levels within the family improved
- children were helped to cope with their relative's death.

Wyer concluded that families found the programme effective in normalising the grieving process. Children were aware that they were not alone – and that there were other children like themselves. They realised that it was OK to show their feelings and to talk about how they felt.

What parents said about their children

'He's a completely different person. In the car he was talking all the time. He's been so quiet since the death, it really brought it out. I was able to talk to him as well. Before camp he never talked about it.'

'They are a lot better in themselves: meeting other children in the same situation really helped. They've really settled.'

'He's a lot more open. He wouldn't talk about it much before and he doesn't wet the bed so much.'

'There are no more nightmares or tantrums.'

'It's not only me that's noticed the change – everybody has.'

'It was like something had been laid to rest.'

What children said about Camp Winston

'The doctor's questions helped me to understand.'

'I learnt how to cope with it. I don't just remember the sad times … I remember the fun times. I used to cry every night, now I don't. I felt it was my fault, now I understand.'

'I learnt about what happened to others; you knew it wasn't just you.'

'I learnt it's all right to talk about it and it's not always a bad thing to cry.'

Dear Camper

I hear that you're going to the Winston Wish Camp. I thought you might like me to tell you all about it. When you get there We were given this great Jumper which had winston on it. We do lots of exciting things like: Salt Sculptures, games, Angry wall and exciting things like that. At the end we have a candle light ceremony which is when all of us form a circle and one by one we Say who has died in our lives. This is a Special moment. Winstons Camp is very helpful because it made it easier to talk about the special person we had all lost, and it was nice to Know that our helpers cared So much. I'm Sure you'll have a wonderful time. With best wishes Lois

'The weekend was absolutely brilliant even though it did not feel so at times.'

A never-ending journey. Here, a child is captured as they are leaving, equipped with their memory bag and a Winston bear to remind them of their experience on Camp Winston.

What parents said about the parents' weekend

'It's lovely to meet people. You are searching for people in the same situation as yourself: you don't feel you are the only one.'

'I found it did help. Everyone was at different stages. It made me realise there is more to life after all. After two days you've shared everything with these strangers, it all comes out naturally … we all had tears and cried on each other's shoulders at some stage.'

The following letter was received in April 2003, and expresses in more detail the depth of the therapeutic process from a parent's perspective.

Dear Winston's Wish

Having attended camp with you guys I always knew I would write to you and in my head I imagined it would be on the Monday and that I would write of 'happy clappy' things! Instead of that it is now Thursday evening and I have only just got used to the emotions and thought process your sessions triggered in me.

The weekend was absolutely brilliant even though it did not feel so at times. I came away feeling completely shattered and raw emotion was flowing through my blood stream. Now I am beginning to feel positive again but somehow a different positive person. I know not to hide that raw emotion, I know how to start to re-build and I know how to care and to continue to grow with David without Paul. Thank you. You do a wonderful job and must help so many people. Take care.

Stephanie

So often parents respond to the death of a partner by becoming 'super parent', filling the gaps and busying themselves to ensure family life continues. As this mother conveys, the experiences at the parents' weekend can sometimes be an intense emotional release, but one which enables the parent to establish a much more secure foundation on which to support their child.

This chapter has described in detail the Camp Winston group intervention which is at the heart of the Winston's Wish community-based service. Through 10 years of developing and refining the programme we have found that the intervention:

- seems to suit the majority of bereaved families
- has an extremely high attendance rate, unlike many mid-week after-school group formats which report high drop-out rates
- can operate over a wide age range
- can accommodate large numbers of children and parents which then allows the service to have open access to any child bereaved of a parent or sibling
- offers a whole-family experience which is at times intense and, at other times, hugely enjoyable but, above all, is a memorable intervention that gives confidence to both parents and children.

'Some people come into our lives
and quickly go. They stay for a while
but leave footprints on our hearts.
And we are never, ever the same.'

Unknown

Chapter Six

Diversions on route

Planning therapeutic interventions for parents and children when mourning becomes complicated

In this chapter, we identify the services required when the assessment indicates that a child's or parent's reactions of grief may be adversely affected by a complicated mourning process. The intervention involves face-to-face individual work and is based on a short-term psychotherapy model, usually involving between six and eight sessions. It is estimated that approximately 25% of all families referred to Winston's Wish benefit from a course of individual work either before or after a group intervention. The provision of an individual work programme allows us to offer a more flexible, family-centred approach for those at risk and for those families needing extra support.

A helping hand can give a child the confidence to navigate the route that lies ahead.

A flexible and family-centred approach

Individual work may be offered before, after or instead of a residential or group intervention. Sometimes, for example, there may be some confusion within a family about what happened on the day the person died. The child may have a very mixed-up notion of what happened, which would make it difficult for them to tell their story in a group environment. Individual work may be offered to parents to help them think through the messages they are giving their children and find ways to improve communication within the family. The child may be included in a session so that the practitioner can support the parents in talking clearly with the child about the death. It may then be useful for the child to have some individual work with a practitioner to make sense of this information, and incorporate it into their own story of what happened.

Therapeutic model

Like all interventions, individual work aims to build on the five primary clinical objectives (see page 33). However, as we employ a multi-disciplinary team of practitioners, the therapeutic model depends to some extent on the practitioner who is offering it. Our current practitioners are qualified in a variety of disciplines including clinical and counselling psychology, social work, mental health nursing, integrative arts, psychotherapy, education and the voluntary sector. This means that most practitioners have a professional background in therapeutic work with children and families before they come to Winston's Wish. However, as an important component of our continuing professional development, we have case management meetings to share practice and develop a model for individual work that is consistent with the aims and values of a community-based service.

The approach for individual work is non-pathological, respectful of the unique mourning process of the individual, and mindful of the individual as part of the family and the wider community. Practitioners aim to have a warm, friendly and human approach as they seek to work alongside either the child and/or parent. The practitioner models an openness to talking about death and grief, and demonstrates an acceptance of whatever feelings and responses someone experiences.

Individual work aims:
- to help unravel information needed to increase an understanding of what has happened
- to develop a coherent story of the death
- to address ambivalent feelings or difficulties in relationships
- to express feelings and identify negative thinking patterns
- to build self-esteem
- to work with symptoms of trauma, depression and anxiety
- to act as an advocate for the child or parent when communicating with other family members or, for example, in school or at work.

The assessment process aims to identify factors which may complicate the natural grief process. This is often referred to as 'risk assessment' in the bereavement literature (Stroebe et al 2001). For example, the mourner's perception of the death as preventable is considered a significant risk factor for any bereaved parent (Rando 1993). Similarly, the nature of the death, and the nature of relationships or key events before the death, can also have a profound effect (Parkes and Weiss 1983). Therefore, assessors will need to carefully consider all the 'determinants of grief' (see page 40) before deciding if someone may benefit from individual work.

A child's sense of 'self' comes from knowing they are valued by people in their family – alive or dead. Children love to anchor this sense of family 'completeness' through artistic representation.

Supporting parents as well as children
The Child Bereavement Study identified that one of the strongest predictors of risk two years after a parental death was *the adjustment and psychological well-being of the surviving parent*.

'The functioning of the surviving parent is the most powerful predictor of a child's adjustment to the death of a parent. Children with a less well functioning parent will show more anxiety and depression, and sleep and health problems. Bereaved children will have fewer emotional/behavioural problems if discipline is consistently administered and if the surviving parent perceives the child's needs and behaviour in a way that is similar to the child's perception. Inconsistent discipline and perceptual discrepancies will lead to high levels of anxiety in the child.' (Worden 1996: p95)

Given these findings, it is essential to ensure that both parents *and* children have access to individual sessions if there are factors and issues likely to intensify their grief.

Individual work is offered as a therapeutic contract, and usually involves between six and eight one-hour consultations of structured work focusing on

'The functioning of the surviving parent is the most powerful predictor of a child's adjustment to the death of a parent.' Worden 1996

bereavement issues. Our current practitioners are likely to use a combination of therapeutic approaches:

- cognitive restructuring (cognitive behavioural therapy)
- systemic (family therapy) interventions
- treatment for post-traumatic stress disorder
- art therapy
- person-centred approaches.

'He who knows
others is wise.
He who knows
himself is
enlightened.'

Lau-Tzu

Sessions are usually organised outside the home, occasionally in school but most often in a consultation room which is comfortable, private and age-appropriate.

When is it offered?

After the home assessment, practitioners discuss the recommendations at a case management meeting and, if individual work is recommended, then the most appropriate practitioner (or practitioners) is allocated to the family.

Although we usually invite families to a group at least six months or so after the death, individual work needs greater flexibility and depends on the needs and issues to be addressed. For example, the father of pre-school children whose partner has just died in an RTA may need some regular support for the first few months. This support may simply be focused on helping him cope with his own grief and that of his children, while making funeral arrangements and dealing with the inquest and the publicity it generates. It often takes a longer period of several months before an adult or child is ready to commit to a series of 'therapy' sessions with someone in a location outside the family home.

Criteria for offering individual work

We use the following criteria to assess whether or not individual work is appropriate:

- if the issues are complicated and would not be sufficiently or appropriately addressed via a group experience
- if the nature of the death might predict a complicated grief reaction: for example, if the death involves suicide, murder, witnessing a violent/traumatic death
- if there was a previous history of cumulative losses, which led to symptoms of severe depression or anxiety
- if the child/parent/family is not willing to participate in a group intervention but we feel they would benefit from some therapy or support on an individual basis

- if some individual sessions might help the child/parent/family to get more benefit from coming to a residential group
- where children are aged 4 or under, we currently offer individual work to the parent(s).

Criteria for not offering individual work – onward referral

On occasion, the team decides that it is not appropriate to either offer individual or group work within the Winston's Wish programme. In such circumstances referral to a more appropriate agency would be advised. The exact reasons can vary depending on the complexity of the family situation and our current staff complement. However, the circumstances in which we would tend not to take on individual work include:

- if the person would benefit from a psychiatric intervention by a mental health team (for example, there was evidence of an acute psychosis/schizophrenia)
- if there was evidence of a recognised psychological condition (such as clinical depression or acute anxiety disorders) which required an intervention over a longer period by an appropriately qualified professional (for example, treatment for a severe obsessive compulsive disorder may take weekly sessions for many months)
- if change would only be achieved via a long-term residential intervention (for example, a teenager who had severe drug or alcohol addiction)
- if the child is not in a stable or consistent home environment (for example, a child who is at the point of entering short-term foster/residential care)
- if change could only be achieved by establishing a weekly long-term psychotherapeutic relationship. After 6–8 sessions the client may only just be ready to establish a trusting relationship. Termination at this point could be counterproductive (for example, a parent who had been seriously abused as a child and also in her marriage may find it difficult to trust within a short-term psychotherapy timescale).

Generally speaking, mourning is complicated because things have occurred to complicate the thoughts, feelings and behaviour of the grieving individual. So, before launching into a discussion about risk assessment and indicators of complicated grief, it may be helpful to consider a model which seems to hold true for many bereaved people.

'I rage inside the dark and call her name; I hide inside the dark and close my eyes. The winter of my life is frozen pain. The longing for my mother never dies.'

Elizabeth Kim (*Ten Thousand Sorrows* 2000) who witnessed her mother's death at the hands of her father and brother

75:25 In a typical month, over 75% of assessments lead to an offer of a place at a group, and over 25% lead to an offer of individual work with one or more members of the family.

Providing a therapeutic framework for understanding grief and mourning

One of the strengths of an effective bereavement practitioner is the ability to help an adult or child find their way through the many diversions of their bereavement journey and, at the same time, provide reassurance about the overall route map. This is important because so often the public perception is that you will get over it, get better and, even as Freud (1961) intimated, become slowly detached from the loved person. For many people, the expectation that the pain of grief will simply shrink day by day until it can be declared that they have 'come to terms with it' is out of kilter with their experience.

In *Growing Around Grief* Tonkin (1996) suggests another way of looking at grief and recovery generated by a bereaved person. Tonkin suggests it can provide a useful framework for doing individual work with some clients. The model offers relief from the expectation that their grief should largely go away. 'It explains the dark days, and also describes the richness and depth the experience of grief has given to their lives … clients have felt comforted using this model, that they can do so without the sense of disloyalty to the deceased that so often holds back bereaved people. In this way they continue the process of integrating the loss with their lives and moving forwards.' (Tonkin 1996: p10)

Figure 18 is an adaptation of Tonkin's model. It shows that it is unrealistic to expect that the pain of grief will simply shrink and that one will soon be 'over it'. The case study opposite provides a vehicle to understand the model outlined below.

Figure 18: 'Message in a bottle'

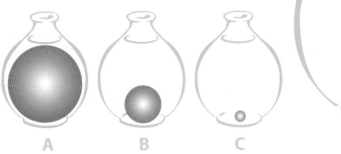

A   B   C   D

Case study Rebecca (aged 49)

Rebecca's husband had died 10 years before in a violent street attack in which he was stabbed. The attacker was never apprehended. Rebecca witnessed his death, with their sons, then aged 5 and 8. At the time of his death she felt her grief consumed her totally (see bottle A) filling every part of her life, awake and asleep.

She ruminated constantly on the fact that the attacker had simply walked away and she was also troubled by the (secret) knowledge that, as a couple, they had been struggling. They had even discussed the possibility of divorce. She had imagined (and been told by everyone around her) that as time progressed she would 'get over it'. Her grief would diminish (see bottle B) and eventually become neatly encapsulated in her life, in a smaller, more manageable way (see bottle C). However, Rebecca's actual experience was different. Her grief was intense and enduring. After three years she was eventually referred, and subsequently offered a series of eight individual sessions. The practitioner aimed to help Rebecca identify various recurrent thoughts that were proving unhelpful, for example:

'I should never have asked him for a divorce.'

'I am a useless wife and mother.'

'What's the point of doing anything with my life? It won't bring Tony back.'

'A happy person is not a person in a certain set of circumstances, but rather a person with a certain set of attitudes.'

Hugh Downs

Using a cognitive behavioural model the evidence for these beliefs was gently challenged and together they worked on evolving thoughts/beliefs and behaviour which facilitated a more adaptive coping style. Rebecca slowly felt she was making progress. She felt a greater sense of control and could face the possibility of expanding her life experience to accommodate the death of her husband, while making space for new things (see bottle D).

In time, her 'new' life involved embarking on a different career, forming new friendships and, after six years, meeting a new partner and eventually becoming a step-mother to his three children. Increasingly there was 'space' in her 'bottle' to experience new things other than the all-consuming grief. However, there were still times when Rebecca felt her original sense of loss just as intensely. Although it remained upsetting, she felt this model for understanding her grief gave her confidence that it was OK and natural to revisit her original experience of loss while enjoying the new life she had allowed herself to create.

How individual work is presented is crucial to the uptake and subsequent success of the intervention. This model can be helpful to engage people who need a framework to understand the rationale for committing to a series of sessions.

Individual work with parents

Individual work with adults at risk requires practitioners who have been professionally trained and have gained experience under careful supervision. This section provides a very brief introduction and directs readers to the many excellent texts which can offer practitioners a thorough understanding of the treatment of complicated mourning in adults (Rando 1993).

Figure 19: Distinguishing between 'bereavement', 'grief' and 'mourning'

- **Bereavement** – the objective state of having suffered a significant loss.
- **Grief** – the subjective reaction to loss.
- **Mourning** – the conscious and unconscious intrapsychic processes, together with the cultural, public or interpersonal efforts that are involved in attempts to cope with loss and grief.

(Corr 2000: p21)

In Chapter 1 we looked at a definition of grief as being 'a natural, healthy predictable set of responses to loss' which we believe underpins the Winston's Wish approach. When considering individual work the focus extends to encompass the premise of complicated mourning. Mourning tends to reflect how bereaved people try to cope with loss and grief. In terms of situations involving a death, coping may be directed to the primary loss of the person who has died, the secondary losses that are associated with the death (for example, the consequences of moving home), and the grief reactions that are experienced. As Corr (2000) concludes, therapeutic work is enhanced when practitioners have clarity on the differences between grief and mourning. This is especially relevant to practitioners when they aim to provide individual therapeutic interventions for people whose mourning is 'complicated'.

Rando (1993) describes in detail a framework for providing treatment of complicated mourning. In Figure 20, Rando outlines a set of indicators which, although not exhaustive, provide a useful guide to assist practitioners.

Rando continues by classifying complicated mourning into seven key syndromes – absent, delayed, inhibited, distorted, conflicted, unanticipated and chronic – and gives guidance on the treatment approaches that can help with these particular issues.

Figure 20: Clinical indicators of complicated mourning

- 'A pattern of vulnerability to, sensitivity toward, or over-reaction to experiences entailing loss and separation.
- Psychological and behavioural restlessness, over-sensitivity, arousal, over-activity, and perception of being 'geared up', along with the need always to be occupied, as if cessation of movement would permit the surfacing of anxiety-provoking repressed or suppressed material.
- Unusually high death anxiety focusing on the self or loved ones.
- Excessive and persistent over idealisation of the deceased and/or unrealistically positive recollections of the relationship.
- Rigid, compulsive, or ritualistic behaviour sufficient to impinge on the mourner's freedom and well-being.
- Persistent obsessive thoughts and preoccupation with the deceased and elements of the loss.
- Inability to experience the various emotional reactions to loss typically found in the bereaved and/or uncharacteristically constricted affect.
- Inability to articulate, to whatever capacity the mourner has, existing feelings and thoughts about the deceased and the loss.
- Relationships with others marked by fear of intimacy and other indices of avoidance stemming primarily from fear of future loss.
- A pattern of self-destructive relationships commencing or escalating subsequent to the death, including compulsive care giving and replacement relationships.
- The commencement or escalation after the death of self-defeating, self-destructive, or acting-out behaviour, including psychoactive substance dependence or abuse.
- Chronic experience of numbness, alienation, depersonalisation, or other effects and occurrences that isolate the mourner from herself and others.
- Chronic anger or some variation thereof (eg annoyance) or a combination of anger and depression (eg irritability, belligerence, intolerance).'

(Rando 1993: pp152–153)

Despite the complexity in understanding the various 'syndromes' Rando suggests that in all forms of complicated mourning, 'the mourner attempts to do two things:

a) deny, repress or avoid aspects of the loss, its pain, and the full realisation of its implications for the mourner and

b) hold on to and avoid relinquishing the lost loved one … no matter what type of treatment is employed, it will need to address these two issues.'

(Rando 1993: p149)

Given limited resources to offer individual work (and bearing in mind key findings from the Child Bereavement Study relating to parental well-being) we ensure that we offer individual work to both parents *and* children. This enables the parent to be in a better place to provide on-going support for their children.

Case study — Mary (aged 48)

Mary has a 12-year-old daughter whose father died two years ago. Mary had an unusual relationship with the father of her child. He was married to someone else and so was not always available to be with Mary's family. She loved him enormously and, now that he is dead, feels as though 'the light has gone out of my life'. As the 'other woman', she was unable to attend the funeral and feels disenfranchised in her grief. She has lived for a long time with depression and hardly goes out of the house. She feels that no-one understands her and she is terrified at the idea of meeting other parents in a group setting. The assessment team felt that Mary's daughter would really benefit from a residential weekend and that it would make a big difference to the family if Mary could come too. They offered some individual work to Mary to explore her feelings over the death of her lover and advised on anxiety management to help with her agoraphobia. After a series of five sessions, Mary recently decided that she will attend a residential weekend with her daughter.

Individual work with children

When life issues are unexpressed or unacknowledged they become locked in what Goldman (1996) calls 'frozen blocks of time'. Many situations that breed fear, shame and terror cut off the grief process and can result in children being caught unexpectedly in these frozen blocks of time. Children at risk usually feel unable to break free from overwhelming feelings experienced at the time of their trauma (see page 82). They become imprisoned in these feelings if they are not given the freedom to work through grief.

If a child is offered individual work, he/she will generally be identified as at risk and showing signs of persistent 'psychological distress'. Worden (1996) recommends that the focus should not simply be on the presence of a symptom, behaviour or thought, but on its *duration*. He identifies 10 'red flag' areas which indicate that a child may require individual work before being able to benefit from a group intervention.

Figure 21: Red flags to identify bereaved children at risk

- persistent difficulties in talking about the dead parent
- persistent, un-containable aggression
- persistent symptoms of anxiety, shown by a refusal to go to school and extreme clinging to the surviving parent
- persistent somatic complaints
- persistent sleep difficulties and/or nightmares after a year
- persistent changes in eating patterns
- marked long-term social withdrawal
- school difficulties or a serious decline in academic performance, continuing after nine months
- persistent self-blame or guilt (indicative of clinical depression)
- self-destructive behaviour or a desire to die: in this case, a child should be offered individual work immediately regardless of how long ago the death occurred.

(Worden 1996: pp147–150)

When reviewing the findings observed in the Harvard Child Bereavement Study, Worden (1996) suggests that 33% of bereaved children have emotional or behavioural problems sufficient to warrant 'some type of counselling intervention' during the first two years of bereavement. Our experience indicates that if families attend a residential weekend during this period fewer children go on to require individual work. This has important resource implications for those developing child bereavement services.

Situations that breed fear, shame and terror cut off the grief process and can result in children being caught unexpectedly in 'frozen blocks of time'.

Dream catcher.
Children who are
experiencing sleeping
difficulties can be
given strategies
to challenge
nightmares.

Methods when working individually with a child

There are many texts which describe a range of therapeutic approaches when working with an individual child (for example, Smith and Pennells 1995). This section looks very briefly at some of the techniques.

Visualisation

Visualisation techniques allow children to create positive images, healthy thoughts and reduce anxiety. Visualisation or guided imagery can empower the child to develop their own internal ways of dealing with painful or disturbing feelings or fears. Then, by guiding their imagery, they can begin to substitute more positive visual memories and find inner resources for strength. The combination of imagination, fairy tales and metaphor creates a powerful tool for change.

Example

An adventure is described which takes place in a magical, mystery land where there are enchanting yellow trees sprinkled with sparkling strawberry-flavoured sweets and brightly coloured beautiful birds. There is however a large, deep river which separates the child from his mother *(who has died)* and a fierce, terrifying monster that guards the bridge, not letting anyone cross. *(The river is the barrier to the dead person and the monster represents the child's fears and scary thoughts!)* A magnificent, marvellous white eagle comes to help the child cross the river and be with their mother. *(The eagle symbolises inner strength that can soar above fears.)* Together the child and eagle create a spellbinding, cherishing cloak which protects the child and allows him to pass the monster unnoticed and cross the bridge. *(The cloak is faith in oneself.)* The magnificent, marvellous eagle can be called upon at any time when visiting the magical, mystery land.

Role-playing techniques

Bereaved children who are struggling often have great difficulty expressing their feelings directly. Shock, rage and terror often arise from how the person died, and block the flow of feelings.

Plays, puppets, clay, drawings, sand trays and dolls' houses are valuable tools which allow younger children to project raw feelings more openly.

Telling their 'story'

Encourage a child by sharing your curiosity, asking questions which will help them tell their version of what happened.

For example:

'How did you find out about dad's death?'

'What do you think happened when Jess was taken into hospital?'

We sometimes give children blank pages which look like the frames from rolls of film. They are encouraged to draw out their understanding of what happened frame by frame. They are later encouraged to think of the film as a video which can be rewound and the tape put away. See page 108 for more information about this activity. For children struggling with intrusive images it can give them a sense of mastery over the continual replaying of traumatic images.

Filmstrips are a useful technique to help children convey their story.

Music/creative writing/poetry

These are powerful forms of communicating, especially for teenagers (see, for example, Natasha's poem for her father on page 90 and Ryan's letter to his mother on page 43).

Activity books

Some individual work may take the form of following a structured framework as set out in activity books: for example, *Muddles, Puddles and Sunshine* (Crossley 2000). *Fire in my Heart, Ice in my Veins* is an excellent workbook aimed at teenagers (Traisman 1992).

Plays, puppets, clay, drawings, sand trays and dolls' houses are valuable tools which allow younger children to project raw feelings more openly.

Five More Minutes

If the person who died could come back for just five minutes, what would you tell them?

If you could come back just for five minutes.

If you could come back just for five minutes ...

You could write a message on some paper and attach it to a helium balloon, and let the balloon go.

Write a message on the tag.

30

It can sometimes be helpful to let children verbalise what they would ask or tell someone if they could come back ... just for five minutes.

Cognitive restructuring

This can be an effective way to help a child to address thinking which has become very rigid or guilt-laden.

Example (a child who was full of rage and felt abandoned following his father's death from alcohol abuse)

Child: *'My dad was a really bad man, I hate him!'*

The practitioner may begin by getting the child to think of things they believe are signs of an 'OK' dad.

Child: *'Someone who is kind, goes to work, works hard, takes care of their family, plays with their children, doesn't hit them if they are naughty, takes the children on holiday'.*

Practitioner: *'So your dad didn't do any of these things?'*

Child: *'Well I suppose he did work hard and we always had nice holidays and I suppose he did always ring us to say goodnight if he was away working ...'*

Practitioner: *'Why do you think he used to ring?'*

Cognitive work obviously builds and builds until the child and practitioner have achieved a more balanced set of beliefs which the child can hold on to, to ease them through (in this particular case) the pain of rejection generated by the father's excessive drinking.

Example (following several sessions of cognitive-based therapy a child may express his beliefs in a more balanced way)

Child: *'I am so angry that my dad carried on drinking – he can't have been thinking straight – I know he cared about me because he used to call me to say goodnight when he was away working – we also had a great holiday together in France. I miss him so much it hurts. I have made a special book of photos of dad and me to remind me of the good times'.*

Memory work

Memory books, memory boxes, photos, videos and tape recordings can all be useful in helping a child to retain a healthy continuing bond. Creating a box of memories that includes 'linking objects' can provide symbolic representations on which the child can focus and clarify their feelings. (Memory work is described at greater length in Chapter 4.)

Case study Laura (aged 8)

'It's not the answer that enlightens, but the question.'

Eugene Ionesco

Laura's mother died last year of an accidental drugs overdose. Laura had a very unsettled life because of her parents' drug use and both of them had served sentences in prison. Before her mother died, Laura had been relocated via social services (due to concerns over neglect) to live with her step-grandmother. At the family assessment it became clear that Laura found it very difficult to speak openly and had a confused story of her mother's death. The practitioners felt that Laura and her older sister would gain a lot from coming to a residential weekend, but that Laura might find it difficult to tell her story to other children. They also felt that her mourning was complicated by the alleged earlier neglect and repeated separations from her mother.

Laura worked with a practitioner for six fortnightly sessions, focusing on her life story and on her self-esteem, slowly building up a picture of her understanding of her mother's death. After the sessions she was much more able to talk about her mother and about the pain she felt when her mother was in prison. The sessions also helped Laura to build a picture of her mother which was less dominated by the family's drug culture of recent years. It was now 10 months since her mother's death. She was enthusiastic about meeting others at Camp Winston, which she subsequently attended with her sister and grandmother around the first anniversary of her mother's death.

Case study Mark (aged 5)

A year ago Mark's father murdered his mother at home before killing himself. Mark now lives with his maternal grandmother. Even before the deaths, Mark is thought to have witnessed a lot of violence at home. The day after his mother's murder he moved house and school to live with his grandmother. The assessment team felt that direct entry to a residential weekend was not an

Memory books, memory boxes, photos, videos and tape recordings can all be useful in helping a child to retain a healthy continuing bond.

After several sessions of individual work, Ben was able to share how lonely he felt being 'the only child alive in my family'.

appropriate intervention at the moment. Mark and his grandmother appeared traumatised by such significant losses all at once. Mark's grandmother was very willing to work with us in supporting Mark as well as she could. We offered both Mark and his grandmother a course of six sessions – four separately and two together – to explore how they had both been affected by these deaths. Their sessions included some trauma work to help with intrusive and recurrent violent images and nightmares experienced by both Mark and his grandmother: it was the grandmother who actually found the bodies of her daughter and son-in-law. Individual work is continuing, however, and we hope that some time in the future Mark will come to camp to remember both his parents and that he will be accompanied by his grandmother. It is thought that this may be more appropriate when Mark makes the transition from infant to junior school.

Case study   Ben (aged 10)

Ben's older sister Amy (11) died from cystic fibrosis. Amy's health had been slowly deteriorating and the adults in the family shared an understanding that Amy could die soon. Understandably, Amy's deteriorating condition and hopes for a heart and lung transplant became the focus for family, friends and school. Ben was perceived by the family as not particularly caring about his sister, often picking arguments and jealous of the treats that came her way. When she died Ben showed marked mood swings – he was often withdrawn and emotionally distant and on other occasions he would get angry and abusive, over seemingly small things. His parents tried hard to support him but became bewildered when he said things like: 'You wish Amy had lived and not me!' Ben's behaviour at school was becoming a problem and his academic performance declining. The school suggested that the family make contact with Winston's Wish. The parents were initially reluctant, but decided to proceed because Ben's behaviour was becoming intolerable. Having assessed the family it was felt that Ben needed some space to really articulate the build-up of feelings and thoughts that he harboured in relation to his position within the family and, more recently, his grief following Amy's death. He was offered six sessions of individual work. On the fifth session Ben agreed that it would be good to share his 'Ben book' (prepared during the sessions) with his mum and dad. The book represented Ben's journey over the past five years and on one page he described in detail how lonely it was to be 'the only child alive in my family'. It followed with a long list of things he wanted to remember about his sister and a moving letter which he had written to Amy ('up in heaven'). We invited Ben's parents to write a letter to their son which picked up some of the dilemmas he had expressed in the book. The parents brought the letter to the last session – dad shared their thoughts out loud and it was later added to the final pages of 'Ben's book'. The parents had sensitively communicated their love for him and acknowledged that they had unwittingly not sensed his isolation, particularly in the last three years. They ended their letter to Ben powerfully by saying that they are still a family of four and that Ben remained their 'number 1 son'. Two months later the family attended Camp Winston and remained actively involved with Winston's Wish for a further three years.

'Healthy grief does not involve a denial of the past any more than it involves a refusal to embrace the future.'

Ann Kaiser Stearn

Case management meetings and clinical supervision

Practitioners work daily with grieving families: being alongside intense feelings and hearing many stories of death is part of a normal working week. The emotional and psychological impact of this should not be underestimated: team and individual supervision is one way of providing support and monitoring practitioners' work. We have tried various models of clinical and personal supervision. Different practitioners prefer individual supervisors who understand their particular professional background so, as we have developed into a multi-disciplinary team, we have been challenged to develop an appropriate model that suits everyone. We currently have a model which gives practitioners a choice of external supervisors according to their professional training. This has the advantage of supporting the clinical specialisms within the team, and allows practitioners the opportunity to choose someone they feel they can relate to. It means that monthly supervision sessions are provided off site: practitioners need time to travel to and from their sessions and there is a cost implication.

Case management meetings take place weekly. These are a form of team supervision in which practitioners discuss the families they are working with and, where relevant, canvass opinion on cases they feel are more complicated. New referrals are processed by the Family Services manager and administrator at a weekly allocations meeting.

'It takes a long time to become young.' Pablo Picasso

An additional
consideration in
offering individual
work is the
importance of
presenting
the service as
non-pathological,
balancing the need
for 'therapy' while
accepting grief as a
'normal' reaction
to loss.

Referral onto specialist mental health services

This book is written from a UK perspective. In North America there is an impressive network of 'not for profit' child bereavement centres. These services are largely based on an established 'peer support' model pioneered by the Dougy Center in Portland, Oregon. The extensive range of open-ended group programmes run by the Dougy Center is available to families who choose to attend a programme if it seems to fit their needs. If family members need a more therapeutic mental health intervention, the Center provides a list of approved independent therapists who may be able to help. This means that referral outside the Dougy programme is not uncommon and, in turn, means that perhaps less emphasis is placed on the assessment process as described in Chapter 3. It also means that families will have to access funds or insurance cover to pay for individual work.

The provision of individual therapeutic work can be a costly intervention for community-based bereavement services. However, in the UK, referring on can be problematic for two key reasons. Firstly, many families do not have health care insurance to fund this intervention. Even if they do, most mental health professionals work within the statutory sector and are therefore unable to see patients privately. Secondly, even if a referral is made to child and adolescent mental health teams (CAMHS), professionals are currently so stretched that they often have long waiting lists and will only see children or parents who present with extreme symptoms. While the proposed National Service Framework for Children (Department of Health 2003) offers some hope, because of these constraints to date we have tried to develop a service which can accommodate families whatever their grief journey. Only in rare cases, where there are severe mental health issues (outlined on page 139), would we refer a family on. This approach requires a major investment in terms of professional staff and needs strict criteria for individual work so that it does not become untenable, resulting in the long waiting lists which are currently found in the statutory sector services.

An additional consideration in offering individual work is the importance of presenting the service as non-pathological, balancing the need for 'therapy' while accepting grief as a 'normal' reaction to loss. This requires our practitioners to tolerate a juxtaposition which is balanced somewhere between self-help and mental health models – with the overall intention of promoting the well-being of parents and children.

This chapter has considered the place of individual work in a community-based child bereavement service. Adults and children can express their grief and mourning in many different ways. The differences in intensity and longevity are caused sometimes by personality factors, sometimes by situational or social factors, and at other times by frightening deaths or multiple or long-term debilitating illnesses (Sanders 1999).

Whatever the reason, there are times when an individual responds in a way that does not appear helpful to the individual or in a way that is not acceptable to the family or community in which they live. Very often these complications in the mourning process initially need an individual approach to maximise the benefits of a group intervention. Various different techniques have been presented, as well as a guide to the issues which may help a practitioner to recognise the factors which indicate complicated mourning.

'Not everything that is faced can be changed, but nothing can be changed until it is faced.'

James Baldwin

Chapter Seven

Beyond the rough rock

Offering a specialist group for families
bereaved by suicide

In this chapter, we consider the particular needs of those bereaved
through suicide and describe a group intervention which builds on the
therapeutic processes described in Chapter 5 while responding to the
particular needs arising for families when suicide is the cause of death.

'For years we'd coped
with his dreadful
mood swings – one
minute everything
would be OK, the
next he'd be
smashing things. I
admit when I first
heard he'd died I
thought: "Thank God
it's all over". Of course
it wasn't all over, but
I did feel relieved
that none of us were
in danger any more.'

Karen

Coping with a double blow

A death through suicide delivers a double blow to families – not only do they have to cope with a sudden, often unexpected death, but they also have to deal with the way their relative has died. They may feel very alone in their grief, but sadly more people are affected by suicide than most of us realise. In the UK, on average, someone takes their own life every 80 minutes (Wertheimer 2001). Suicide accounts for 9% of all the children we see in Gloucestershire. Suicide is the second most frequent cause of death mentioned in calls to our Family Line and accounts for 20% of calls. It is estimated that in the UK 50,000 family members are 'profoundly' affected by suicide each year (Royal College of Psychiatrists 2003). For every suicide it is claimed that, on average, six people suffer intense grief (Clark and Goldney 2000). With around 5,000 suicides a year in England and Wales, the impact of suicide is immense.

The death of someone important can cause great grief and sadness, whatever the cause of death. However, families bereaved by suicide are recognised as significantly at risk of complicated grief. They can often face agonising questions and intrusive public scrutiny when they are feeling confused and vulnerable. For both adults and children, it can take a long time to trust others again, and this includes placing trust in a child bereavement service provider.

Those affected by the death of someone by suicide are often plagued by self-blame and thoughts of 'what if' and 'if only'. This is part of the process of trying to make sense of the suicide death and attempting to curb the prevailing sense of powerlessness. When a child dies by suicide, parents have to deal with the additional issue of responsibility. If they were aware of their child's intentions, and their efforts to stop the child were unsuccessful, then they have to deal with the weight of feeling responsible in some way. If there is a difference in the grief of parents whose children died by suicide, and that of parents whose children died of other causes, it is the degree to which parents feel guilt and are blamed – by themselves and others – for what happened (Silverman 2000).

The 'tyranny of silence'

Because a death through suicide is one of the most painful and complicated types of bereavement families can experience, families are left asking many unanswerable questions. Families feel isolated within their own community as a result of the stigma attached to this type of death, even though the numbers of people affected by suicide are significant (Hawton and Simkin 2003). Individuals within families are left isolated as the pain is felt too great to bear and permission to talk and share thoughts and feelings is not given. Many families have difficulties being open about their thoughts and feelings after a bereavement through natural or accidental causes. With the added dimensions of secrecy, shame, guilt and distortion associated with bereavement through suicide, communication within families is further hindered. The result is individuals and families who feel alone in their grief, and powerless to mobilise the support they need to negotiate the path ahead.

Bereavement through suicide clearly has unique elements that warrant specialist attention. Placing children and parents bereaved by suicide in a heterogeneous group of bereaved individuals 'represents a potential obstacle that could over-ride the anticipated benefits of group membership' (Webb 1993). Therefore, we have developed a programme of services for families where suicide is the cause of death. The programme specifically aims to recognise and address the trauma and stigma surrounding this type of bereavement.

In order to tackle the 'tyranny of silence', the programme is founded on the belief that suicide deaths are best addressed by an intervention that incorporates both a focus on the individual and the family. For many family members it is the first time they have been with others and heard the word 'suicide' spoken openly and without apology. It is usually also the first opportunity for children and parents to share their experience and have their feelings and thoughts acknowledged and validated.

'The day after, I was walking around as if nothing had happened. It couldn't be real, could it? Surely I would wake up and find it was a dream ...'

Mick

Aims of the residential group

The aims of the programme for children and parents are very similar to those for Camp Winston and also for all the services we deliver. They are underpinned by our primary clinical objectives (see page 33).

Specific aims for this group are to provide opportunities to:
- meet others who are also bereaved through suicide
- talk about the death and the specific circumstances of the suicide in a safe and accepting environment
- explore the reasons why someone might take their own life
- understand that they are not responsible for the death
- acknowledge and express a range of powerful feelings
- remember the person who has died, and acknowledge both positive and difficult characteristics and events
- explore positive strategies for coping with distress and difficulties by developing personal resources.

80

In the UK, on average, someone takes their own life every 80 minutes.

'Simply knowing we were not alone made a huge difference.'

Jill

Who attends?

The group for families bereaved by suicide is a stand-alone intervention and not purely a forerunner or preparation activity for attendance at Camp Winston, although some families who have participated in the suicide group are also subsequently offered the opportunity to experience Camp Winston where they will focus on the person rather than issues about how they died.

All the families who join the group have been bereaved by suicide and all members of the family will know this by the time they attend.

We recommend a group size of no more than 20 children and around 10–12 parents. The children are allocated to small groups according to their ages: there are between four and six children in each small group.

This family intervention involves children and parents being divided into separate groups, but they take place in the same venue. This is important as time is built into the programme to allow children and parents to join together to share some of their experiences in a structured way. For a multitude of reasons, communication within families bereaved by suicide is often fragmented. The focus on opportunities to be together and take part in joint activities is not necessarily about talking about the suicide or their thoughts and feelings. Rather, the aim is to facilitate time (such as meal times) when family members can be together and have a positive experience of communicating openly.

The team

The residential group is co-ordinated by four members of staff, two taking responsibility for the parents' group and two for the children's group. For the children, each small group is led by an experienced member of staff, assisted by two volunteers who have received additional specialised training on issues associated with bereavement through suicide. For the parents, the staff co-ordinators will usually have the support of two or three of these volunteers. A practical helper offers support with the day-to-day running of both the groups.

The role of the team in facilitating effective group work is described in Chapter 5.

The venue

Because the programme is residential and spans two days for both parents and children, we use a venue where family members can stay together overnight and meet for some meals.

The venue needs to have:
*   sufficient rooms for families to stay together overnight
*   rooms for the staff and volunteers
*   a mixture of small group rooms and two rooms large enough to accommodate all the children and all the parents
*   a room large enough to accommodate all participants
*   a dining room and kitchen
*   sole use during the group programme
*   space to let off steam outside
*   a therapeutic atmosphere and attractive surroundings.

Preparation and planning

Great care goes into considering the programme for the group and into considering the needs of those attending. Even after running over 10 groups specifically for those bereaved by suicide, we still try to make small improvements to the programme that will further enhance the quality of the service and ensure that practice relates to a clear theoretical model.

Summary of the programme

While the group experience has significant differences to the Camp Winston programme described in Chapter 5, it still aims to mirror a non-pathological model.

The format for the children's group involves a combination of small group work and whole group activities. As at Camp Winston, activities such as 'telling the story of what happened' seem to work best in relatively small groups where the children are of similar ages and where group leaders can focus their attention on individuals. In this way trust is fostered and an environment of intimacy grows which supports the sharing of personal, difficult information. Other larger group sessions – such as 'talking about suicide' – mean that participants can benefit from the thoughts, ideas and questions of a larger number of people affected by similar circumstances.

As the programme shows, the format for the parents' group is similar to the parents' programme at Camp Winston but also incorporates sessions which focus specifically on the issues associated with a death by suicide.

There are specific times in the programme – beginnings and endings of each day – that are facilitated times for families simply to be together having fun and relaxing.

'For months I thought it was all my fault for suggesting a divorce. Meeting the others enabled me to understand that I cannot be responsible for his death any longer.'
Chris

For a multitude of reasons, communication within families bereaved by suicide is often fragmented.

Programme for residential group for children bereaved through suicide

Day one

9.30	Families arrive
10.15	Welcome and introductions Rocky rocks Outline of programme Warm-up exercise
10.45	Parents and children move to their meeting rooms
10.50	Introductions to the children's team Memory table and lighting the candle Getting to know you games
12.00	Lunch
12.45	Large group work – talking about suicide
13.15	Small group work – telling the story of what happened
14.30	Break
15.00	Large group work – exploring difficult feelings
16.00	Small group work – debriefing the last activity
16.30	Break
16.45	Candlelight ceremony Coat of armour
17.30	Break
17.45	Preparation for sharing with parents
18.00	Sharing – parents and children
18.30	Supper
19.00	Free time with optional activities

19.30	Story-teller
21.00	Bedtime for younger children
22.00	Bedtime for older children

Day two

8.30	Breakfast and packing
9.30	Welcome back Warm-up activity
9.50	Parents and children go to separate rooms
10.00	Large group work – exploring 'why' Jenga
11.00	Break
11.30	Large group work – developing alternative coping strategies
12.30	Large group – beginning to say goodbye Wool web
13.00	Lunch Activities
14.00	Closing ceremony – with parents
15.00	Event ends

Welcome and introductions

Careful attention is paid to welcoming families as they arrive: we recognise that most are probably feeling highly anxious. Families are registered and shown to their family rooms where they can briefly settle before having refreshments.

With parents and children together, staff and volunteers introduce the two-day programme. On all our groups, we use the metaphor of 'rocky rocks'. It is acknowledged that the two days are likely to be a challenge for everyone at times. However, there will also probably be times when they will have a laugh or remember something special about the person who died. The rocky rocks concept uses three stones – a smooth, rounded pebble; a jagged, sharp, small rock; and a polished gemstone – to represent the different types of memories or feelings people might have about the person who has died. The smooth pebble is intended to represent ordinary, everyday memories or feelings. The sharp rock is intended to represent more difficult times and memories or feelings, perhaps a reminder of the way the person chose to die. The gemstone – smooth, bright and polished – is intended to represent really special memories or feelings. This activity can help people look beyond the 'rough, sharp rock' (for many this represents how the person died and the pain of rejection) and to find a balance between the good, difficult and everyday memories that are a natural part of family life.

We then read out a story called *There's No Such Thing as a Dragon* (Kent 1984) which illustrates the fact that families find some things difficult to talk about openly. However, even if ignored, sometimes the issues grow bigger and bigger (like the dragon in the story) causing problems if family members do not have the opportunity to share their thoughts and feelings with each other.

After a warm-up activity for fun, we then explain that children and parents will be doing separate activities for the rest of the day, but will see each other just before the evening meal when a brief organised sharing session will take place.

The programme for children

For the full timetable, see pages 160–161, Programme for residential group for children bereaved through suicide. The main activities are described in this section.

Day one

Introductions

The children are introduced to the adults (staff co-ordinators, group leaders and volunteers) who will be working with them throughout the two days. Children are asked to say their name and who they have come to the group to remember. Then the children are invited to gather around the memory table and a candle is lit. The memory table is a designated area in the children's activity room where they place a photo of the person they are remembering, plus a memento if they wish. This provides an opportunity for the children to focus together on the reason why they are at the group and to remember their important person who died. It also gives the children a symbolic opportunity to reflect quietly, with the candle and their photo providing them with a visual image to strengthen the connection.

'Getting to know you' games and challenge activities

Children then take part in several energetic games and activities which enable them to get to know each other and to build trust within the group. For more information see 'Winston's wilderness challenge' in Chapter 5. These activities are designed to build group cohesion and to enhance self-esteem.

Talking about suicide

This session is a facilitated discussion with the whole group which aims to get the children talking about suicide generally. Everyone sits in a large circle and within the circle is a large piece of paper and lots of felt-tipped pens. The discussion is prompted by asking the group to say all the different words and phrases they know of to describe 'suicide' and the different ways people can die by suicide. As children voice their ideas, they are encouraged to write their word or phrase on the paper in the centre of the group.

'Until Gill and Luke went to the group, I think they thought they were the only children whose daddy had died in this way. Gill was able to express her feelings and ask questions that were obviously on her mind. As a bereaved parent I only want to do what is best for my children and myself. But it is very difficult to cope with my own loss as well as the great loss the children have had.'
Parent

Some of the words and phrases that children and young people use are 'topped himself', 'killed themselves', 'ended it all', 'took his own life', 'done himself in', 'chosen to take their own life', 'committed suicide' and 'suicide'.

The co-ordinator can prompt discussion about the words by asking the following questions:

- Are certain words better than others?
- How does it feel to use those words?

If ignored, sometimes the issues grow bigger and bigger – like the dragon in the story.

'At times sorrow
floods my mind –
and drowns me.'
Jola created this
moving artwork and
quote to express her
grief following her
partner's death by
suicide. 'I think that
children surviving a
parental suicide have
the most terribly
complex grief …
furthermore it is
compounded by the
grief, guilt and
spiritual abyss which
their surviving
parent is left alone
to climb out of.'
Jola

- How does it feel when someone else says the words?
- Do you talk with friends, family or teachers using these words?

The co-ordinator brings the discussion to a close by summarising the different elements raised and acknowledging the difficulties we have in talking about death – particularly a death where the person took their own life.

The co-ordinator links this to the next activity and explains that there will now be the opportunity to share our story with others in smaller groups.

Telling the story of what happened

In this session, the children are asked to draw pictures that represent each of the following four stages:

- What was life like *before* your relative took their own life?
- *How* did they die?
- What was family life like *after* they died?
- What is life like *now*?

The children are then asked if they would like to share what they have drawn with the others in their group. Everyone is encouraged to talk through their story. Older children sometimes prefer to skip the drawing stage, and simply tell their story verbally.

Exploring feelings

This session begins with a story which aims to provide information on the range of emotions associated with the death of someone important. The story needs to illustrate that different people often have different feelings in response to painful experiences.

After the story, the group is invited to describe the different feelings they have felt and also those they have seen in others. This session is facilitated in the large group. The group sits around a large piece of paper – the 'graffiti wall' – and members are given pens to record their ideas. After the session, the paper is mounted on the wall, and kept visible for the rest of the programme.

The next part of this session is a physical, largely non-verbal activity where children have the opportunity to work with clay while focused on a particular feeling. In this session, feelings such as anger, guilt, confusion and sadness are acknowledged as part of the process of grieving the loss of someone important. Initially children are asked to think about a feeling or feelings they have in relation to the person who died. They are given some clay and invited to use it and play with it and, if they wish, to make a shape or shapes that represent that feeling. We emphasise that this is not a competition to construct an object – it does not have to be recognisable as an object. They can just play with the clay, and feel it in their hands, while thinking about that emotion. Equally, if they prefer to make something recognisable they can. Some children continuously change the shape of the clay as they describe their feelings.

'I light a candle on my dad's birthday and on Christmas day.'

Towards the end of the session children are given a number of options for what they can do with their clay shape. For example, they can take it home, recycle it, they can throw it away, they can squash it, they can throw it noisily into a metal bin or they can choose to change it into something else.

Candlelight ceremony

The children have had opportunities up to this part of the programme to meet others, play games and participate in activities designed to help them get to know each other. They have shared their individual stories with each other, and have talked about and had opportunities to express their feelings. Now the focus turns to remembering the person who has died in a quiet, reflective mode. It is important for children to be able to access memories about the person who died and not just 'how' they died. Their memories are an integral component on which their self-identity is developed. Opportunities to remember are often reduced because of the stigma associated with deaths through suicide.

The process is similar to the ceremony described in Chapter 5. We explain that the next activity is a quiet time so they can reflect and remember the person who died.

The candlelight ceremony then follows the same format as on Camp Winston (see page 112).

Coat of armour

This is a brief activity which takes place after the candlelight ceremony. It is designed to offer children a concept or strategy for self-care when faced with difficult situations and difficult feelings. Children are introduced to the concept of a protective armour and invited to think about an imaginary protective shield that they can 'put on' when faced with difficult situations and feelings. We offer some

Children are invited to think about an imaginary protective shield that they can 'put on' when faced with difficult situations and feelings.

suggestions and ask them to think about what they would like their armour to look like. Once they can imagine it, we invite them to walk round the room wearing their shield – to practise what it feels like. They are then asked to take it off, and then put it back on again. They are reminded that this is a strategy they can use when faced with something they find difficult to do or difficult to cope with.

Joining together and sharing
A brief, energetic and fun game is played to facilitate, in a structured way, the parents' and children's groups joining together at the end of day one. After the game, a team member from the parents' group and one from the children's group briefly summarise activities from the first day.

'How do you tell a child their mum has died and that she decided to end it all? It didn't seem fair to burden them with it ... but then again I thought, above all, they now needed to be able to trust me completely.'
Bob

Organised evening activity for families
Families have their evening meal together. There are organised activities for those who want them, including a story-teller. Parents are also given the opportunity to have a relaxing foot, hand, neck and shoulder massage.

Parents take responsibility for the care of their children for the evening and bedtime process. Children know our bedtime rules in advance, which takes some pressure off parents and ensures uniformity across families. The co-ordinators meet for a debrief on the day, to consider the programme, the families and any issues arising.

Day two
Welcome back
Everyone gathers together for a warm-up activity and a broad outline of the day is given. A relevant story may be read. Once again the children's and parents' groups separate.

Exploring why someone might take their own life
The day begins with a review of day one. The review then links to a discussion of why someone might take their own life.

We begin by saying that as we start to talk about 'why' someone might take their own life it can leave us feeling like we're in the middle of a whirlpool. We ask the children to tell us what they know about whirlpools and link this to feelings such as lack of control and confusion. We draw a large whirlpool and then ask the group for any reasons they can think of why someone might take their own life. It is important that the language is generalised so the children do not feel they have to contribute personal, specific reasons. Instead, they can speculate more broadly on the reasons.

We bring the discussion to a close by summarising the many different reasons why someone might take their own life. Importantly, we emphasise that there is never just one reason. And the answers to the 'why?' question more often than not leave us feeling unsatisfied.

Jenga

The group is given a short introduction to this session which conveys that they will be looking at the different kinds of reasons that might lead someone to choose suicide.

We explain to the group that they will be told the story of a young boy's life. Positive and negative life events are included in this story (we try to include circumstances that are represented in the stories of the children in their group).

As negative or challenging life events are described, the two members of staff who are playing the game take turns to remove the Jenga blocks and place them on top of the structure. This process continues until the tower becomes so unsteady that it tumbles over. The group is asked to think about what caused the structure to collapse.

Worries pile up until the tower tumbles down …

We talk to the group about how this game can be seen as a metaphor for the challenges life can present. Life is made up of a range of events and circumstances – 'good'/positive and 'bad'/negative – with the negative ones often bringing balance and recognition to the positive ones. Often one brick will be seen as the main reason why the tower fell, whereas in reality there were a number of bricks that contributed. We explain how Jenga can be used to think about the way individuals deal, or don't deal, with difficult life events and how previous events and risk-taking behaviour may contribute to the suicidal risk and action that leads to death.

When using Jenga in this way, the two co-ordinators playing the game need to be aware of the script the narrator is using. The players need to ensure that the focus does not become the 'winning' of the game; rather they are facilitating a powerful metaphor. The tower needs to stay standing long enough for the narrator to tell most of the story leading up to the suicide. So, when the tower eventually tumbles, the narrator explains that this is the point when the character in the story took their own life.

It is important that those watching recognise that there is never just one event that causes someone to take their own life but that it can be any number of unresolved issues and pressures which finally became unbearable.

Developing alternative coping strategies

This discussion starts with a brief introduction about the importance of having problem-solving strategies and finding ways that help us deal with difficult times. To illustrate the concept we blow up a balloon and talk about the stress the balloon is under as it gets more and more air pushed into it. Eventually it pops! Then we blow up another balloon and release some air – talking about releasing pressure – and then blow it up a bit more. The balloon is able to keep taking more air in and not pop as long as, every now and then, some air is released. We suggest that this is just like us humans – we too need to look after ourselves.

Working in small groups, the children then generate ideas about the things they can do for themselves to help cope with problems and with feeling stressed.

The groups are then called together and the session concludes with a light-hearted activity which may help children to visualise and manage their worries. We give each child a bubble blowing kit, gather outside, and suggest that they think about any worries they have and blow them individually into the bubbles, and then watch the worries floating away.

First aid kits

In the small groups, and using some of the responses generated in the previous discussion, we talk about the concept of first aid kits. Children and young people can experience a wide range of emotions and behaviour when someone important to them has died. This activity aims to identify different ways of coping. One example might be: 'If I'm angry I can kick a ball in the garden'. The children are then encouraged to make tiny models: so, in this example, a 'ball' is made out of fimo (polymer clay modelling material) which is then fired. The symbolic objects become a series of prompts to remind them in the future of their ways of coping. The models are kept safe in a miniature decorated box – their first aid kit.

Saying goodbye to the group

To acknowledge the importance of saying goodbye and facilitating endings appropriately, this session provides the group with the opportunity to say positive things to each other and about each other. This is also the start of bringing the group to an end and gives the small groups a chance to start saying goodbye by acknowledging each other and what they enjoyed about the two days. One way of doing this is through the 'wool web' activity described in Chapter 5 (see page 115).

Closing ceremony

Children and parents come together for the closing ceremony. A fun game is played to facilitate this coming together in a structured way. Families are asked to sit together and share with each other the parts of the group that they had liked or felt they had learnt from. They are also asked to think of something they will take from the group. These comments are written down and placed on the wall. Two of the co-ordinators summarise and share these comments with the whole group. This is an opportunity for the co-ordinators, volunteers and families to acknowledge the achievements everyone has made over the past two days.

We then tell the group a story called *Apache Tear*. It is said that the stone known as the apache tear represents the tears cried by the families of Native Americans when their braves were killed in battle. When the stone is held in the palm of the hand it appears opaque (impenetrable by light) just as at times it seems difficult to imagine getting through some of the feelings of grief. When the stone is held up to the light we see that it is translucent. We explain that the light penetrates the stone but it remains clouded. In life it is possible to learn to live with your grief, though your life will always be affected by the death you have experienced.

The event finishes with the celebratory bearduation ceremony (see page 116) where each family is asked to come up to receive a Winston bear and receive acknowledgement and loud applause from the group.

'After attending the group I found I can live with his life and I can live with his death … I can go forward.'

Kathy, aged 15

Watch the worries floating away.

Programme for residential group for parents bereaved through suicide

Day one

9.30	Families arrive
10.15	Welcome and introductions Rocky rocks Outline of programme Warm-up exercise
10.45	Parents and children move to their meeting rooms
10.50	Introductions to the parents' team and programme Memory table and lighting the candle How am I feeling? Individual introductions
12.30	Lunch
13.30	Small group work – telling the story of what happened
15.00	Break
15.30	Large group work – exploring difficult feelings
16.30	Break
16.45	Candlelight ceremony
17.15	Time to reflect on the day
17.45	Break
18.00	Sharing – parents and children
18.30	Supper
19.00	Free time with optional activities

19.30	Story-teller Massage
21.00	Bedtime for younger children
22.00	Bedtime for older children

Day two

8.30	Breakfast and packing
9.30	Welcome back Warm-up activity
9.50	Parents and children go to separate rooms
10.00	Exploring 'why' Jenga
11.30	Break
11.45	Looking after yourself First aid kits
12.30	Beginning to say goodbye Wool web
13.00	Lunch Activities
14.00	Closing ceremony – with children
15.00	Event ends

'In some ways
Jack seemed less
bothered about the
way he died – he did
ask me, if he loved
him why did he do it.
I felt weary having
to explain it over and
over again. Eventually
he found a way of
understanding about
depression and now
his questions are
more about his dad
as a person.'

Kate

The programme for parents

For the full timetable, see pages 170–171, Programme for residential group for parents bereaved through suicide. We provide an abridged version here, as the therapeutic process is similar to that described in detail in Chapter 5.

Day one

Introductions

After the family introductions, parents go to their group room and the leaders facilitate a 'setting the scene' session. In this session, participants begin the process of getting to know each other. This can be done in a variety of ways. One simple method is for group members to draw a face or write a few words that describe how they are feeling at this moment. Group members often feel anxious, nervous and distressed – providing space to name these feelings right at the start of the group in a non-threatening, non-verbal way can allow some of the intensity of the feelings to disperse. It also gives group members a very clear message that others are feeling the same.

Group members are then asked to jot down a few facts about themselves on a piece of paper which they can use to help them when they introduce themselves to the group. The group co-ordinators facilitate this process by drawing out similarities which may emerge within the group.

The group is then introduced to the concept of the memory table where, if they wish, they can place their photograph. Co-ordinators have a heightened awareness that not all parents will have had a positive relationship with the person – a significant number may have had difficult or estranged relationships with the person who took their own life. Consequently, they may not wish to take part in activities which for them seem to be about remembering the person in a positive light or imply that they have certain feelings for them.

Lunch

The programme is designed so that the parents have a separate lunchtime from the children.

Telling the story of what happened

One of the co-ordinators starts by reading out the poem *The Elephant in the Room* by Terry Kettering (as cited in Grollman 1993). This reinforces the importance of

The Elephant in the Room

There's an elephant in the room,

It is large and squatting, so it's hard to get around it,

Yet we squeeze by with "How are you?" and "I'm fine",

And a thousand other forms of trivial chatter.

We talk about the weather,

We talk about work,

We talk about everything –

Except the elephant in the room.

There's an elephant in the room,

We all know it's there,

We are thinking about the elephant as we talk together,

It is constantly in our minds,

For, you see, it is a very big elephant,

It has hurt us all,

But we do not talk about the elephant in the room.

Oh please say her name,

Oh please say "Barbara" again.

Oh please let's talk about the elephant in the room,

For if we talk about her death,

Perhaps we can talk about her life?

Can I say "Barbara" to you and not look away?

For if I cannot, then you are leaving me

Alone …

In a room …

With an elephant …

by Terry Kettering

*Reprinted with permission from Bereavement Publishing, Inc
(+1 888 604 4673)*

'Ten years ago my
father killed himself
with a shotgun, and
I never got to ask
him why.'
Toni, aged 19

people telling their story and acknowledges that it is a very
common experience for those bereaved by suicide to feel they do
not have permission to do so with friends and family. This session is
vital in conveying the message that participants can find support
from others and can talk about what has come to be seen as
'unmentionable'. In sharing the details of the death participants are
enabled to put words to their experience, the very thing they try to
shield others from. In keeping the details of their experience to
themselves the trauma is perpetuated and the healing cannot begin.

Groups of up to four parents are formed, along with one or two
co-ordinators and volunteers. Where possible, parents are grouped
according to similar types of suicide or other common factors. Being
able to share their story with someone who shares elements of their
experience can help build trust and create a sense of reduced isolation. Each person
is encouraged to tell their story using a structure that includes details about what
was happening in their life before the death, the details of the death, life after the
death and what is happening in their life now. The co-ordinator's role is to model
effective listening and, where appropriate, to comment on the common threads
running through the stories.

The whole group then comes together to 'debrief' from the experience.
Participants are asked to share how they are feeling and to comment on how they
found the experience of telling their story.

Break

Where suicide is the cause of death, the experience of sharing individual stories
can be intensely emotional for participants and a scheduled break provides a
much-needed change of pace and energy.

Exploring feelings

A death by suicide leaves the survivors facing a complex mix of feelings and
thoughts (including those in the 'if only' category). The purpose of this session is to
acknowledge the difficult feelings – including guilt, anger, relief and shame – that
are commonly experienced. There is also time to explore the different aspects of the
relationship they had with the deceased. This activity follows a similar format to that
used in the children's programme (see page 164).

Closing

Time is given for the group to reflect on their experience of day one. The co-ordinators ask participants to comment on how they're feeling now and how they've found the experience. Parents then have a short break before getting back together with the children's group to share a summary of the day. The evening meal is taken together, followed by free time.

Day two

Welcome back

Children and parents begin the day together with a warm-up activity and a broad outline of the day ahead. A relevant story may be used, if appropriate.

Considering the question 'why?'

Considering why someone might take their own life can plague those who are bereaved by suicide. Significant time is devoted to considering the questions people are left asking: many people will not have had the opportunity to voice these questions before. As with the children's group, the game of Jenga is used to illustrate the issues. Jenga provides a simple metaphor to show how stressors build up in our lives. It shows how some people's outlook on life becomes skewed (demonstrated by the Jenga tower becoming so unbalanced that it collapses) and how some people see their only way out as taking their own life. This session is run in a similar way to the children's session (see page 167).

Looking after yourself

This session focuses on the importance of self-care and offers practical ways that participants can look after themselves physically and emotionally. We explain the concept of the first aid kit (see page 168) as a way of thinking about the different activities that can help nurture ourselves through the grieving process and more generally in life.

Following this exercise the delightfully illustrated children's story *Five Minutes' Peace* (Murphy 1998) is read out as a way of reinforcing the importance of getting time to ourselves and the difficulties family members face in finding time and space for themselves in their everyday lives. A small token gift of bubble bath is then handed out as one suggestion of an activity that can relax and replenish.

'At first I felt I should be easy on them because of all they'd been through. But what they really needed was to see that somehow we could get on with ordinary family life.'
Parent

Sharing the story of a relative's death by suicide can be hard to tell and hard to hear.

The session ends with a 'goodbye' activity such as the wool web (see page 115) as this is the last time that the parents will be alone as a group. The children and parents join together for the closing ceremony.

Team debrief

After the families have left, the co-ordinators and volunteers from the children's and parents' groups meet together to debrief about their personal experiences of the groups and to give feedback on family issues. The programme itself is reviewed formally about 10 days later using a structured evaluation format.

'Now we can look at his photo and think about him as a person. He will always be part of our family ... regardless of how he died.'

Issues that may arise

Of course, as noted before, not every group runs perfectly smoothly, however carefully planned and executed the programme may be. Some of the issues that may occur and therefore need to be considered are listed in Chapter 5 (see pages 118 and 129).

Follow-up with families

We telephone families within 10 days to ask how they have been as a family, to find out about any difficulties or challenges they have encountered and to arrange a follow-up visit. The purpose of the visit is to provide the family with an opportunity to reflect on their experience. Each person is also given some individual time to talk privately about their experience of the weekend, and how life has been for them since the group.

This chapter has explored our response to families bereaved through suicide and outlines a residential group intervention. Three key points are raised:

- **Bereavement through suicide may be best addressed in a group setting if all those attending have been bereaved in the same way.**
- **The nature of a bereavement by suicide lends itself to a whole family intervention.**
- **Co-ordinators need to be sensitive to the often ambivalent memories participants may hold of the person who has died.**

Suicide accounts for 20% of calls to the Family Line.

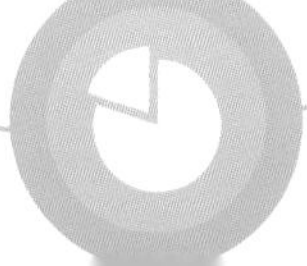

'The life of every person who dies
needs to be commemorated if we
are to teach young people that all
lives have value.'

Sandra Fox

Chapter Eight

School – the constant carer?

Enabling the school community to respond positively to a death

In this chapter, we emphasise the crucially important role a child bereavement service has in supporting schools after the death of a pupil, pupil's parent or sibling, or indeed the death of a staff member. School life can represent a familiar and constant environment, and a child needs to feel that their grief is acknowledged and can be expressed in this setting. The effects of bereavement on academic performance and behaviour are well documented (Holland 2001). It is important that head teachers have the information they need to support the children, parents and staff directly involved.

'Kind words can be short and easy to speak but their echoes are truly endless.'

Mother Teresa

A shared responsibility

Not surprisingly the vast majority of children referred to Winston's Wish attend either a primary (46%) or secondary (40%) school. It is therefore essential that we develop a respectful and collaborative relationship with our colleagues in education.

Over the past 10 years we have approached this in a number of different ways. In the early years we employed a teacher who had a natural affinity with school life and of the pressurised environment many teachers operate within. In his paper, Gisborne (1995) identified some key observations on the relationships that need to be fostered to support a bereaved child in their school environment. The issues raised are endorsed in an excellent government report which describes good practice guidance on promoting children's mental health within the early years and in school settings (Department for Education and Employment 2001).

While there has been a growth of 'death education' initiatives to help teachers feel more confident about this 'taboo' subject, teachers seem to value the opportunity of having support *when* a death actually affects their school. Although most schools are keen to respond positively, they also seem to value the fact that they themselves can refer on to a community agency. Therefore a *shared* responsibility involving the family, the child bereavement service and the school appears to offer the best approach for both the bereaved child and the school community (L Rowling 2003).

Working in partnership with schools

Building a meaningful partnership between schools and a community-based bereavement service will take time to evolve.

Initially, our clinical work involved spending time with teachers, facilitating staff meetings and providing outreach work in school. This led us to develop a manual which sets out a strategy for schools (Gisborne et al 1995). The manual covers three key areas:

- a resource pack for schools affected by the death of a pupil
- a resource pack for schools affected by the death of a pupil's parent or sibling
- a resource pack for schools affected by the death of a teacher or other staff member.

Each resource pack gives ideas on:
- informing staff and governors
- informing pupils and parents
- special considerations for sudden or traumatic circumstances.

The packs include sample letters, case histories and practical ideas, such as guidelines for an assembly. All are deliberately simple and easy to use. The pressure on head teachers is immense so we recognise that they need resources to access easily as soon as a death happens. Often a head or deputy head will first call the Family Line where we can complete a phone assessment followed by preliminary guidance and information relevant to the particular experience of their school. If a school community can be helped to feel confident in handling one death, this provides invaluable learning should future deaths occur. While we occasionally facilitate 'Inset' training days when requested, we put our main emphasis on providing services that can respond within 24 hours of a school contacting us about a recent death.

In Gloucestershire the service is now well recognised within the school community. Most schools know and trust the service for a variety of reasons:
- The majority of schools have had a child who has benefited from the Winston's Wish programme. Over 2,500 children were referred over a 10-year period.
- Schools are keen to make direct contact with us in the event of a pupil's death. While rare, a child's death remains the most challenging death which can fragment all aspects of the school community.
- We have helped a number of local schools to develop memorial projects to remember people who have died.
- Children choose to do educational projects about Winston's Wish. For example, one woodwork project made a money box and a business studies project looked at how the charity raises funds.
- Many children suggest Winston's Wish as the beneficiary of school fundraising activities.
- Whenever possible we will try to go to a school assembly and thank children for their fundraising, which also gives us an opportunity to talk with pupils about our work and engage them in exploratory discussions about death and related issues.

'Emily, a pupil of mine, returned to school today. She had been off for two weeks after her brother died. I didn't like to mention it in case it upset her.'
Winston's Wish Family Line, April 2002

This was a teacher who phoned the Family Line to talk about a 15-year-old pupil who had been absent from school following her brother's death by carbon monoxide poisoning. The teacher had initially instructed the tutor group 'not to mention it'. The teacher returned to school the next day and apologised to Emily for not talking about her brother the day before. After that they chatted frequently and Emily subsequently asked her teacher to read out a poem she wrote for her brother at his memorial service. It would seem that the honesty of her instinctive apology meant a lot to both of them. All the teacher needed was timely support to give her confidence that she could respond as a respectful human being, genuinely concerned for a pupil under her care.

Children choose to do educational projects about Winston's Wish. For example, one pupil made a memory box as a woodwork project.

- With parental permission, we write to schools before and after key interventions such as Camp Winston or individual work. This alerts staff to work we have done with a bereaved pupil and the role the school can have in continuing this work.
- We have developed a partnership scheme with school nurses who provide therapeutic services in school under the supervision of a Winston's Wish practitioner (see page 189).

It is not uncommon for schools to have bereavement videos and books and other resources on their shelves (for example, *Wise Before the Event* (Yule and Gold 1993) or *Good Grief* (Ward and Associates 1993) are both excellent resources). In an ideal world such resources will have already supported in-service training initiatives. However, when a crisis occurs, most head teachers seem to prefer to telephone immediately and engage in action planning which is specific to the current challenge. A trusting relationship is crucial as our practitioners may need to ask penetrating questions to establish the impact of this particular death, at this particular time, for this particular school. The practitioner will usually follow up the conversation by sending sample letters and other support material from the resource packs by e-mail or fax. We may also send through simple checklists and can offer confidential support to key staff.

We do not generally recommend textbooks at this time: what is required is a practical, meaningful and rapid response to the immediate crisis. The head teacher may also be shocked and feel vulnerable, and is therefore unlikely to have the concentration or time to read dense text during the crisis itself. Any suggestion to do so may only create or heighten a possible sense of inadequacy. Everyone is anxious to 'do the right thing' when a tragedy occurs. The practitioner will try to boost the head's confidence to cope, and reassure them that they know their school best. It is also acknowledged that the head teacher can retain an effective leadership role at the same time as knowing that they are a human being wrestling with their own feelings and emotions.

We aim to ensure that the school community feels it has pulled together, worked as a team and included everyone at a time when it could inadvertently create a blaming, distant and potentially divisive team.

The case example opposite demonstrates how one Gloucestershire school worked with us after the very sudden death of a pupil.

Case study Child in Year 8 dies: one school's story

A deputy head of a local secondary school called to say that a child in Year 8 (aged 13) had died very suddenly from a previously undiagnosed heart defect. The call lasted 30 minutes. The practitioner established key details which would help to structure our response. As with any assessment it was vital to understand the impact of this particular death, at this particular time, for this particular school in this particular community. The deputy explained that the head teacher was absent at a conference and was not due back for two days. However, she explained that the head had already been informed and he had asked the deputy to ring Winston's Wish for advice. The phone call broadly focused on the following issues:

- It emerged that the child had complained of headaches at school the previous day. 'It was winter and many children were under the weather.' However, the deputy head believed that the pupil's teacher now appeared to feel a sense of responsibility because she had not noticed anything unusual.
- The deputy head also explained that today was the day of the long-awaited and popular school disco. The pupils were very excited and the deputy head was unsure if it would be disrespectful to allow the event to go ahead.
- The deputy head wanted feedback on a letter she had drafted to inform parents. She also asked for guidance on how to tell the class involved and then the whole school.
- Finally discussions turned to the child's sibling who was not in school today. The deputy head expressed her dilemma about how to contact the family, explaining: 'I don't want to be intrusive at a time like this'.

Later we agreed to e-mail guidelines for a school assembly and also sent through template letters which could be personalised by the school. The practitioner arranged with the deputy head to come to the school to help facilitate a staff meeting. A discussion took place on who would be the most appropriate staff to attend. They also discussed ways to include the wider staff team, such as the dinner time staff, cleaners and office staff who would also be affected by the death and would have a part to play in the school's strategy. The staff meeting was arranged for the following day, at lunchtime. It took the form of a debrief to check everyone's understanding of what had happened and their associated

'The liaison role Winston's Wish had with the school was very valuable – if other children in class and the teachers can be given the confidence to acknowledge the death, then many feelings of shame/abnormality can be avoided.'
Feedback from parent, Service Evaluation 2003

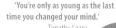

'You're only as young as the last time you changed your mind.'
Timothy Leary

The children generated some really creative ideas to honour the memory of their friend.

thoughts, feelings and behaviour as a consequence. The staff were available for 45 minutes. Ideally, more time is needed for a debrief, but everyone needs to be sensitive to the school curriculum and environment. Two school governors, including a parent governor, were also present. The session involved a problem-solving approach to develop a mutually agreed action plan. The teachers and governor agreed that they would:

- hold a special memorial service in six weeks
- develop a plan to offer on-going support to the sibling throughout their remaining years at school and in their transition to further/higher education
- create a large memory box for children to post messages and memories (this would later be given to the parents of the child who died, possibly at the memorial service)
- develop a pebble pond water feature: each child in the class would be invited to paint a pebble with a symbol that reminded them of their classmate
- ask the pupils if they had any further ideas (not surprisingly they had lots!)
- agree to hold a review meeting with staff in 2–3 months to feed back on the school's response, any lessons learnt and reflect on what they felt had gone well.

We then explained that the Winston's Wish support programme would be available for the pupil's brother and parents. We gave all the teachers information about our Family Line and encouraged them to telephone the helpline if they had any queries which may emerge over time.

We spoke to both the head and deputy head in the lead-up to the memorial service. The children had generated some really creative ideas to honour the memory of their friend. The staff group spoke warmly of the closeness they felt in school on the day of the memorial service. The bereaved parents were nervous about attending 'in case they became too upset'. However, the pupil's year tutor made sure they were fully involved with the event and had visited them on four occasions to bring them mementos and messages from school. The parents later told us that 'the school had been brilliant'.

Sadly, later in the same year, the school had to face further tragedy.

A sixth former died in a road traffic accident. They did call the Family Line, primarily to touch base and to refer the pupil's younger siblings to Winston's Wish. This time the school was self-assured, clearly demonstrating a capacity to be genuinely affected by the sadness of a further death without feeling utterly overwhelmed. On this occasion it wasn't necessary to visit the school and the deputy head personally facilitated an excellent debriefing with staff.

Case study Father of Year 4 pupil dies: one primary school's story

This is an account of how a large Gloucester primary school responded to the sudden death of the father of a Year 4 pupil (aged 9).

Early on a Monday morning the head teacher rang for some guidance as she had heard that the father of a Year 4 pupil (Becky) had died after a brain haemorrhage during the weekend. As we spoke, she understood that Becky was on her way to school. The head was clearly surprised that she was coming back to school so soon after her father's death.

We were able to talk to the class teacher and reassure her that the child's attendance at school so soon after the death of her father was not necessarily a bad thing considering the turmoil and upset in the family home. Some children crave the predictability of the school routine.

We discussed the need to acknowledge the death with Becky on her arrival and talked about how this could be done. We agreed on a simple statement like: 'I am really sorry to hear about the death of your dad, Becky – would you like to tell me what happened?' Arrangements were made for another teacher to take the class registration so that the class teacher and Becky would have some time to talk privately in the school library. Becky said she would like the head teacher to let people know what had happened, but was worried that everyone would be looking at her.

After talking to Becky's mother (Mrs Brown) on the phone, the head teacher, mum and Becky agreed that it would be best to inform the rest of the children in the junior school to avoid rumour in the playground and to send a short letter to parents of all children in the school. The children in Becky's year group would also take home information for their parents on talking about death, taken from our school strategy. Extra copies would be made available if parents of children from other classes wanted some information too. We spent some time talking

'Even at 5 years old a child can become ashamed of their loss and shrink from mentioning it outside the family.'
Feedback from parent, Service Evaluation 2003

The school made a pebble pond water feature: each child painted a pebble to remind them of their classmate.

with the head trying to identify who in the school might be most affected by the death – obviously including the class and class teacher but also others. Primary schools are often part of a close-knit community and, in this instance, it transpired that the school secretary knew the father as they had acted together in the village panto. Other children in different classes knew Becky's dad as he took football practice with the after-school group. Another factor which was considered was that there might be other children in the school who had previously been bereaved and that Becky's situation would trigger their grief again. It emerged that four other children in the school were bereaved of a parent and one of a sibling.

Case study **The class teacher's story**

'We were told on Monday morning that Becky's father had died of a brain haemorrhage at the weekend. I was able to speak to a member of the Winston's Wish team, who gave me some ideas about what to say and do when the children arrived. I was shocked and terribly sad that such an awful thing should happen to a child.

'Cover for my class was arranged while I talked to Becky alone about what had happened and how she was feeling. She was able to cry (and so was I).

'The teacher who covered my class stayed with us in the classroom while Becky and I told the rest of the children that Becky's dad had died. It was very difficult to tell them and it was supportive to have another adult there. The children could see that Becky and I had been upset, and were very kind: one child offered me his snack for playtime and Becky's close friends were genuinely attentive, holding her hand and sending reassuring notes.

'The head teacher visited each class to tell the other children and staff. He organised letters to be taken home to explain the situation and to avoid rumour and gossip.

'With support, I felt able to discuss the death openly with all the children and they felt confident enough to respond to their bereaved classmate "normally". Becky said that she had been worried about what everyone would say, but was glad that she had come to school because the other children had made her "feel better".

'Many classes, children and parents sent cards and messages to Becky and her mother which they both greatly appreciated.

'Looking back, I was really pleased to be able to phone the Winston's Wish Family Line just to chat things through. Often, I was on the right track, but you need to be so careful not to make things worse. I feel proud to be part of a school which can openly recognise such an important event in a child's life. I was 12 when my mother died. My teacher didn't mention a word – even my friends avoided the subject. Becky's experience brought out the very best in her classmates. I feel we all learnt something today.'

Summary of action taken

- Class teacher given guidance in talking with the bereaved pupil at the start of the school day.
- Cover arranged for class to allow the class teacher and pupil to talk privately.
- Simple statement agreed with class teacher: 'I am really sorry to hear about the death of your dad, Becky – would you like to tell me what happened?'
- Class teacher explains that it might be a good idea to inform the class together – in doing so she explored the pupil's thoughts and concerns, allowing the child a sense of control over how information is shared.
- Class informed by the teacher, accompanied by the child.
- Head teacher visits each class to inform staff and children of the news.
- Factual letter prepared for pupils in Becky's class to take home.
- Information prepared for parents on how to talk to their children about death. All pupils in the school year of the bereaved child take this information home. Information for other parents is available in the school office should it be requested.
- Letter of condolence sent to the family from the school.
- Bereaved child was given the opportunity to talk when the need arose, such as gentle preparation for and information about the funeral.

'I think it would be a good idea for parents to write to the head teacher saying that their dad is talked about freely at home; that teachers should not change lessons to avoid issues – but ask that a bereaved child is given prior warning and if they do get upset they can leave the room with a friend.'
Feedback from parent, Service Evaluation 2003

'Looking back, I was really pleased to be able to phone the Winston's Wish Family Line just to chat things through.'

GLOUCESTER PRIMARY SCHOOL

<Date>

Dear Parents

Mrs Wood had the sad task today of telling the children that their classmate Becky's father died suddenly from a brain haemorrhage over the weekend.

We felt it was appropriate to inform all children in the class. The children have been told that their teachers are willing to try and answer their questions at school. Answering children's questions about death can sometimes be difficult, so we enclose some information which I hope will be helpful to you as parents.

I know your thoughts will be very much with the Brown family who are somehow trying to make sense of this terrible tragedy.

Yours faithfully

<Name>

Head teacher

GLOUCESTER PRIMARY SCHOOL

<Date>

Dear Mrs Brown

Following our telephone conversation this morning, we were pleased to make arrangements to support Becky in school. We have enlisted the help of Winston's Wish, a service that has experience of supporting bereaved children and their families.

As Becky may have explained, she and Mrs Wood had a good chat and together they decided to tell her classmates about the death of your husband.

We were shocked and deeply saddened to hear the news this morning and many staff and children have sent their good wishes to support you at this difficult time. You will now be making plans for Rob's funeral, and I will give you a call in the next day or so to see if we can be of help. Equally, if you have any concerns whatsoever about Becky, please feel free to call me. With kind regards.

Yours sincerely

<Name>

Head teacher

These letter formats were used by the school when writing to the parents of children in Becky's class and also to Becky's family. They are based on samples we supplied to the school which were personalised by the head teacher.

Partnership scheme with school nurses

As part of our service to support bereaved children in schools we set up a partnership scheme with school nurses in Gloucestershire. Working with the local National Health Service primary care trust, we recruited a group of six school nurses who represent different geographical areas and who were interested in being involved in bereavement work. We designed a training and supervision programme to build their skills and confidence in offering a series of one-to-one sessions with bereaved children in schools. The primary care trust agreed that a small proportion of the nurses' time could be spent on this work and provided funding for training and supervision. Referrals come from the schools themselves or sometimes from Winston's Wish. The children offered a service in this scheme are usually those who fall outside the referral criteria for Winston's Wish, for example a child whose friend or grandparent has died. Often these children were at risk because of experiencing difficulties at school before the bereavement.

School nurses have found the six-session structure in the activity book Muddles, Puddles and Sunshine *a useful vehicle for supporting a child in school.*

Case study   Jessica (aged 5)

Jessica was 5 years old and in her second year at school. Her reception year had not been smooth when she had presented significant behaviour problems. Recently her behaviour became so difficult to manage in school that the special educational needs co-ordinator (SENCO) suggested she should be referred to a community paediatrician. Jessica was diagnosed with dyslexia and mild dyspraxia. It transpired that these neurological difficulties meant that she was acutely aware of her poor co-ordination in sports and lacked the confidence to write. As a result she had very low self-esteem and a high fear of failure. Jessica was the youngest

of four children and had spent a great deal of time with her grandmother. Six months before, her grandmother had died suddenly from a stroke. Jessica chose not to attend the funeral. She was angry with her grandmother for dying and 'did not want to say goodbye'.

Her grandmother's death triggered a significant deterioration in both behaviour and concentration. She refused to continue sessions with an occupational therapist to help with her dyspraxia, even though she had been making good progress. The school acted promptly. It arranged for Pat, the school nurse, to offer Jessica some support in school. Pat followed the six-session structure outlined in the activity book *Muddles, Puddles and Sunshine* (Crossley 2000). This aimed to help Jessica express her feelings about her grandmother's death and achieve a greater understanding of how and why she died. Jessica's mum and dad were fully involved and helped to gather various mementos: a photo of Jessica on holiday with her grandmother, granny's lavender soap, her scarf and so on.

Jessica made good progress with the school nurse and by the end of the six sessions her anger outbursts had reduced and she was regularly attending her occupational therapy sessions.

After the last session a more confident Jessica shared the contents of her activity book and memory box with classmates who were captivated to hear about the special relationship Jessica had enjoyed with her grandmother.

How our response to bereavement in schools relates to performance

In the UK, the government has introduced rigorous testing (SATS) which give us closely scrutinised league tables. These tables highlight 'successful' schools and, by contrast, those which are 'failing' to meet (purely academic) standards.

Goleman (1998) suggests that since the onset of intelligence (IQ) testing in 1918 average IQ is rising in developed countries around the world. The reasons include better nutrition, more children completing their education, and computer games and puzzles that generally help children master spatial skills. Smaller family size is also correlated with higher IQ in children.

However, Goleman also suggests that there appears to be a potentially dangerous paradox. As children's IQ grows ever higher, there is increasing evidence that their 'emotional intelligence' is on the decline. In a fascinating study, Achenbach and Howell (1993) instigated a large-scale survey of parents and teachers. Their findings indicated that the present generation of children is more emotionally troubled than the last. On average, children are growing more lonely and depressed, more angry and unruly, more nervous and prone to worry, and more impulsive and aggressive. In Achenbach and Howell's study, the rate of decline in emotional intelligence was the same across all economic groups.

It is highly likely that every head teacher will come across bereavement and loss on a regular basis. When a death affects a school community, this offers a crucial opportunity for everyone involved to develop what Goleman defines as emotional intelligence: 'Our capacity for recognising our own feelings and those of others, for motivating ourselves, and for managing emotions well in ourselves and in our relationships' (1998: p317). A community-based child bereavement service is well placed to foster these skills and reinforce the need to give time and resources to staff who genuinely want to support pupils as they try to assimilate death into their on-going lives. For a bereaved family to say: 'The school was brilliant ... they couldn't have handled it better!' should result in instant elevation on the achievement tables. Emotional literacy programmes, 'Citizenship' and personal, social and health education (PSHE) all become somewhat irrelevant if the school feels ill-equipped to cope with a death *when it happens for real*. An appropriate response becomes a powerful role model which pupils will remember – a role model which will possibly influence the rest of their lives.

This chapter has explored the various approaches a child bereavement service can take to work in partnership with schools to promote the well-being of a child who has been bereaved. The benefits of including and empowering the school to feel confident in this area are significant. Practical interventions are suggested which aim to educate and promote inclusion. The bereaved child and their family can then relate to the school as an environment where their teachers and friends understand and appreciate the impact of death on their lives.

As children's IQ grows ever higher, there is increasing evidence that their 'emotional intelligence' is on the decline.

IQ

'Give sorrow words.'

Shakespeare

Chapter Nine

Whispering into someone's ear

Providing guidance, information and support over the phone

Telephone support is likely to be a part of every bereavement service.
In this chapter, we consider the way in which bereaved parents and adult
carers can receive support and guidance over the telephone. We identify the
issues involved in providing telephone support, and describe a day on the
Winston's Wish Family Line.

'It was as though he
listened, and such
listening as his,
enfolds us in a
silence in which we
begin to hear what
we are meant to
hear.'
Lau-Tzu, from the
Tao Te Ching

The advantages of telephone support

The concept of helplines is over 50 years old (when Chad Varah founded The Samaritans) but it has only been in comparatively recent years that the general public has thought of using the telephone to reach out for information, advice, guidance and, especially, emotional support. The phone offers several advantages to someone who is seeking help:

'I came off the phone and thought for the first time – I can do this. I felt understood and confident to be there for my children.'

Caller to the Family Line

- **You are in control. You can ring off at any time – even before speaking.** In face-to-face encounters, even with strangers, it would be rare for someone simply to walk away from a conversation.
- **You can be completely anonymous – all that anyone needs to know about you is a guess at your gender as revealed by your voice.** In face-to-face encounters, you can feel 'labelled' or 'known' by your clothes, your age, your size, your ethnic background, your physical ability, your health, your wealth and so on.
- **You can make immediate contact when you need to.** Face-to-face encounters are usually subject to an appointments system, sometimes with long waiting lists. You can respond immediately to a crisis.
- **You can choose when to make contact (at least within limits).** You don't have to make an appointment nor do you need to cancel one – there's no pressure to attend at a specific time.
- **You can have easy access to information, guidance and support even if you live at a distance from any service.**
- **You don't in the future have to meet the person to whom you have told your deepest secrets at the club or at the school gates.** You don't therefore run the risk of laughing at a joke at a barbecue three years later and having that person turn to you and say: 'Well, there was a time when I never thought you'd laugh again'.
- **You don't have to consider how the other person is feeling or reacting to the call – the focus is on you, your family, your grief.** You don't have to play conversational 'ping pong' … I say this and you say that and then I say this and …

Some people think that it must feel impersonal talking to a helpline; in practice, most callers find a special intimacy in talking over the phone to someone who makes the time to listen and is felt to care. A caller once described it as 'whispering your pain into someone's ear'.

What kind of helpline?

Helplines have a variety of functions. Some or all of these
services may be offered:

- emotional support
- befriending
- guidance
- advice
- information
- practical ideas.

Helplines come in three particular styles:

- **self-help** – those who have direct experience offer the
  support (for example, parents answering Parentline
  Plus, some cancer self-help services)
- **professional counselling and guidance** – 'expert'
  support and advice from someone who has a
  professional knowledge and experience (for example,
  NHS Direct)
- **volunteer support** – someone who offers support
  without reference to any of their own personal
  experience (for example, The Samaritans, Saneline).

Are you caring for a bereaved child?

Winston's Wish Family Line offers support, information and guidance to all those caring for a child or young person who has been bereaved.

Winston's Wish **Family Line**
guidance and information for families of bereaved children

0845 20 30 40 5
voice and text phone
Calls are charged at the local rate.
www.winstonswish.org.uk

At the funeral people were saying to Jack: 'You're the man of the house now ... be brave for your mum's sake.' He looks so lost and confused. I want to help: what can I say?

Winston's Wish
supporting bereaved children and young people

Charity registration number 1061359
Winston's Wish Family Line is supported by Swiss Life (UK) plc

Swiss Life

The Winston's Wish Family Line

After nearly a decade of offering services to bereaved children and their families in
Gloucestershire, Winston's Wish was offered an opportunity to reach thousands
more bereaved children throughout the UK. This opportunity was realised when we
opened the Winston's Wish Family Line in February 2001. In its first two and a half
years, we spoke to over 10,000 people on the helpline and estimate that we,
therefore, indirectly supported over 20,000 bereaved children.

Early intervention

The Family Line offers a new twist on the concept of early intervention in bereavement
and trauma support. It is more traditional to see early intervention as a face-to-face
interaction between the bereaved person and the practitioner. Thirty minutes of
information, guidance and support from a person with experience and expertise

'Even when I thought
I was doing the right
thing it was great to
have the advice and
reassurance, as at
the time I felt very
alone.'
Feedback from parent,
Service Evaluation 2003

In its first two and a half years, we spoke to over
10,000 people on the helpline and estimate
that we, therefore, indirectly supported
over 20,000 bereaved children.

'Getting it right for
the children seemed
so important – I
didn't want to let
Stuart down, he was
such a great dad.'
Caller to the Family Line

can make a huge difference to bereaved children and those who care for them. Through the Family Line we are able to offer this timely connection and provide supportive guidance and advice to many more families than we could meet face to face. We perceive this as a highly effective early intervention for many families.

Aim

The specific aim of the helpline is to offer a timely and appropriate intervention for bereaved children by providing anyone caring for a bereaved child with:

- experienced and skilled guidance, information and advice
- support, reassurance, encouragement and validation
- appropriate resources
- access to other services (both those provided by Winston's Wish and those provided by the wider child bereavement network).

The experience we gain from operating the helpline is also used to reflect the needs of bereaved families in the development of our services.

Outcomes

The principal desired outcomes for the helpline are that:

- the concerned adult making the call feels more confident to support a bereaved child

and therefore:

- the bereaved child or young person will be better able to manage the impact of death on their life.

Other outcomes for bereaved children, young people and their families relate to our five primary clinical objectives (see page 33).

Who answers the phone?

We decided that our own staff would answer the Winston's Wish Family Line. This ensures that every call from any caller is answered by an experienced practitioner. That is, the calls are answered by the same person who, later in the day, will get down on the floor to draw with a 6-year-old, the same person who will co-ordinate Camp Winston, the same person who can go alongside an angry adolescent or despairing parent or carer. This skills base ensures a credible response for parents, carers and professionals.

The staff on the Family Line offer emotional support, information on subjects such as grief reactions and children's developmental understanding, guidance on supporting children in grief and many practical ideas.

Defining our potential callers

Primary audience

Our publicity carries the line: 'Are you caring for a bereaved child?' This allows potential callers to define our primary audience for themselves in terms of their relationship to the child under concern and the child's relationship to the person who has died. We expect to receive more calls from family members than any other group.

In fact, in our first two years, calls from family members made up 77% of our calls. More mothers called than fathers, with grandparents and step-relations being the next largest groups of family members. Twenty-four familial relationships were described by callers, for example great aunt, second cousin.

Secondary audiences

These include:

- health and social care professionals: doctors, nurses, health visitors, social workers, paid carers
- teachers and educational workers: educational social workers, school counsellors as well as teachers and classroom assistants
- police family liaison officers
- faith leaders
- counsellors and befrienders
- members of voluntary organisations.

Other potential audiences

These include bereaved children and young people.

While recognising that we may receive calls from children and young people at any time, we have deliberately not aimed the Family Line service at young callers. Young people are encouraged to call ChildLine over any concerns (and just over 1% of calls to ChildLine are about bereavement). In addition, there is a special service for young people aged 12 to 18 operated by Cruse.

'No period in history has been more child-orientated than ours, nor produced parents who regard themselves as so inadequate. After generations when they could do no wrong, many parents now feel themselves incapable of doing anything right.'

David Lewis

Thirty minutes of information, guidance and support from a person with experience and expertise can make a huge difference.

30

'It has been a lifeline to us all, making me believe in what I am doing for the children and that I should trust my instincts on how best to support them.'
Feedback from parent, Service Evaluation 2003

What we can offer

This includes the following:

Emotional support:
- listening to the feelings of the person who has called.

Information on:
- children's developmental understanding of death
- children's responses to grief, death and loss
- grieving 'processes', stages and reactions
- funerals and other practical processes
- Winston's Wish publications and their appropriate use.

Guidance on:
- children's responses – how to help them
- involving children in plans and events
- describing what happened to the person who has died
- handling troubled behaviour
- ideas for memory work.

Contacts for:
- other bereavement services nationally and locally
- statutory services
- other voluntary services
- other individuals: for example, accredited counsellors.

Tone of the service

We set the desired tone as caring (but not cloying), approachable, trustworthy, informed, professional with a small 'p', and supportive of callers' choices and actions.

Helpline number

We use a 'lo-call' number (0845) that is, we believe, sufficiently memorable: 20 30 40 5.

The advantages of lo-call are that the lower tariff encourages people to use the service and reduces a barrier to seeking help. It also makes the service geographically imprecise so callers don't think: 'Oh, they're in Gloucester and I'm in Bootle, so they're not for me'. It also reduces the incidence of inappropriate calls. The disadvantages are that the number would show on a phone bill, inappropriate calls are not completely deterred and it's not yet a universally recognised prefix.

Meeting the need

The helpline hours are currently 9.30am to 5pm, Monday to Friday. Being consistent about opening hours is essential, principally for the sake of potential callers but also to make it easier to advertise the service.

While we have run trials of weekend and evening opening, in practice few calls are made outside our opening hours reflecting, we presume, our callers' assumption that we operate within normal office hours.

Support for practitioners

Practitioners work alone or in pairs on the helpline but are in the same building as the rest of the organisation. A nominated 'on call' person (one of the managers, or the director of the Family Services team) is on hand for support, consultation and guidance. Additional support can be offered by other colleagues if required.

Policies

The helpline follows policies that apply to the rest of the work in Family Services, and include:

- confidentiality
- child protection
- equal opportunities
- complaints
- health and safety
- lone working
- record-keeping, including data protection
- police checks
- insurance.

'You provided us with a space that helped us to feel we weren't alone – and that we were special because of what we went through.'
Feedback from parent, Service Evaluation 2003

We set the desired tone as caring (but not cloying), approachable, trustworthy, informed, professional with a small 'p', and supportive of callers' choices and actions.

A day on the Winston's Wish Family Line

Perhaps the best way to convey the service is to share some of the types of calls made to the Family Line in a day. The following 'log' has been compiled from calls received on the helpline although details have been changed and some elements of the stories created to illustrate the types of calls we receive. What has not been artificially created however is the range of calls we receive in any one day, nor the truth and intensity of the interactions between the Winston's Wish practitioner and the person who needs us at that time.

Brendan and Kat are answering the helpline phone on this day: this is what happens during their shifts. Some calls last 10 minutes; some last over an hour. We receive around 15 calls a day.

 Brendan is answering the helpline phone this morning. He's also one of the most generous tea makers in the office – so he's making a quick round for the fundraisers and the other practitioners before he settles into the dedicated helpline room to take the first call of the day. We always promise to keep his caffeine level topped up in return – a drink and a friendly smile from a colleague can be very supportive when taking a demanding call.

 The Family Line is now open. Brendan checks the answering machine for any messages left overnight. While the majority of calls come in during our opening hours of 9.30am to 5pm, people sometimes leave a message. This morning, there's a message from a head teacher asking for a call back during mid-morning break time. Brendan makes a note and checks for other messages left by colleagues. However, the phone rings ... and it continues to do so with only short gaps between calls for the rest of the day.

 Brendan answers the phone to a grandmother, Florence, who is concerned for her 6-year-old grandson, Matt. His mother died four months ago of breast cancer and Matt is now living with his father and his paternal grandparents over 300 miles away from Florence and his 'old' home. His father, and his father's family, believe in the 'stiff upper lip' school of coping and have decreed that his mother will not be mentioned in the hope that Matt will 'get over' her death quickly. Florence has different beliefs about expressing emotions and wonders how she can support Matt from a distance.

Brendan explores ways she can keep in contact with her grandson and how she can play a vital role in helping preserve memories of his mother (her daughter). Brendan suggests that she begins to write down some stories about his mother as a child, being naughty, favourite subject at school, meeting dad, telling granny about being pregnant with Matt and so on. With some old photos from gran's drawer, this will form a life book of his mum that will be treasured as Matt grows up. Brendan also suggests activities that might help Matt that Florence could try – even from a distance – and suggests a couple of books Florence could post for Matt to read. He also explores with Florence her own feelings about her daughter's death and how she might find gentle ways to engage her son-in-law so they can both help Matt establish an appropriate 'continuing bond' with his mum.

Activity sheets can give parents practical ideas to cope with difficult anniversaries and days which are usually 'celebrated'.

Angela rings the Family Line for ideas on how to celebrate the tenth birthday of her surviving twin son, James. His twin died of leukaemia about nine months ago. Angela feels that James is entitled to have fun at his party but knows that it will be extremely difficult as it's the first birthday he has not shared with David.

Brendan encourages Angela to talk about how hard this birthday will be for her too. Brendan then shares some ideas on how to celebrate David's life in a fun way – recognising that the friends at the party, as well as the family, will be grieving for their friend. Among the ideas is to make jars of memories – using coloured salt swirled together to represent each child's memories of David. They could decorate biscuits with icing faces to represent how each one is feeling right now and the children could write a birthday message to David to tie to a helium-filled balloon released at the end of the party. He agrees that his birthday will always be a hard time for James; that's how it is when someone dies. There's no magic wand to make everything better. The best that can be hoped is to find a way to move forward into the future, with the precious memories of the past. Brendan says he will post activity sheets about the ideas they discussed.

Callers can order
memory boxes from
us in which each
child can keep
mementos of the
person who has died
– such as photos,
shells from a special
holiday, aftershave
or perfume, tickets
to see a film,
birthday cards and
indeed anything else
which will act as a
trigger for memory
retrieval.

Almost missed the time to call the head teacher! Mr Lloyd is very concerned about a 14-year-old pupil in Year 8, Sean, whose work has recently deteriorated and who is beginning to get into trouble for his angry outbursts at children and staff. Sean says it's because his brother died two years ago and he hates the world. Mr Lloyd and his staff want to be supportive but wonder sometimes if he is using the bereavement as an excuse.

Brendan discovers that the brother was a star student, two years older than Sean, who was knocked off his bike and killed when they were out riding together. It strikes Brendan that Sean is now the age his 'golden' brother was when he died, and he recognises that, like many siblings, Sean may even feel he should have been the one who died. They discuss ways in which the school can support Sean, and Brendan checks that Sean's mum is aware of the head contacting Winston's Wish.

The next call comes from Jane, a friend of someone whose husband died last week. She is glad to talk to Brendan about ways she can support her friend's children. The funeral is in two days and Jane is wondering how the two children will cope.

Brendan explores whether the children will be attending and if Jane feels she could take on the role of supporting them during the ceremony to allow her friend to grieve freely. They discuss some suggestions for ways in which the children (aged 17 and 6) can be involved, for example, by choosing one of their father's favourite pieces of music or writing a poem for him. Jane decides to order two memory boxes from us in which each child can keep mementos of their father – such as old photos, shells from a special holiday, his aftershave, tickets to see a film, birthday cards and anything else.

Andrew calls about his daughter Kate, aged 13. They always used to be 'best friends' but since her mother's death a few months ago Kate has changed totally and is now very 'stroppy' according to Andrew. Andrew is exhausted and is really struggling after his partner's long illness and recent death. He said he is at his wit's end. He feels Kate can't love him or her mother because she doesn't ever want to talk about her and slams out of the room at the slightest provocation. Andrew's voice shakes throughout the call – he is afraid that Kate will begin to 'get into trouble' with drugs or drink.

Brendan listens to Andrew, encouraging him to share the pain. Sometimes, a caller needs our presence and our attentive listening more than our ideas, guidance and information. When it seems right, he helps Andrew consider how he and his daughter are grieving separately and differently; maybe there's also a place for them to communicate how they are feeling to each other. He offers some very simple ideas (notes stuck to the fridge saying: 'I love you and I know you're hurting', for example) as a beginning but he feels this family might benefit from attending Camp Winston. After ascertaining that Andrew and Kate live locally, Brendan tells Andrew that he will ask a colleague to arrange a home assessment to discuss how we can best support them.

Book for children about cancer, *The Secret C* and the booklet *As Big as it Gets*, written for adults supporting a child when someone in the family is seriously or terminally ill.

 It's been a busy morning with no time to sip the tea we at last remembered to make him!

A hospice in Blackpool calls to order some of the publications which Winston's Wish produces. They ask for our book for children about cancer, *The Secret C* (Stokes 2000) and the booklet *As Big as it Gets* (Stokes and Crossley 2001) written for adults supporting a child when someone in the family is seriously or terminally ill. The hospice has a mother with young children as an in-patient.

Brendan takes the order and after a brief assessment discusses how they might use the publications with this family.

 Kat takes over, tidies up the booklets and directories of information, waters the plant and reads the messages. Kat and Brendan are part of a team of experienced practitioners who take turns answering the Family Line while also supporting families through our other services. Their direct experience with bereaved young people gives a unique depth and breadth to the guidance and support they are able to offer callers throughout the UK over the phone.

 Kat's first call is from a health visitor concerned about a 7-year-old girl she sees when visiting the family. The little girl won't go to bed at night and

Words can be
confusing to a child:
'If you can die in your
sleep, there's no way
I'm going to risk
going to bed'.

becomes very distressed and hysterical if the family tries to make her do so – she ends up falling asleep exhausted on the sofa. Her grandmother died recently and the health visitor wonders if there may be a connection.

Kat enquires what the child has been told about her grandmother's death and learns that 'her mother simply told her that granny died in her sleep'. Kat explores how confusing these words could be to a child: 'If you can die in your sleep, there's no way I'm going to risk going to bed'. The health visitor immediately grasps the point and plans a visit to explain to the little girl that her grandmother died because she was ill and elderly. Kat also offers to describe on another occasion some other ideas that may help if the little girl is still afraid of sleeping. They agree that it might be helpful for the child to complete an activity book to consolidate both her understanding and her need to commemorate the relationship with her grandmother properly.

 Janet calls. Her two children, Ben (10) and Anna (8), came to one of our residential weekends last year after the death of their father. The children had responded well to Camp Winston and had seemed more settled afterwards. Recently, though, Ben is having trouble with stomach pains; he says he's worried about passing the entrance exam to secondary school.

Kat remembers Ben and Anna from the residential group the previous spring; she's glad Janet took up the offer to ring as part of an on-going support network. In exploring together what may have changed for Ben, Kat learns that the school for which Ben is sitting the exam is his father's old school. She wonders if Ben feels pressure to follow in his father's footsteps, even to take his father's place in the family. Janet had seen the chance as a positive way for Ben to keep a sense of contact with his father but she says she will make it really clear to Ben that he does not have to replace his father in any way.

 Kat notices a new e-mail that has come in to the central enquiry address for Winston's Wish and forwards it to the colleague who responds to e-mail questions asked through our website (at www.winstonswish.org.uk). We regularly receive e-mails, often from young people using their preferred way of finding information and asking the questions they find impossible to ask when face to face with someone. The questions can range from: 'I'm 16 and I've just learnt that my mum killed herself when I was 7. I was always told she'd had a car accident. She must have really hated me, mustn't she?' to the heart-breakingly simple: 'Why my friend?'

 The manager of a nursery calls for advice. At 'news time' today, a 3-year-old who attends the nursery full-time had said: 'My news is that my daddy died on Friday'. The manager was looking for advice, both on how to support the child and also on how to handle questions from interested playfellows. She added that the staff had also been at a loss when the young boy had then asked one of them if his dad would be picking him up at the end of the day as he often did. Later, the child's mother told the nursery that her ex-partner had killed himself.

Transferring to secondary school is proving a daunting challenge for Ben, following his father's death.

Kat explains about children's growing understanding of death and dying, and how this child will neither understand the permanence of death nor even properly what death is. Finding out that the nursery is in Oxfordshire, she suggests that they contact SeeSaw, their local service. Finally, Kat agrees to send out a booklet which gives guidelines when supporting a child bereaved by suicide (Crossley and Stokes 2001). She sends it by first-class post so it will arrive the next day.

 A neighbour of a woman with three children whose husband has just died suddenly of a brain haemorrhage rings to ask if there's a service like Winston's Wish in their part of the UK.

Kat checks our information but finds that as yet there is no similar service within 50 miles. She gives the number for the Childhood Bereavement Network, a co-ordinating body which brings together individuals and organisations providing services to bereaved children, in case there is a local individual with experience of bereavement support. She also arranges to send the neighbour some information about the Family Line and the other services we provide for all families.

 Kat's last call today is from a young mother, Emma, with a 5-month-old baby girl. Her husband was diagnosed with cancer on the very day they discovered she was pregnant. Despite great efforts on everyone's part for him to survive long enough to see his baby born, he died just three weeks before her birth. Emma feels she went straight from the funeral to the delivery suite – everything in-between is a blur. She is worried about being a bad mother since she finds herself crying desperately while she is feeding the baby and, in particular, she wonders how she can ever make her husband seem like a real daddy to Alexandra when she will have no memories of him.

This is a demanding call and Kat gives Emma every ounce of her attention. After listening carefully, and checking whether anyone else is supporting her, Kat explains a little about how children remember things. Kat suggests that as Alexandra grows up, Emma talks openly about Mark, that his picture is around the house, and that as Alexandra develops she tells her stories that help her to understand how excited Mark felt about her arrival. For example, she could say something along the lines of: 'When daddy knew we were going to have a little baby to love, he hugged the doctor and almost kissed the woman in the bread shop he was so excited!! He had some funny ideas of names for you – would you like to have been called Rainbow? – but we chose your beautiful name together'. Kat has several other ideas but feels that, for now, it will be best to encourage Emma to ring us whenever she wants to or needs to. This may be over many years, when we can hopefully offer on-going support and some suggestions for creating and preserving memories.

'He had some funny ideas of names for you – would you like to have been called Rainbow? – but we chose your beautiful name together.'
Simply talking to children is an effective way of creating and preserving memories

The last call had been very poignant and Kat is glad that Sarah pops in to check how she is feeling as her shift nears the end. Informal support among colleagues counts for a lot when you are working with and supporting those affected by grief and loss. Sarah and another colleague Edward will be answering the Family Line tomorrow and Kat told her to expect the call from the mother whose friend had called Brendan earlier.

The Family Line closes for the night. Any night-time callers can leave a message that will be responded to first thing in the morning. It's been a fairly typical day. We receive more calls from mothers than from other relatives; the person who has died is most frequently the father of the child under concern. The most frequently mentioned causes of death are cancer, suicide, heart problems and road traffic accidents. Professionals concerned about a child or children make up around 23% of our callers.

Depth and breadth of support

With two children experiencing the death of a parent every hour in the UK (around 20,000 children under 18 every year) and many more experiencing the death of a sibling, a grandparent or best friend, the Family Line is providing a vital, accessible and appreciated service. Our callers are supporting bereaved children – through family members, carers and professionals – who call with a great variety of questions and concerns.

Drawing on their direct experience of working with bereaved families, our Family Line practitioners offer callers significant depth and breadth of support. They take time to listen carefully, and to help callers make sense of questions and concerns. They also know that some questions can never be answered.

This chapter has explored the use of the telephone in the provision of support to bereaved families and those caring for them. Four key points are raised:

- A timely and therapeutic intervention can be successfully made over the telephone; for some families, this support may be all that will be required.
- Easy, immediate and direct access to those with expertise and experience of supporting bereaved children and families can make a great difference to a child's journey through grief.
- For some families, telephone support may be the 'gateway' to face-to-face services.
- The Family Line number can be given out by developing child bereavement services, which may have limited resources and find it difficult to respond at short notice.

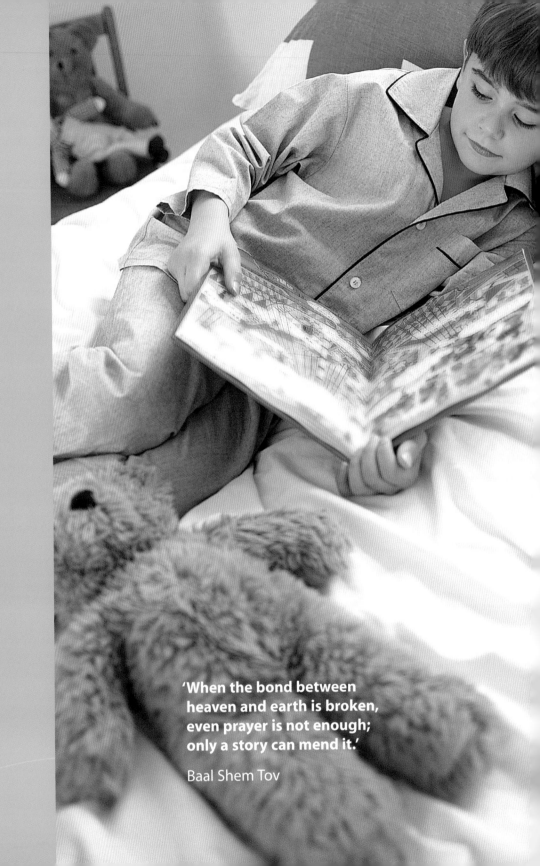

'When the bond between
heaven and earth is broken,
even prayer is not enough;
only a story can mend it.'

Baal Shem Tov

Chapter Ten

Convincing text messages

Using words and images to provide travellers with a good route map

'Imagination is more important than knowledge.'
Albert Einstein

In this chapter, we consider the ways in which we can reach bereaved families using publications, videos and the web. The therapeutic use of books and story-telling metaphors is also explored.

Goodbye God Bless

'I'm not really a
group person myself,
but I found I
watched the
documentary over
and over – each time
I noticed something
different. It gave me
confidence to know
that I wasn't doing a
bad job in bringing
up the kids.'
John, talking about the
Everyman documentary
Goodbye, God Bless, a
joint collaboration with
BBC television which
features three families
who were supported by
Winston's Wish (first
screened BBC 1998)

Communicating consistent messages

A comprehensive support programme will ideally offer both 'direct' services (for example, individual and group work) as well as a range of indirect services (for example, a helpline, a website, publications, memory boxes and other resources). The availability of booklets and other publications is a cost-effective and far-reaching way to communicate consistent messages. Families can get a sense of the service from our resources, and can gauge whether we might offer a 'good match' for their own experience and needs. Indeed, for some families, simply having a written resource or watching a video will bring them into contact with other bereaved people, in a way that feels safe and reassuring. For some, this intervention in itself is enough.

Getting messages across

The written word is a very powerful and visible way of getting messages across. Many people will gain their first impressions of an organisation from reading one of its publications. We aim to translate our vision and mission into all aspects of our work, including the production of publications and other resources.

We offer a range of books, booklets, leaflets, activity sheets, memory boxes and other resources. Written for children, and the adults supporting them, the booklets cover issues such as how to understand cancer, and how to explain serious illness or suicide to a child.

We strive to produce publications which are attractive and easy to read. An overly pious and serious approach is not necessarily the best trigger to engage a lively child. Although publications need to be respectful of the serious subject matter, we also try to respect the reader's need to be engaged by what they read.

The range of publications and resources has been developed from our conversations with thousands of bereaved parents and children. Comments and ideas generated in these discussions help to inform the development of publications, and fine-tune the final text and design. They enable us to check out assumptions, clarify the needs of the target audience, and double-check the approach and presentation. Many judgments are 'tightrope' decisions, and discussions with bereaved parents and children allow us to gauge the impact generated through our publications: is the approach honest or brutal, is it authoritative or authoritarian, is it empathetic or patronising? We aim, above anything else, for the messages to be both received – and understood.

Publications for parents – plain English, powerful design

Our intention is to produce publications which are informative, without being overwhelming. The booklets are designed carefully so that a parent who may be finding it difficult to concentrate can still absorb key messages simply by flicking through. Publications offer benefits in the form of privacy (material can be read by someone on their own), anonymity and the time to absorb the information at leisure (publications can be used flexibly – a little at a time). We have developed a house style which makes extensive use of quotes and 'eyes to camera' portrait photographs. Feeling as though you connect with another person's thinking has an important role. People's hunger to belong is at the very heart of human nature. All too often bereaved people become aware of their 'isolation' and 'different-ness'. Booklets can help this sense of belonging while also providing a gentle prompt to challenge the grieving person's vulnerability to fear and negativity.

'I would just like to express my thanks. My husband took his life a month ago. I had just received an information pack which included Beyond the Rough Rock. I read it cover to cover that night. The next morning my son (who is 5) woke me and asked me "how did daddy die?" so I told him the truth ("overdose with antidepressants and vodka"). I would not have known what to say or had the knowledge or courage to tell him if I had not read that book. I express to you my heartfelt thanks from myself and Michael; you have all made such a difference to our lives. Just now, by your information and help we are finding this journey so much easier to travel.'
Mother aged 30 and son aged 5

Much creative energy, thinking and teamwork go into the development of our publications, and in working with the editor and designer to develop the best possible brief. As an example, we set out the background to our booklet *Beyond the Rough Rock* (Crossley and Stokes 2001). The objective was: 'to look at some of the issues affecting families bereaved by suicide and to help a parent to support a child affected by suicide'. We defined the primary target audience for this booklet as: 'a parent whose partner has recently died by suicide – a distressed parent who wants to talk to their child in a sensitive way about what has happened'. The secondary audience was seen as largely professional (for example, coroners, clergy, police).

We identified several particular editing and design challenges: we wanted the booklet to be accessible, practical, readable, and look copy-light with key messages emphasised. We wanted it to be very visual, with freshness and sensitivity. We did

Books, videos and the web can be a private yet powerful vehicle to bring a bereaved person in contact with others who share their experience.

'When I read it I realised I wasn't the only parent whose partner was dying. Although it was hard to read in places – I realised for the first time that my questions had been asked by others.'
Mother of Jack (aged 6)

not want it to look dense, sombre or quirky. We wanted the design to reflect the fact that families affected will already feel different and alienated. We also wanted to show a range of culturally diverse and strong images, reproduced large, with quotes. As newly bereaved people often describe immense difficulties with concentration, it was part of the brief that these photos with captions would 'tell the story', and highlight the most important key messages contained in the booklet. We wanted a format that would enable readers to scan through the publication and pick out issues of interest to them, using lots of headings to highlight points of interest, and short paragraphs to make it easy to assimilate the information. We hope this format not only makes material easier to read and digest, but also means that it can cater for different information requirements and different levels of literacy.

Some of the key words in the brief – both for the text and the design – were about credibility, trustworthiness, holding attention, getting across key messages, accessibility, comprehensibility, readability, legibility, reassurance and empowerment.

A major part of the brief was to write the texts in plain English. The Word Centre describes plain English as a way of writing that gets the meaning across clearly, concisely, and with the effect you want, to your intended reader. Plain English writing should be clear, concise and human (The Word Centre 2002).

The booklet – *Beyond the Rough Rock*, about suicide (Crossley and Stokes 2001) and another booklet in the same series *As Big as it Gets*, about serious illnesses (Stokes and Crossley 2001) – won a Plain English Campaign award at the end of 2001. The Plain English Campaign award judges look particularly at how appropriate the document is for its audience, and take into account the resources available to the writer. Some of the specific questions they ask when judging the awards are listed here:

- Is the language clear?
- Is the tone appropriate for the intended audience?
- Will any jargon terms be understood by the intended audience?
- Is the intention of the document clear?
- Is the style and size of the text suitable?
- Does the layout and design of the pages make it easier to read the information?
- Is the information clearly sign-posted through clear and appropriate headings?

- If colour is used to aid design, is this done consistently?
- Has the writer anticipated the questions the reader is likely to ask as they read the document?
- Is it clear how the reader can contact the organisation that produced the document if they have any further questions?

The citation for the award Winston's Wish received was as follows:

'These booklets help kids to come to terms with tragedies in their lives such as the serious illness of a family member, bereavement or the suicide of someone close to them … *As Big as it Gets*: the use of personal reference, everyday words and active verbs all combine to make the information easier to read. *Beyond the Rough Rock*: this booklet's use of short direct sentences, a clear design, logical structure and using pictures to break up the text all make a difficult subject more accessible.' (Plain English Campaign 2002)

Effective communication comes in all guises of course. Having explored the importance of sharing information through published booklets for parents, we now consider how we might try to connect with a younger audience through story books and metaphor.

Close your eyes and a child's imagination can take them on the most magical adventures … of course, a few old dressing gowns and a plastic sword help the Jedi monks to develop their powers …

Story-telling: engaging a younger audience

The imagination of young children has no limits. This is why children are consistently captivated by stories. A story has permission to go anywhere, on any delicious, even scary adventure. Its characters can have any powers and do anything they like. The child rarely experiences the story as an observer – very often they will identify personally with characters. With stories and metaphor, the wonder and imagination of the child can be awakened and engaged. For some time much of the death educational literature operated within factual boundaries and is understandably careful to be respectful of the multiplicity of religious and spiritual beliefs, which have different views on 'the meaning of life and death'.

More recently we have seen an expanding range of books often addressing similar issues, but presented more creatively, which fully engage the child in the therapeutic process. There are several excellent catalogues which provide a range of stories for children of different ages.

With stories and metaphor, the wonder and imagination of the child can be awakened and engaged.

Anything and everything is possible in a story. The longing of a child lives in the realm of pure possibility.

In 1996 we worked in partnership with our local school library service to produce a catalogue of books available for loan to Gloucestershire schools (Yendall 1996). Not only did David Yendall (a team librarian) produce a beautifully illustrated catalogue, he then actively encouraged schools to borrow the books and include them in relevant curriculum planning.

A recent publication (Jones 2001) reviews the use of bibliotherapy with bereaved children. The book demonstrates how young people can help themselves work through their grief by reading fiction. Compassion Books (www.compassionbooks.com) has collected an inspirational range of stories for bereaved children. Many people have also been inspired by the work of Alida Gersie who has written the helpful guides *Story-making in Bereavement* (1991) and *Reflections on Therapeutic Story-making* (1997) which explore the use of stories with groups and individuals.

A story can give the child the choice to act with a power and a strength which challenge the reality focus of 'dead is final'. Anything and everything is possible in a story. The longing of a child lives in the realm of pure possibility. Sometimes a child will prefer to reflect on a death from an indirect vantage point.

Books such as *No Matter What*, shown on page 216, enable subsequent conversations to evolve naturally about issues that many parents might feel are too upsetting or 'inappropriate' if tackled head on.

For older children we see an equally impressive range of fiction books which are comfortable dealing with bereavement and loss themes. For example, in the hugely popular Harry Potter series we see Harry growing in his awareness of what he has lost following the death of his parents, and his journey through grief gradually builds in each book. 'His growing understanding and gradually widening circle of trusted friends and adults gradually make it safer for Harry to find words, feelings and images which create continuity and meaning, from babyhood through the complex, difficult present to a foreseeable future.' (Harris Hendriks 2002: p11)

In the first book, *Harry Potter and the Philosopher's Stone* (Rowling 1997), Harry discovers the mirror of ERISED ('desire' spelt backwards). The mirror shows the deepest most desperate desires of our hearts, but it can give neither knowledge nor truth. Harry's trusted mentor, Dumbledore, suggests that he does not dwell on dreams and forget to live in the present. One has to know about the past *in order* to live, not simply to avoid the present and future.

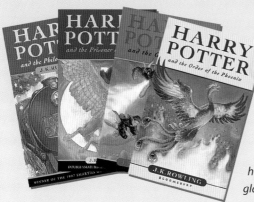

In JK Rowling's 'Harry Potter' series (Bloomsbury Publishing Plc), Harry Potter's journey through grief gradually builds in each book.

Reproduced with permission

Illustrators: Thomas Taylor, Giles Greenfield, Cliff Wright and Jason Cockcroft

Harry 'could die in book 7'

By Jack Malvern

FOUR THOUSAND children gasped in unison yesterday as J K Rowling told them that Harry Potter might not survive beyond the last volume in the Harry Potter series.

At a packed interview and reading at the Albert Hall, Ms Rowling said: "People often ask me if I will write about Harry when he has grown up. I always say you will have to wait and see whether he survives."

Children from Clifton High School said that they would cry if Harry died. Ella Rothwell, 10, said: "I think he'll probably die really horribly at the end of book seven. I wouldn't be very pleased."

But Ms Rowling, who said that the screaming crowd made her feel like a Beatle, said that she was trying to confront death in the books.

She compared the death in Harry Potter to the British soldiers killed in Iraq. "There you are with your friends sitting next to you, and the next moment he is gone," she said.

"What I was trying to do with the death [in Harry Potter and the Order of the Phoenix] was to show how arbitrary and unfair death is."

Asked by a child what she would see in the Mirror of Erised — in which one sees one's greatest desires — she said she would see her mother again, a scientist inventing a healthy cigarette and a journalist being boiled in oil.

She joked that she had not written about Hermione's parents in detail because they were dentists.

"They're not very interesting," she said.

Reproduced with permission

Jack Malvern Copyright *The Times*, London, 27 June 2003

'Mum?' he whispered. 'Dad?'

They just looked at him, smiling. And slowly, Harry looked into the faces of the other people in the mirror and saw other pairs of green eyes like his, other noses like his, even a little old man who looked as though he had Harry's knobbly knees – Harry was looking at his family, for the first time in his life.

The Potters smiled and waved at Harry and he stared hungrily back at them, his hands pressed flat against the glass as though he was hoping to fall right through it and reach them. He had a powerful kind of ache inside him, half joy, half terrible sadness. (Rowling 1997: p153)

Reproduced with permission

Copyright © JK Rowling 1997

JK Rowling firmly believes that children cannot be protected from the reality of death. 'What I was trying to do with the death (in *Harry Potter and the Order of the Phoenix*) was to show how arbitrary and unfair death is.' (JK Rowling quoted in an article by Jack Malvern: *The Times* 27 June 2003) With one in 28 Britons buying the book on the day of its release (*Guardian* 24 June 2003) Harry has become an important vehicle to carry 'death education' to adults and children alike. Following media interviews, children throughout the world are now processing the prospect that, like other mortals, even super hero 'Harry' is not routinely granted the pleasure (or pain) of everlasting life. Whatever the outcome for the beloved Harry, such fiction books have been, and always will be, a captivating way of enabling children and young people to confront their own meaning of life (and death).

The beautifully illustrated book *No Matter What* by Debi Gliori (1999) tells the story of 'Big' (a parental figure portrayed as an animal) and 'Small' the inquisitive offspring who is finding it hard to know just how grumpy he can be before 'Big' will stop loving him. The book takes the child on a gentle yet magical adventure of unconditional love. It culminates in allowing 'Small' to ask perhaps the biggest question of all.

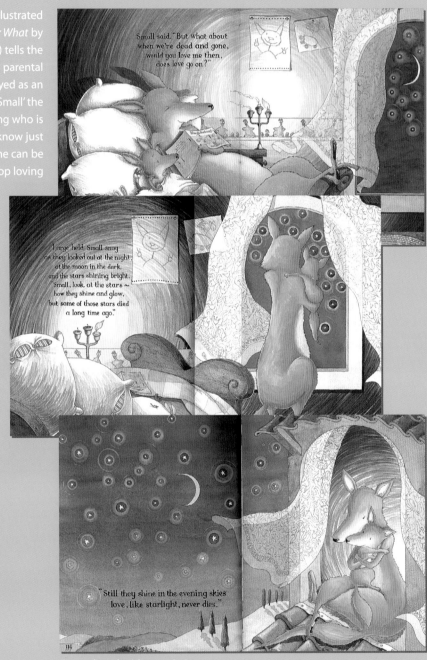

Small said, "But what about
when we're dead and gone,
would you love me then,
does love go on?"

Large held Small snug
as they looked out at the night,
at the moon in the dark,
and the stars shining bright.
"Small, look at the stars ~
how they shine and glow,
but some of those stars died
a long time ago."

"Still they shine in the evening skies
love, like starlight, never dies."

Using metaphors

Whatever adventure a story-teller will develop to strengthen a 'continuing bond', the child will also need to live with the 'real' ending which is that their loved one can no longer be physically present in their living life. However, if we can somehow as adults be comfortable with our role in accompanying children on these creative adventures with the meaning of life, then we may witness first hand the child's self-healing ability.

'Mum, you can be the silver band that keeps us all together.'
James

Case study   Mum's magic ring – using metaphor to enhance resilience

A mother explained about a family story which started when her eldest son demonstrated a desperate longing to be close to his grandfather. His grandad died when he was 4 years old. They had enjoyed a rich and imaginative relationship which often involved inventive story-telling. When James was told that his grandad had died from a heart attack, his very first question was: 'Will you die too?'

Suddenly, and brutally, the security of his inner world was under interrogation. Later, when looking in the coffin, he was faced with indisputable evidence: 'People I care about can die'. Over the coming months he struggled to find ways of feeling secure. Central to his adjustment to his grandfather's death was his need to feel close to his mother. So she explained how their story of the 'magic ring' evolved. 'He knew my ring was a special wedding day gift from his dad and therefore already symbolised a strong sense of security for his family. He decided that the most prominent and beautiful amethyst stone could represent him, the iridescent opal could be his younger brother, the silver flowers were his younger sister and the silver leaves would be dad. We decided together that if either of us ever needed to feel close to each other then I would gently press my finger on his gemstone. He felt reassured, and went on to add: "Mum, you can be the silver band [meaning the shank] that keeps us all together". In his own inner world he had created a fantastical formula to help reduce his fears of sudden and permanent separation. The metaphor of the magic ring has become a family story which all three children use to remind themselves of family unity.

Children can be helped to engage in imaginative solutions to help them manage their fears.

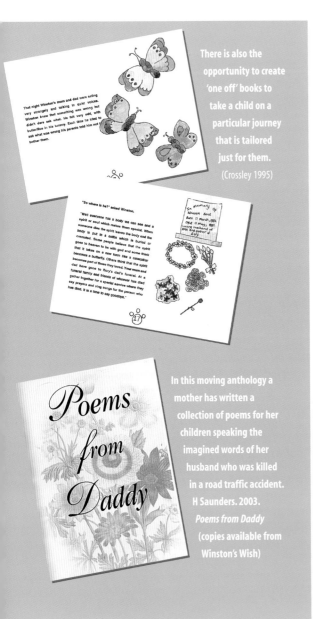

There is also the opportunity to create 'one off' books to take a child on a particular journey that is tailored just for them.
(Crossley 1995)

In this moving anthology a mother has written a collection of poems for her children speaking the imagined words of her husband who was killed in a road traffic accident. H Saunders. 2003. *Poems from Daddy* (copies available from Winston's Wish)

Bespoke stories: special stories for special circumstances

Developing a published book for children is not always possible or appropriate. Sometimes a unique person requires a unique story book, so there is also the opportunity to create 'one off' books to take a child on a particular journey that is tailored just for them. For many years we have been fortunate to have the talents of creative story-tellers on our staff team. As well as presenting stories verbally some have also created individual story books for children struggling with specific issues.

In one such story a wise and wacky Australian aunt was created for Winston (Crossley 1995). This aunt was able to pick up on some particular issues involving HIV and AIDS which a young child was struggling to understand. The child's mother had died from AIDS and she herself was infected with HIV. A bespoke story enables the practitioner to carefully narrate the child's journey while also providing some additional diversions such as humour, new characters with special powers, characters who have the confidence to blurt out exactly what's on their mind, and places to escape where they can be protected from fear, unpredictability and loss of control.

www.winstonswish.org.uk – using the web to reach young people

One of the real challenges for a child bereavement service is to engage children, young people and their parents by finding a variety of communications that will work for all ages. Towards the end of our first decade, we took a critical look at our services and judged that our communications for children were mainly geared towards a primary age group. We also recognised that many bereaved 12 to 18-year-olds might not be receiving help in a medium which fitted their lifestyle.

Why a website?

The expanding world of e-technology seemed a natural route to explore in reaching and supporting this older age group (Slater 2003). We are therefore developing an interactive and moderated website, which we hope will particularly appeal to teenagers.

Web pages have many potential advantages for bereaved young people providing:

- anonymity – nobody knowing who is accessing the pages
- privacy – nobody looking over your shoulder at your emotions
- ease of access – no appointment system or library check-out to negotiate
- immediacy – there at the click of a mouse
- accessibility – accessible to all regardless of physical ability, race, culture, gender – and no need to travel

- availability – available 24/7
- one-to-machine – no obvious contact with another person
- freedom of expression – no need to feel bad if you rush off somewhere else or swear vehemently
- a culturally relevant environment – meeting young people on their own 'ground'.

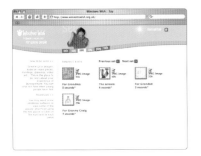

The youth pages of the website will develop as an integral part of the services that Winston's Wish offers, and contribute to realising our vision that all bereaved children receive the support they need to manage the impact of death in their lives. Additionally, they may also provide an insight into young people's responses and reactions to a wider audience, for example their parent(s), professionals and students.

While many 12 to 18-year-olds have access to a personal computer at home, and 100% have access through schools and libraries, not all young people have private access to the internet. This means the development of a website does not remove the need to develop and deliver other direct services for bereaved teenagers. Also, using computers is of course not appropriate for all young people. However, we are developing our site so that it will be accessible to those with impaired sight or hearing, to young people with low literacy levels and to those for whom English is not their first language.

Website structure

Like most organisations, the Winston's Wish website provides a wider window to the range of services available. We strive to make the standard features of these 'corporate' pages clear and striking for interested parties and potential supporters. Here, however, we concentrate on the section of the website that is specifically designed for young people.

We recognise that if the web pages for young people are to be successful, they must be vibrant, engaging, relevant and fresh.

The primary objectives identified for the web pages are closely aligned to those for the whole service, that is to offer support and encouragement to bereaved 12 to 18-year-olds using an appropriate means of communicating with this hard-to-reach audience.

We plan to achieve this by:

- encouraging emotional expression
- encouraging communication within the family
- enabling bereaved young people to communicate with each other
- enabling bereaved young people to ask questions about death
- informing and raising awareness among all young people of death, dying and grieving
- offering guidance and information sensitively and appropriately
- offering contact details and links, where appropriate, to other suitable services
- encouraging young people to take up other aspects of the Winston's Wish services
- encouraging young people to re-visit the site.

Design approach and tone

The whole design of the youth pages is intended to be attractive to young people who are, firstly, very internet-literate and critical and, secondly, likely to reach the site with at least some of the following thoughts:

- reluctantly – 'I don't want to be someone who is bereaved'
- ready/poised to click away – 'Don't dare patronise me'
- cautious – 'Are you going to preach?'
- diffident – 'I don't need any help'
- angry – 'No-one can help'
- prickly – 'Get away from me'
- isolated, both emotionally and physically – 'Am I on my own with this?'
- anxious about future/new responsibilities – 'I'm the eldest: everyone expects me to cope'.

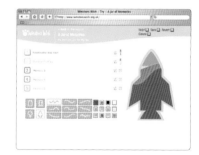

We assume that our audience will probably *expect to be*:

- patronised
- offered false comfort
- told 'there, there'
- told what to do
- told what to do to feel 'better'
- bored
- met by a host of fluffy bunnies and teddies.

We therefore set the tone of the youth pages with the following qualities:

- warm
- caring, but not cloying
- approachable
- accepting of people's feelings, choices, lifestyles
- supportive of web user's choices and actions
- trustworthy and reliable
- informed and factual
- clear
- competent and professional with a small 'p'
- kind
- confidentiality and security conscious.

Because of the audience, the youth pages can afford *not* to be too safe, polite, serious or worthy.

To sum up the desired tone, we hope that these web pages sound and even look like a bereaved young person's *ideal* big brother or sister.

We are also considering how to encourage bereaved young people to return to the site, being very aware that this audience will be looking for any excuse to click away to another site. Our hope is to build in sufficient helpful features so that a young person might say to themselves:

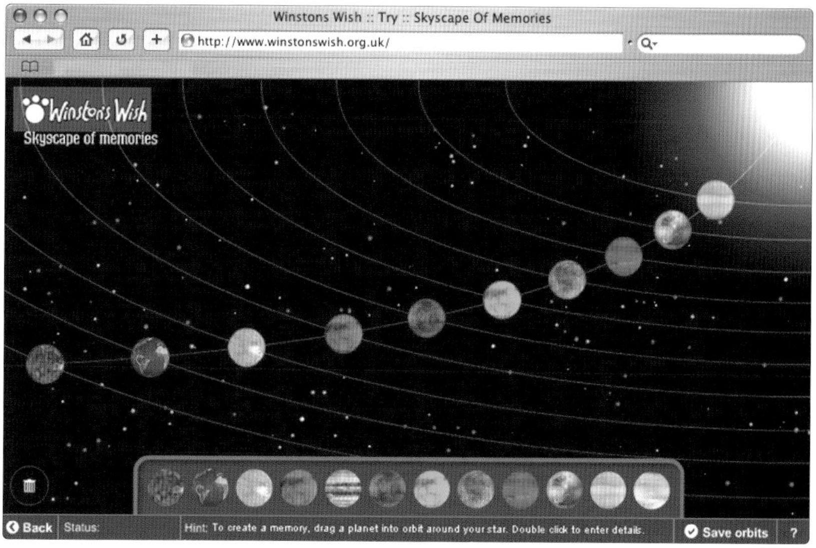

- 'It was cool.'
- 'I want to finish the piece of "work" I was doing on the site.'
- 'Actually, I don't like to admit it, but I felt a bit better afterwards.'
- 'I talked to mum about dad for the first time since he died.'

Content

Through this area of the site, bereaved young people are able to:

- **Remember** – easily accessible from both the youth pages and the rest of the site is our 'skyscape of memories'. The concept is a simple one, based on that of memorial quilts and the 'in memoriam' pages often found in local newspapers. Anyone can write their personal dedication which is linked to a star and solar system.
- **Ask** – any question about death, dying or bereavement and receive a personal reply next day. They are also able to look through some answers to frequently asked questions. We currently receive about 15 e-mails a week from young people with specific concerns and questions.

'In one of the stars I shall be living
in one of them I shall be laughing
and so it will be
as if all of the stars were laughing
when you look at the sky at night
… and there is sweetness in the laughter
of all the stars
and in the memories of those you love.'
Antoine de Saint-Exupery, *The Little Prince*

- **See** – a changing gallery of art submitted: pictures, drawings and, hopefully, video art too.
- **Say** – read through a 'library' of young people's words, stories, poems and song lyrics.
- **Try** – some of the resources that we find helpful in our work (for example, the notion of first aid kits: see page 168) as interactive exercises that young people can do on-line and then come back to when they want.
- **Talk** – via a 'message board' or discussion area where young people can talk to each other about their common and their unique experiences of bereavement and thereby support each other. This area is fully moderated by one of our staff to ensure young people's safety and security, and we also promote Talk Safe rules for web communication safety. There will also be a small, lightly moderated chat room facility for those young people that we know personally through group or individual work. This will be by invitation and password-protected. We hope this may be helpful in continuing supportive friendships among teenagers.
- **Play** – a link to a variety of (non-violent) computer games simply to make the point that young people may choose to have a break from the more intense aspects of the site.

Interactivity is not restricted to the young people's pages: the research area of the site offers opportunities for researchers to post their own papers and communicate with each other through a message board. Some pages are geared towards parents, while others are concerned with fundraising using some interesting ways of communicating with our supporters.

This chapter has shown that in supporting bereaved families we should be prepared to think and respond using a variety of creative outlets.

- Firstly, it discusses how carefully constructed booklets and videos can effectively support a bereaved parent and also seek to inform others (such as professionals and relatives) of the issues they face.
- Secondly, it considers the place of imaginative story-telling with younger children, exploring the possibilities of creating metaphors which promote memories and which positively strengthen connections with the person who has died.
- Finally, we describe a developing project using the web to reach 12 to 18-year-olds. It shows how the use of technology may be a more appropriate early intervention for some bereaved young people than face-to-face work. Moderated message boards are one way for bereaved young people to exchange thoughts, feelings and responses with others in similar situations and thereby reduce the isolation experienced.

'There are only two lasting bequests we can hope to give our children. One of these is roots, the other is wings.'

Hodding Carter

Chapter Eleven

Success is a journey, not a destination

Creating a context which offers services to families for as long as they need them

'Life is a succession of lessons which must be lived to be understood.'
Helen Keller

Previous chapters have outlined a series of interconnecting services which join together to make up a grief support programme. Since it is now widely accepted that bereavement is not something you simply 'get over' within a finite period of time, a child bereavement service will at least need to consider the possibility of having an on-going 'open door' policy. This chapter looks at the issues involved in accompanying families for as long as they need to stay.

Maintaining close connections

Currently, families can remain in contact with the service:

- by telephoning the Family Line, Mondays to Fridays, 9.30am to 5pm
- through crisis intervention, usually resulting in a re-referral for individual work
- by receiving *Pawprint*, our newsletter for all supporters of Winston's Wish
- remotely, by reading about the charity in the local or national press and occasionally through television coverage.

Pawprint, our newsletter for all supporters of Winston's Wish.

In addition, we arrange three specific social-therapeutic events each year which families can come to for as long as they find the connection helpful:

- Winston's birthday party (spring)
- Summer fun day (summer)
- Christmas ceremony, party and pantomime (winter).

In January each year we write to families inviting them to let us know if they want to remain on our database. The covering letter is carefully worded to ensure that those families who want to keep a close connection do not feel they are a burden and, similarly, those who feel it is time to move on can do so comfortably. The database is then updated and communications only sent out in accordance with parents' wishes. In the early years we observed a trend for families reliably to 'forget' to send the form back: some then experienced an acute sense of rejection when invitations no longer arrived in the post. We want families to feel there is stability and reliability to be found at Winston's Wish without fostering an unhealthy dependency. Before making their record inactive on the database a further communication is sent to say that as we have not received their form we will assume they no longer wish to be involved unless we hear from them to the contrary. This process provides a useful safety net for forgetful parents.

Experience shows that the majority of families choose to attend the social-therapeutic events for 2–3 years. However, when planning the events programme the practitioners are sensitive to the fact that, within the group of people attending, many will be at different places along their bereavement journey. Some families will be facing the utter desolation experienced in the early months of a bereavement. Others, who faced their bereavement many years ago, may arrive at an event in a social and buoyant mood, keen to catch up with old friends. Occasionally a parent will be tentatively involving a new partner/step-parent, who themselves may be nervous with the dynamic that Winston's Wish has in 'representing' the deceased parent or child. Because these events usually involve 300 or more people from all the situations described, staff and volunteers are carefully briefed on the families attending and designated workers are asked to link up with any particularly vulnerable family groups.

The younger the children, the more likely the family is to attend social-therapeutic events. Mothers are more likely to attend events than fathers. If a surviving parent forms a new relationship this is often a transitional point for a family to end contact. However, for some families the introduction and involvement of a new partner in social events is a subtle (and often unconscious) process to see whether the new partner can find a way for the deceased to have a continuing place in the family unit. This means that we need to be sensitive to a new partner's sense of apprehension, and make sure that they too receive a warm welcome. One mother said: 'When I brought Tom [new partner] to the summer fun day I almost felt a bit disloyal to Ben [husband]. It was as though our relationship with Winston's Wish came about through Ben's death and maybe it was not right to be there now I had met Tom. I sense that the kids would be really upset if we didn't go; Gemma has already asked; "Now Tom's here will we have to forget our dad?"'

Children meeting up with friends at Winston's birthday event.

Planning social-therapeutic events

Organising a successful social-therapeutic event for a large number of people, including children and young people of all ages, is a challenging task. It has all the usual constraints of budgetary limitations, unpredictable numbers and accommodating individual preferences. On top of that, the programme needs to reflect appropriately the bereavement issues that bring this collection of families together. Most families attending will have experienced individual work and/or a residential weekend, which is a structured and intimate experience. It can therefore seem like a significant culture shift to move from that experience to a large venue with many unfamiliar faces. It is easy to be lonely in a crowd. We therefore work hard to try and manage families' expectations and experiences when they attend these social-therapeutic events. We give particular thought to activities on arrival which will promote integration and give families an opportunity to talk with and meet others while they settle in.

There is insufficient space here to describe all three events, so we outline the essence of our annual Christmas event, which attracts the highest numbers and is the one event that families often choose to attend for many years.

2–3

Most families choose to attend the social-therapeutic events for 2–3 years.

Tom, aged 7, came to
Winston's Wish after
the death of his
mother from cancer
in 1997 aged 34. Tom
says that when he
lights his candle he
likes to 'think about
mummy and her
smiley face and all
the nice things we
did together'.

The Christmas event

Of our three social-therapeutic events, the Christmas ceremony, party and panto remains the most popular. It usually attracts more than 300 children, young people, parents, relatives and friends. These large events present a significant challenge to a service provider, and are potentially costly, particularly in relation to the structured entertainment required to occupy and amuse such large numbers. At Christmas, we need to create a range of activities that will be satisfying for people across all age groups, encompassing everyone from energetic toddlers to anxious grandparents who may be experiencing the service for the first time.

The Christmas event usually takes place early in the build-up to the festive season. Parents are often extremely apprehensive about how they will cope and make Christmas sufficiently 'special' for their children. The event is therefore structured to address both a social and a therapeutic agenda. Families have a choice of coming to all three parts of the Christmas event, or just one or two. The majority do attend the ceremony, party and pantomime: however, those families with very young children usually decide to go home after the early evening party ends.

The ceremony is carefully designed to allow time and space to remember, while the party and panto which follow also acknowledge that it is OK to have fun. This message seems particularly meaningful for children who are sensitive to the strain they perceive in their parent(s), yet throughout the festive season are constantly reminded by TV adverts, past experience and so on that Christmas equates with fun, excitement, magical experiences and presents. Not surprisingly, parents are often far removed from the magic, acutely aware of their children's expectations, and desperately keen for 'the whole thing to be over'.

We find that everyone particularly engages with our 'skyscape of stars' activity (see pages 232–233). Children, parents, grandparents and friends are all invited to write their messages on silver stars. These may be pinned on to a large piece of blue material, which is then hoisted up to simulate a star-laden sky. It is a moving, memorable and engaging ritual for everyone.

On some occasions children have read their own poems. One year, a father read out a poem called *That's Normal* which provided a real connection for parents who struggle with the high expectations of making Christmas 'good' while also wanting to collapse in a heap.

That's Normal

If you think you're going insane –
that's normal.

If all you do is cry –
that's normal.

If you have trouble with most minor decisions –
that's normal.

If you can't taste food or have any semblance of appetite –
that's normal.

If you have feelings of rage, denial and depression –
that's normal.

If you find yourself enjoying a funny moment and immediately
feeling guilty –
that's normal.

If your friends dwindle away and you feel like you have the plague –
that's normal.

If your blood boils and the hairs in your nose curl when someone tells
you it's God's will –
that's normal.

If you can't talk about it but you can smash dishes, shred old phone
books or kick the garbage can (preferably empty) down the street –
that's normal.

If you can share your story, your feelings, with an understanding
listener, another bereaved person –
that's a beginning.

If you can get a glimmer of your child's or partner's life, rather than
his or her death –
that's wonderful.

If you can remember your child's or partner's smile –
that's healing.

If you can find your mirrors have become windows and you are able
to reach out to other bereaved people –
that's growing.

Adapted from a poem by Edith Fraser

Skyscape of stars – messages from children and parents

'Daddy. I remember all the stories you would read me and riding on your lap in your electric wheelchair!'

'She would stand a few steps up on the stairs and say "Ciara … can fly" and she'd jump down and I would catch her in my arms.'

'My precious memory is: doing girly things with my mum.'

'Pete. I remember his love of music and the funny way he danced. I remember how he could talk for hours about history. I remember how he carried Stephen and wrestled with him. How he loved us all. X'

'I loved your outrageous teases, wrapped in adoration; your magic and your magnetic laughter.'

'I would like to remember the "normal" times when we were all together as a family. Luv Phillipa.'

'My favourite memories of daddy: He was funny. He was kind. He loved me and I loved him.'

'I miss you so much and wish I could see you again. I remember practising bringing up your breakfast on weekends for when I was older but I won't be able to do that now.'

'To my darling Emma. Remembering you always and keeping you close to my heart. Your hugs and smiles are missed but felt always. Loving you always – Love Mum xxx'

'My Dad x
I love you, and my biggest memory is that you love me too. I will never forget you and never stop loving you! I just want you to know I love you. I miss you. You are my Dad. Love Beth xxx'

'Your love shines in our lives and gives strength to enjoy our future. Missing you still, but able to look forward now. Rosie'

'My precious memories are still as strong as our "power rope". That holiday. Tug of duvet. Your smiles. Your smelly socks. Miss you. Love you forever.'

'I hope that I will always remember you Dad xxxx'

'I remember … making a snowman on the corn field. Love you always my darling.'

'Reece. Always on my mind. Forever in my heart. Too many precious memories to write, but they are all in my heart and mind. Love and miss you so much. Why aren't you here? Everlasting love Alice xxxxxxxxxxxx'

'My precious memory of my lovely son Jack; His beautiful smile. His chubby knees. His special hugs and wet kisses. His huge appetite for life. The love he gave to us.'

'I enjoyed playing with my Dad because he has been kind to me in all my life.'

'Watching Chris sing carols outside shops with the school, dressed as an Xmas present and really wanting her to win the prize. AND SHE DID.'

Winston appears
with 'Mr Brog' at one
of the birthday
events at a local
theatre.

The rest of the programme is equally magical, involving music, story-telling and appropriate festive touches.

After this opportunity for memory and reflection, it is then time for tea! The Christmas event is usually supported by local companies or schools which help with the catering. Locations vary. One year we chose a beautiful modern church in a central location, close to the pantomime venue. Choosing a church as a venue can be off-putting for some families: however, we are careful to make sure the programme concentrates on spiritual rather than overtly religious themes. Another year we were given wonderful hospitality at a secondary school. Many sixth formers came in for the afternoon to help set up the party and serve the party tea.

After the tea party families then make their way to the local theatre to see the panto, where 300 seats are reserved for Winston's Wish families. Younger children usually bring their own Winston bears to watch, sometimes dressed to match the theme of the show. The theatre, like other community organisations, readily embraces the cause and chooses to offer significantly reduced ticket prices. We now ask families to contribute towards the ticket price: previously, when tickets were provided free, some families would routinely request them and sometimes not turn up. While we encourage friends and extended family to accompany parents and children to the ceremony, restricted resources mean that the panto tickets are limited to the nuclear family group. This is a purely practical resource issue.

New partners and step-families

Life is a series of transitions. The bereavement journey, like all journeys, may involve junctions which, if taken, could lead the family on an altered route. Here we consider the issues for a service if a parent forms a new relationship. Families who become involved with a child bereavement service do so to receive support, and maintain or resolve fractured connections with key people in their lives who have died. However, research (Worden 1996) shows that some parents, mostly fathers, are likely to reach out for some kind of new attachment early on, a replacement for the lost spouse who was their primary source of support.

In the Harvard Child Bereavement Study, it was found that 37% of parents dated in the first year. At year two, 17% of families had a parent who was either engaged, living with someone or remarried. We have no comparative data at Winston's Wish although the majority of parents attending Camp Winston have not established new relationships. However, it seems that families in which parents find a new

partner fairly soon after the death feel less need to maintain a connection with our service. Here, the transition to leave the service early on seems to happen fairly easily. Perhaps where the transition becomes more complex is for those families which have become attached to the service for two or more years before a potential new partner has arrived. In some ways, 'Winston' seems to be a vehicle to 'continue the bond' with the deceased relative. A potentially difficult transition can occur when the unsuspecting bereaved parent falls in love but is sensitive to the possibility that their new partner may feel overwhelmed and/or threatened by the memories of a previous partner. Since Winston's Wish actively encourages memories the change process can be sensitive. The challenge perhaps is to try and create a situation in which the new partner feels actively welcomed and valued. This is a vulnerable time for the children too who will also need tangible reminders that they can hold onto a valid and legitimate relationship 'then, now and always'.

In this picture, Laura has the confidence to recognise the relationship with her step-dad Michael, but ensures her paternal father is clearly represented in the picture which communicates her need to maintain a continuing bond.

A new partner can mean a child will need to be reassured that their birth father or mother can remain an on-going part of family life.

Winston makes a
surprise visit at the
wedding of two
families.

Case study **Rob and Mandy**

The couple met each other at a French evening class. Rob was divorced and he and his ex-wife shared custody of their two children. Rob had recently been made redundant and his confidence was low. Mandy's husband had died from cancer five years before and she also had two children. Mandy had been coming to Winston's Wish throughout this period and was well known within the organisation, more recently helping regularly as a fundraising volunteer. The couple started going out and a solid, secure relationship developed between them.

The older children from both families were casually interested in witnessing their parents' budding relationship, the younger ones excited at the prospect of building a new family unit. After eight months together, Rob still seemed reluctant to move into Mandy's family home. Eventually he confided that he found it difficult to be faced with photos and other memories of her dead husband throughout the house. Mandy's children also had mixed feelings. Her eldest daughter liked the stable life they had finally created after dad's death and valued the connection with Winston's Wish. Her much younger sister liked the idea of a 'new dad' but also wanted to remain close and loyal to her 'real dad'. Mandy's in-laws gave the impression that they were surprised that she had become involved with someone. Her own parents were delighted but wanted her to be very careful 'in case she got hurt again'. Mandy was busy trying to keep everyone happy and near to collapsing under the strain.

One morning she phoned the Family Line and rapidly burst into tears. After a 40-minute consultation, we suggested that it may be useful for us to come and meet with Rob and Mandy together. Mandy's mother looked after her children so the meeting could take place in Rob's home, where he might have a greater sense of being in control. The session simply aimed to create a safe environment to address the issues openly and work out the best way forward. Together, we discussed the forthcoming transition period which the couple hoped would culminate in marriage. We all agreed that a gradual withdrawal from Winston's Wish would be preferable for the children. They planned that for the next few years they would just attend the Christmas event as the key time to formally acknowledge the past, while building on the present.

As a marriage gift, Rob gave his step-children a photo frame with three photos. One photo showed the children with their mum and 'real' dad. Another showed the children with the friends they had made at Camp Winston, and a large central photo featured the new family unit with Rob, Mandy and all four children. Rob presented the gift to the children on the day of the wedding. He even arranged for a life-sized costume Winston bear to make a surprise appearance at the reception. This proved to be a sensitive gesture which was appreciated not only for his step-children but also for their paternal grandparents (Mandy's previous in-laws) who understandably experienced a mix of emotions on the day.

We continued to see the family for three more years just at Christmas. Mandy recently wrote 'officially' to say goodbye and thanks. She felt they had completed the part of the journey which needed to involve Winston's Wish – a journey which for them had lasted for eight years.

Coping with re-referrals

A recent analysis of re-referrals shows that there are many reasons why families may make contact with the service again (a re-referral is defined as a child or parent who was no longer involved in group or individual work). Often it is because a child has reached a further developmental stage in their lives with different challenges (such as starting secondary school, sitting exams or being under threat of exclusion) that trigger a destabilising transition period. Sometimes it is due to a further death in the family or, as mentioned earlier in the chapter, due to changes in the family structure such as their parent establishing a new relationship or the birth of a brother or sister. In some cases significant problems such as aggression, disruptive behaviour, anger and withdrawal may have developed and this leads the parent or a professional to look for further support for the child. Alternatively, re-referrals are sometimes made simply because the child was too young to benefit from the service when the death occurred, and they are now older, asking many questions and ready, for example, to attend an intervention like Camp Winston.

Following new assessments for all the children who are re-referred, the most common interventions offered are a series of individual sessions and/or an invitation to attend Camp Winston if they have not been before. In some instances the most effective intervention is to offer individual work with the parent to help them gain the confidence to 'contain' their child's psychological distress. For some children who are re-referred a choice is made not to take up any services. Interestingly, this is most likely to occur when the re-referral has been made by a professional (for example, social services) rather than the family. For others,

'As the children grow they confront problems at school and at home. It is very difficult to know how sympathetic or strict to be – knowing what may be due to their dad's death and what would be happening anyway. On-going contact with Winston's Wish helps put a perspective on what would have happened anyway.'
Feedback from parent, Service Evaluation 2003

Young people will revisit their grief at different developmental stages. Christ 2000

'We have received
thoughtful and
appropriate help
from you ever since
our bereavement.
Through it, and
because of it, the
children have
maintained a fluid
emotional outlook
which has not locked
up their feelings.
Dad has become
someone to whom
they all refer and
whose presence can
be called on, and is
no longer someone
who is not there.'
Feedback from parent,
Service Evaluation 2003

even though appointments are made for a series of individual sessions, it can be difficult for them and their family to commit to the service.

An analysis of all re-referrals from January to September 2002 (excluding people who phoned the Family Line on more than one occasion) pointed up a number of trends. Most children being re-referred were aged between 10 and 16 and the gap between original referral and re-referral varied between one and four years, with the average being two years. In the majority of cases it was the father who had died, with a mother or sibling death being less common. Cancer was by far the main cause of death. Mothers were the most likely to re-refer their children.

Our findings from this small sample of children re-referred are quite similar to others (Winton 2002) and are consistent with the knowledge that children and young people will revisit their grief at different developmental stages and through various life events (Christ 2000). Some children have expressed a feeling of 'security' in working with the same practitioner that they did when they were first referred. While we have to be realistic in terms of a perennial 'open door', our clinical observations suggest that parents feel confident to re-contact the service when problems or questions arise which often means that problems can be responded to quickly and with a relatively brief intervention.

Viability of an open-ended service?

Having a service for as long as people need it is a financial liability that most service providers would naturally shy away from. Yet, market researchers will tell us that 'an extended warranty' (Krauss: in preparation) is reassuring and is a service that 'customers' value enormously: 'We know you will always be there when we need you'. Such principles undoubtedly require significant resources. If an organisation wants to offer some level of service to *any* child who has experienced the death of a parent or sibling, then those services will be determined by balancing the demand and funding resources available. Another approach is to assess those families most *at risk* and offer a comprehensive service to fewer families. As we set out in Chapter 1, we hope to create an open access community-based service. However, this means engaging the community to such an extent that the necessary funds are raised allowing a comprehensive service to be offered to all families.

This chapter has reflected on the need and viability of creating an open-ended service for bereaved families. Service providers clearly need to balance carefully the concept of:

- offering services which are *'preventive'*
- being there when parents/children choose to get in *contact*
- creating services which encourage *independence* (not dependence)
- being realistic in terms of creating *expectations* given the *available resources*.

The model of providing on-going social-therapeutic events is described and the capacity of services to respond to re-referrals is considered.

'If a child is to keep his inborn sense of wonder, he needs the companionship of at least one adult, who can share it, rediscovering with him the joy, excitement and mystery of the world we live in.'

Rachel Carsen

Chapter Twelve

Fellow travellers

Establishing a child bereavement
service which is sustained and
cherished by the community it serves

'The journey of
a thousand miles
must begin with
a single step.'
Lau-Tzu

**In this chapter, we reflect on the way Winston's Wish has attempted
to build bridges with various aspects of the local community to help
construct secure foundations to ensure its survival.** We describe the
importance of having clear and viable fundraising and marketing plans, and
a communications strategy that enables us to connect with all the various
groups and individuals who relate to the service.

'Children come "alive" when they have the opportunity to do something that may help to prevent more grief.'
Feedback from a parent whose child had helped to organise a fundraising event

Constructing secure foundations

As discussed in Chapter 1, Winston's Wish started life firmly conceived and delivered by the National Health Service (NHS). Although the NHS continues to support the service to a limited extent, both financially and in kind, it was clear that if the service was to survive it needed the 'community' to champion its survival.

It has taken many years for the service to become slowly woven into the community fabric of Gloucestershire. The majority of community-based child bereavement services will rely on some degree of public fundraising and will therefore need to embed themselves in their local communities. They will need support from charitable trusts, companies, fundraising events and community groups. However, awareness in the community is not just about generating funds. Greater familiarity will also mean that potential users of a service will be more likely to make contact. A community-based child bereavement service must not be seen as a 'bolt on' to a mental health service. Winston's Wish is simply known as a service for children coping with a family death, which relies heavily on charitable funding. It is not seen as a mental health/psychiatric service. Even though a significant part of our work involves the skills of mental health practitioners great care is taken to present the service in non-pathological packaging (Timimi 2003). This approach seems to be acceptable to families – and makes sense to a variety of potential funders.

Case study **Building community networks**

The position of Winston's Wish in the local community can be illustrated by a number of different conversations which took place at a community fundraising event: the teddy bears' picnic.

This family day out was organised with help from various business sponsors in the local community. It was held in the grounds of a local university. Our staff had regularly given lectures to new teachers on their personal, social and health education curriculum, and four PE students subsequently trained to be group leaders for Camp Winston. On this day, all four energetic volunteers were on hand to provide wet sponges to throw at the mayor. The mayor had chosen Winston's Wish to be his charity of the year, and he, like many other supporters, personally understood the need for our work. So too did the man who emerged from the wood-turning tent. 'I made you this – not sure if it will be of any use. I lost my wife 15 years ago when my daughter Janet was 12. Somehow we made it through – if only there had been something like Winston's Wish then.' Janet was sitting in the corner of the tent proudly bouncing a giggling baby. It was a poignant reminder that this baby's grandmother could not share in the joy of the new arrival. Life does go on, but so too does the longing. He had presented us with a beautifully hand-engraved miniature coffin. He explained that he had read an article in the *Citizen* (a local newspaper) which talked about children's involvement at funerals. He hoped this might help us. It has since been regularly used as an aid when preparing a bereaved child for a funeral.

People in the community help in many ways: this miniature coffin was beautifully made by a local craftsman.

As we enjoyed the sunshine and music from the local radio 'sound bus', a mother tentatively approached and asked if she could pass on a cheque. When asked why she had chosen to support Winston's Wish her eyes filled up with tears as she explained that the son of a work colleague had been killed in a road traffic accident the previous week. We talked for some time and together thought of ways she and other work colleagues could respond. The family concerned was already known to Winston's Wish as the boy's school had been in touch. While ensuring the family's confidentiality, we explained the ways we might hope to help any family in this situation. She seemed reassured and said she would now feel able to call her colleague to offer her support.

Finally, on the way home, someone waved from the car park. (The reason we sometimes get stopped is because we wear bright red fleeces with the Winston's Wish logo on the front!) This time it was an upbeat young man with his wife and three children. He called over: 'You won't know me, but I just wanted to say thanks on behalf of The Royal Oak'. (We remembered that The Royal Oak was a pub which had held a raffle in memory of a member of its bar staff, who had died very suddenly in her 50s.) We were able to acknowledge that the fundraising had a particular meaning because of their loss. He went on to say: 'That certificate you sent was great. We had it framed. It's in the bar and every time I look at it I think of Chris. It helps us talk about her, we all miss her so much … so thanks for that and keep up the good work with the kids'.

So we left for home, happy that we had raised over £4,000 on that day – but equally happy to get feedback on the less tangible, but nonetheless valuable role of a child bereavement service networking within the wider community.

Of course it takes time to become nurtured by any community. It takes even longer for that warmth to be translated into genuine enthusiasm where people feel they can play a personal role in influencing a developing organisation.

'That certificate you sent was great. We had it framed.'

'Friends of Winston'
launching a series of
coffee mornings in a
French patisserie.
Picture courtesy of the
Gloucestershire Echo

Media opportunities

Ambassadors come in all guises. A very few will carry the influence attached to celebrity status and the most persuasive and effective ambassadors are the families which have used the service. It took us some long and thoughtful discussions before we realised that some families actually benefit from having the opportunity to share their story publicly. At first we believed that as practitioners we knew best and should not be involved in any action which may run the risk of exploiting and bringing harm. What we perhaps under-estimated was that there comes a time for some families when they themselves feel strengthened by their ability to offer support to others. We have recently evolved a media policy which aims to protect families while offering them a framework to communicate key messages confidently. Over the years we have been involved in a variety of national broadcast and print media. However, the most important partner for a community-based child bereavement service will probably be local newspapers and radio stations. For example, in Gloucestershire there are several local papers; however, the two main papers (the *Citizen* and the *Gloucestershire Echo*) have a combined estimated readership of 746,000 each day. They therefore present a wonderful vehicle to communicate with the community and invite them to help in our on-going development. An editorial commented on our tenth anniversary:

> *'Hundreds of children and their parents have been helped through the most difficult times in their lives … the county is proud of its [Winston's Wish's] achievements and grateful to have such an exemplary service on our doorstep. It doesn't happen on its own of course. With costs of over £1,000 for each family the money must come from sponsors. So if you're running the London marathon, organising a cake sale, or even writing a will, spare a thought for Winston's Wish – which couldn't wish for anything better than your support.'*
> Editorial, *Gloucestershire Echo*, Wednesday 8 January 2003
> Reproduced with permission

Of course 'the media' can also present a more challenging persona, especially for a bereaved family whose story is thought to be of local interest. Many families have been outraged by inaccurate or insensitive reporting. We decided to try to establish a genuine and positive relationship with local journalists. As these relationships developed it became possible to highlight with journalists the issues that caused distress to some bereaved relatives.

Case study **Building a relationship with the media**

We became aware that increasing numbers of families were telling us about unhelpful media intrusion. This was particularly relevant for families where the death was sudden and traumatic ... and implicitly 'newsworthy'. Families were upset because details like names were often spelt incorrectly, and ages inaccurate. There were sensitivities to the language (for example, 'estranged', 'inconclusive evidence') used which many felt unfairly implied blame and responsibility. We decided to be proactive and phoned the editor of one of our local newspapers. We made it clear that we appreciated their agenda was to fill a paper with news stories and features which were of interest to the Gloucestershire community. Once this had been acknowledged the editor was actively interested in looking for practical ways forward. A number of tangible outcomes arose from this telephone conversation.

'The whole class really enjoyed the fundraising and my daughter was really proud to help her friends understand.'
Feedback from parent, Service Evaluation 2003

We arranged a meeting with the editor, chief constable and chief executive of Winston's Wish to discuss how the police and journalists could build a more co-operative relationship which understood each other's responsibilities and could hold a shared understanding of the needs of families bereaved by sudden deaths.

The editor subsequently invited the chief executive and a parent to come into the newsroom and make an informal presentation to staff. The parent explained the impact of reading coverage of her daughter's accidental death. The child had died in a drowning accident while abroad on holiday. The mother, now several years on from her daughter's death, calmly and carefully explained how certain aspects of the reporting had impacted on the family's grief and presented the community with inaccurate messages which took years to ameliorate. The meeting was collaborative, both parties clearly wanting to make a difference. Many journalists appeared genuinely moved.

Through this meeting relationships were developed on a face-to-face, personal level which has meant that the paper will willingly promote important child bereavement issues (for example, features on Mother's Day and Father's Day) as well as highlighting fundraising activities. Equally, if a news item has caused distress, it has been possible to call the paper to highlight the issue and, where possible, remedial action has followed. A simple phone call from the paper to say 'sorry' can sometimes avoid a bereaved person years of ruminating on the thought that the paper had deliberately sought to cause harm.

It took us some long and thoughtful discussions before we realised that some families actually benefit from having the opportunity to share their story publicly.

A head teacher is 'jailed and bailed' in a fundraising event which involved extensive community networks.

Building collaboration with community groups

'The community' is composed of thousands of community groupings, many with constitutions designed to 'give something back'. Figure 22 gives some indication of the scope of this collaborative work. All these organisations and many more have requested a talk on our work. Since our initial launch in 1992 we have been fortunate to receive regular requests from Rotary Clubs, the Scouts, the Brownies, Women's Institutes, youth groups and others, all keen to know more about what we do – and how they may be able to help. In the early years, practitioners would be asked to make such presentations. We now have a presentation team largely made up of volunteers who are trained to make presentations tailored to each group, take questions as they arise and be comfortable with the likelihood that there may be people in the audience personally affected by the subject matter.

We are invited to make an average of six presentations to community groups each month. Here is a cross-section from a four-month period to give a flavour of the range of community groups. The vast majority of these clubs and groups wanted to hear about our work as they had, or intended, to fundraise on our behalf. In many of the clubs, members knew families who had been bereaved.

Figure 22: Local community presentations about Winston's Wish (January to April)

- Beaufort Swimming Club
- Cheltenham Townswomen's Guild
- Churcham Art Group
- Cirencester Phoenix Majorettes
- City of Gloucester Wine Circle
- Cranham Women's Institute
- Drybrook Ladies Choir
- Elmbank Seniors Club
- First Redding Brownie Pack
- Forest Green Rovers Football Club
- Forest of Dean Golf Club Ladies Section
- France Lynch Friday Evening Group
- Gloucestershire University Students Union (RAG)
- Holy Trinity School
- Hucclecote Metal Detecting Club
- Retired Police Group
- Rotary Club of Stonehouse
- Saintbridge Sports and Social Club
- St Gregory's 55+ Social Club
- Street Youth Project: Gloucester
- Tewkesbury Abbey Mothers' Union
- The Bell Inn Charity Committee
- The Royal Naval Association: Dursley and District
- Three Counties Show
- Woodchester Friendly Circle

Building networks with companies

Like community groups, companies often have a desire to link up with charitable organisations. The motivation to link with a particular cause may be multifaceted. Staff may be interested because of circumstances in their personal background, or there may be a strong cause-related marketing link, and/or it may be an effective way to boost team-building within the staff group and so on.

Case study Company partnership

A large local company which offers financial services selected Winston's Wish as a 'partner' for three years. We were nominated by staff who had read about our work in the local papers and seen a documentary on TV. We drew up a detailed memorandum of agreement to reflect the terms of the partnership and were allocated three senior managers to be our 'sponsors'.

These managers helped us with strategic planning, database development, risk management and relocation of our office accommodation. In addition to a corporate donation of £10,000 each year, the staff also arranged a host of enjoyable fundraising activities which raised further revenue. Each year the company was given a series of 'challenges'. The challenges were suggested by a range of local charities, and staff could choose which ones captured their interest. The nature of the challenges often required more than one person so they became an ideal focus for team-building, usually as out-of-hours work. The gardens outside our offices were transformed over five weekends by members of a committed team who were always motivated to go for a team (building) drink at the end of a strenuous day.

The company also offers an innovative skills sharing scheme, which allows staff the opportunity to share their skills within work time. So far we have benefited from advice on database administration, information technology development and human resources.

Supporters from the community have helped 'Winston' to become part of everyday life. Here, an employee from a local company celebrates his success in raising funds to buy bears for children who attend Camp Winston.

Fitting the pieces together

In building a community-based service, we are repeatedly reminded that it is the community 'networks' which become the real foundations on which a service can be developed. A communications strategy therefore needs to carefully identify all the key stakeholders. This allows us to work out ways in which our values and vision can be plainly articulated, understood and embraced by the various groups.

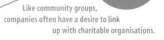

Like community groups, companies often have a desire to link up with charitable organisations.

Figure 23: Building a community-based service – key stakeholders

There are many individuals and groups who can influence the integration of a child bereavement service into the community by acting as ambassadors.

Bereaved child
Trustees
Staff
Volunteers
Community groups
Bereaved parent
Extended family
Work colleagues
Companies
Friends and neighbours
Charitable trusts
Schools
Major donors
Professionals
Media
General public
Childhood Bereavement Network
The statutory sector

Winston's Wish

Pictures courtesy of the *Gloucestershire Echo* and the *Citizen*.

This chapter has highlighted the crucial importance of ensuring that service development is embraced by the community it serves. The growth of many child bereavement services has been witnessed over the past decade. That is truly fabulous. However, in the same period we have witnessed the near burn-out of equally fabulous clinicians who cannot be expected to cope with ever-increasing workloads with no accompanying income increases. In recent years at least three excellent UK child bereavement services have been closed. The difficult question we have to ask ourselves is: can a service be truly 'excellent' if it gives insufficient attention to community networks? Perhaps we shall only really have a feel for the answer to this question when the Childhood Bereavement Network has a chance to reflect on the next 10 years' progress in seeing open access, community-based services becoming established in counties throughout the UK.

'Only those who risk going too far, can possibly find out how far one can go.'

TS Eliot

Chapter Thirteen

A continually evolving journey

Given the distance travelled, are we on the right path?

'Failure is success if we learn from it.'
Malcolm S Forbes

In this chapter, we consider the need to reflect regularly on what we do and why we do it. In particular we consider how we might evaluate the overall impact of an organisation against the longer-term vision we hold for bereaved children and young people. This final chapter also reflects on the organisational structures that have evolved, enabling Winston's Wish to move out of a pioneering mode into a more mature and robust organisation that has the capacity to plan, evaluate and develop its work.

Travelling towards the vision

Our vision is that bereaved children, young people and their families will receive the support they need. Our mission is to provide high quality services – in a creative environment – to grieving children and the community through:

- direct work with children and young people
- parental support
- facilitating peer support
- training, education and research.

'You really brought us together as a family – and Liz is able to understand when we have our good and bad days – most importantly she now feels she is still able to have Paula as her sister.'

Ann

Our key aims are:

- to provide a range of consistently high quality services for bereaved children, young people and their families
- to contribute to public and professional understanding of the needs of bereaved children
- to generate the necessary resources to provide a sustainable service
- to have in place effective financial, information, management and human resources infrastructure to support all activities.

Primary clinical objectives

Winston's Wish has identified five primary clinical objectives for its work. Our services are designed to help bereaved children and families by providing increased opportunities for:

- **support, information and education** – supporting children and families to understand death and what it means to them

- **understanding and expressing grief** – encouraging children and families to share and understand the feelings, thoughts and individual ways of coping with loss

- **remembering** – helping families to find ways of remembering the person who has died

- **communication** – encouraging family members to talk openly with each other

- **meeting others** – providing opportunities to meet other families with similar experiences.

The passing of time is unlikely to alter our overall vision. However, while this vision might be the ultimate goal, it is not easily achievable in the short term. There may be a whole range of multifaceted reasons which complicate the vision being achieved. For example, a child may have a surviving parent who is suicidal, a death may mean severe financial hardship, a death may have resulted in a family needing to move house, the child may have pre-existing mental health difficulties which have intensified since the death and so on. Equally, the availability of limited financial resources will also have an impact on the range of services which can be developed. There are many separate areas to address, therefore, to achieve this vision, and the process of achieving the end result – that bereaved children and young people receive the support they need – may not be straightforward.

The National Council for Voluntary Organisations (Wainwright 2002) shows that it is possible to think of this progression towards a final goal as a journey and, even if the end result is not achieved, some progress will almost certainly have been made towards this goal. The amount that has been achieved in the process is sometimes referred to as '*distance travelled*' and usually consists of '*soft outcomes*'. In the case of child bereavement we need to find ways of identifying the stepping stones or soft outcomes – the necessary achievements en route to the final, hard outcome. For the bereaved child this could include increased confidence, community services which are acceptable and accessible to parents, and evidence of memory retention which improves self-esteem. An organisation's outcomes may also include a capacity to generate reliable income sources, to market itself effectively and so on. As an organisation within the Childhood Bereavement Network we need to be able to demonstrate that something worthwhile has been achieved – that some distance has been travelled on the journey.

Evidence-based services

The path for all statutory and voluntary organisations concerned with health promotion and social care is now firmly heading in the direction of evidence-based services, a route to 'what works'. With increasing pressure on limited resources in the public and voluntary sectors, we need to show that our interventions do have an impact on people's health and well-being (Muir Gray 2000; Davies et al 2000). We also need to monitor and evaluate our services so that we know they are relevant and appropriate to people's needs.

'The whole experience of Winston's Wish has been uplifting, supportive and positive. For the first time since my husband's death I was able to express how I felt about single parenthood and the way his untimely death has changed me. It is great to know that someone out there understands.'
Feedback from parent, Service Evaluation 2003

A controlled trial of family therapy with children bereaved of a parent showed that psychological difficulties (40% morbidity) could be reduced to 20% by a series of six family meetings. Black and Urbanowicz 1987

'Thank you all whole-
heartedly for the
ideas, thoughts, care
and everything
possible in between
that you gave to
myself, Tess and
Anna. I reckon you
have provided us
with the sturdiest,
unwobbliest
stepping stone yet.'

Parent

In the UK, community-based child bereavement services (whether statutory or voluntary) are guided by government strategies for mental health and for children's services. In England, for example, there is the National Service Framework for Mental Health (Department of Health 1999), and the National Service Framework for Children (Department of Health 2003). The Children and Young People's Unit works closely with organisations such as the National Children's Bureau, within which the Childhood Bereavement Network is located.

We are also mindful of the role that child bereavement services might play in reducing inequalities in health, promoting social inclusion and contributing to the healthy schools initiative. All these areas of work require multi-agency partnership, which we can monitor and evaluate to determine the impact on bereaved children.

What does 'measuring impact' mean for child bereavement services?

Before considering the larger question of impact, it may be helpful to look at the more tangible components in evaluation (Wainwright 2002; Charities Evaluation Services 2000; Shaw 2002).

'Inputs' are the resources that contribute to a service: for example, income, staff, volunteers and equipment. After 10 years we are reaching a point where we can accurately define and cost these inputs.

'Services/activities' are what an organisation does with its inputs to achieve its mission. At Winston's Wish this would be the services described in chapters 3 to 11: for example, residential groups, helpline and individual work.

'Outputs' are countable units and are the direct products of an organisation's activities. We are in the process of devising a range of monthly key performance indicators (KPIs) to measure and describe these outputs objectively. For example, Figure 24 shows some of the KPIs relating to a residential group service.

'Outcomes' are the benefits or changes that occur as a result of the work for bereaved families. They are more difficult to measure than outputs, as they will often be less tangible and they may be longer term. For example, an outcome may be an increase in resilience or self-esteem, increased open communication between parent and child, a more robust continuing bond facilitated by prompts to assist memory retention and so on. All these so-called 'soft outcomes' provide the stepping stones to the overall hard outcome that bereaved children will receive the support they need.

Finally, **'impact'** is a widely-used term but is rarely clearly defined in the evaluation literature.

> 'Impact is any change resulting from an activity, project or organisation. It includes intended as well as unintended effects, negative as well as positive, and long term as well as short term.' (Wainwright 2002)

We have tried to increase the impact of our work in a number of ways, for example by encouraging the development of other community-based child bereavement services. Nationally we are trying to do this through training and raising awareness of the needs of bereaved children. However, perhaps the overall measure of impact lies in the prevention of mental health difficulties for bereaved children and the adults (mostly parents) who look after them. 'Success' for an organisation focused on prevention is the absence of symptoms: in other words, something not happening. This can be difficult to evaluate. For example, a service may aim to raise awareness through the local press to increase the number of children referred for support. However, identifying those families who would have developed mental health difficulties had the service not existed is likely to prove impossible to measure.

A decision was taken early on not to measure a reduction of mental health symptoms per se. Instead, the route we have taken is to identify five primary clinical objectives (see page 252) which have been generated from factors which families say are important to them. These objectives are incorporated into all services we develop and are consequently the focus for evaluating impact and outcome (Stokes and Wood 2003).

Services are currently evaluated using the structure outlined in Figure 25. These in-house evaluation reports provide useful benchmarks for before-and-after comparisons. For example, in the past four years our groups for children bereaved by suicide have had a maximum of 12 children; this year the group was significantly larger at 19. It was helpful to read the evaluation from the previous year in order to make careful judgments about how the larger group may have contributed to a different therapeutic process. The benchmark of the previous year was a good baseline on which to focus discussions on the therapeutic process witnessed with the larger group.

From Seb, aged 12, who came to a residential weekend with his mother and sisters.

Dear Jule, Diane and Tim
Thank-you for looking after me and my sisters at the camp. It was great fun and I really liked the challenges. The camp has really helped me sort things out more and I'm definatley coming to the Camp Reunion and Christmas ceremony

I hope you are well

from

Seb

Figure 24: Example of a key performance indicator report for a residential group

Activity: **Camp Winston**		Date: 24/9/03

	Target	Actual
Number of children invited	20 minimum/25 maximum	24
Number of children attended	24	22
Variance between actual and target		-2
Number of parents invited	100% (all children represented by a primary care-giver)	11
Number of parents attended	11	10
Variance between actual and target		-1
Total number of families attended	11	10
Out-of-county referrals	4	4
Geographical location		London, Yorkshire, Hampshire, Birmingham
Funder (for example, primary care trust, self-funding)		Primary care trusts x 3 Self-funding x 1
Number receiving funding prior to residential	4	3
Volunteers involved Male Female From Gloucestershire From outside Gloucestershire	40% 60% 80% 20%	4 (27%) 11 (73%) 9 (60%) 6 (40%)
Follow-up activities Phone call to family Postcard to children Letter to family, school etc Memory books sent out Follow-up family visit Database updated	Within 1 week Within 5 days Within 4 weeks Within 4 weeks Within 8 weeks Within 1 week	✓ ✓ ✓ ✓ ✓ (for 9 families) ✓

Comment and analysis

- The family which did not come decided to wait for a few months until it would be possible to include the youngest child in the family.

- Male volunteers continue to be under-represented and 40% of volunteers travelled from outside the county.

- Demographic analysis of who attended (for example, cause of death, time since death etc) available on request from Allyson.

Figure 25: Service evaluation report framework

Each service is currently evaluated using the following structure for the final evaluation report:

1. **Introduction (to include a description of the service offered and the need observed).**
2. **Aims and objectives of the service/programme.**
3. **Evaluation of the event in terms of the five primary clinical objectives.**
4. **KPI data relating to numbers and efficiency targets (see opposite).**
5. **a) Feedback from children.**
   b) Feedback from young people.
   c) Feedback from parents.
   d) Feedback from staff.
   e) Feedback from volunteers.
   f) Feedback from other relevant parties: for example, supporters, donors and trustees.
6. **Cost-benefit analysis (breakdown of expenditure and staff time involved – for preparation, planning, implementation, debriefing).**
7. **A review of media coverage (if relevant).**
8. **Recommendations/actions.**

(All reports are dated and the author is responsible for ensuring that actions are followed up.)

In our Introduction we referred to the question: 'How can a child bereavement service understand and meet the needs of children and the communities in which they live?' This question remains central. However stretched clinicians are, we need to find enough time to link our practice to the theory, research and resulting evidence base of community child bereavement programmes, and make sure that the evaluation of the programmes devised is robust.

In 1997 we published a paper called 'The Challenge of Evaluating a Child Bereavement Programme' (Stokes et al 1997). At that time the literature on evaluating adult bereavement interventions was becoming more comprehensive, but for child bereavement it was still fairly limited. We raised a number of key points in that paper relating to why, what and how we evaluate and concluded that there is no one way to proceed, recognising the great scope to introduce qualitative and quantitative research methods into the child bereavement literature.

'To be uncertain is
uncomfortable, but to
be certain is ridiculous.'

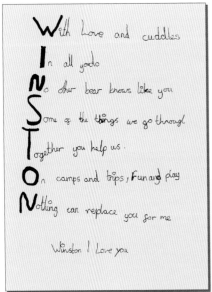

With Love and cuddles
In all yado
No other bear knows like you
Some of the things we go through
Together you help us.
On camps and trips, Fun and play
Nothing can replace you for me

Winston I Love you

From Amy, aged 7, whose dad died suddenly from a heart attack. Younger children often develop a close relationship with 'Winston' who can act as a mediator and indirect link to the person who has died. As Amy poignantly writes: 'Nothing can replace you for me'.

A recent review of the empirical evidence (Curtis and Newman 2001) found nine studies in the UK and USA that demonstrate limited evidence for positive outcomes for bereaved children. However, what they also found were many methodological weaknesses in the studies, such as small sample size, and concluded that there is an urgent need for more research into different interventions.

While others (Harrison and Harrington 2001) continue to question the need for 'specialised bereavement counselling services', this is balanced by those who propose a preventive, non-pathological framework. 'Even children in the most emotionally literate family may value someone outside the family to talk to, since we know that they may well be protecting those who look after them from their most troubling thoughts. These children are not sick, but they are vulnerable and some do need a special acknowledgement of the hard and sad event they are experiencing.' (Winton 2002: p3)

People reading this book are likely to know the wisdom of these words intuitively. However, it remains a responsibility to allocate resources so that we can provide evidence to others who are not in a position to observe the changes Winton describes first hand. Rolls and Payne explain that 'answering the question "do childhood bereavement services work?" is not simple'. The authors are preparing future papers 'designed to look beyond description to more conceptual ways of thinking about service provision, and it is these concepts that may provide a more useful basis for comparison and evaluation'. (Rolls and Payne 2003: p428)

We are committed to making sure that an evaluation is carried out as part of each programme activity and are trying to build in sufficient time to ensure this happens. We aim to build research competence and skills, and to view evaluation as an essential developmental tool for learning, rather than a bureaucratic and time-consuming exercise. We are also actively engaged in finding methods to measure the five primary clinical objectives described and to work with partners worldwide to develop inter-agency evaluation programmes. For example, a sub-group of the International Working Group for Death, Dying and Bereavement is currently identifying factors to assess resilience in bereaved children. The sub-group involves several European and North American service providers.

Quality assurance

'Quality assurance is a systematic approach to identifying and responding to the needs of your users by providing an appropriate service consistently and to agreed standards.' (Charities Evaluation Services 2000)

As a national organisation, we are not only concerned with service evaluation, but also with quality assurance and evaluation of the fundraising, marketing, financial and administrative processes of the organisation as a whole.

The assessment tools incorporate 'quality standards'. They concentrate not so much on the broader aspects of impact but on internal processes within organisations. The focus is on how these processes can be improved to allow smooth running of an organisation, or to increase its efficiency and effectiveness.

We decided to use a self-assessment system called PQASSO – Practical Quality Assurance System for Small Organisations (Charities Evaluation Services 2000).

This system identifies 12 quality areas:
- planning for quality
- governance
- user-centred service
- management
- managing money
- managing activities
- managing resources
- staffing and volunteers
- training and development
- networking and partnerships
- monitoring and evaluation
- results.

The benefits of PQASSO include:
- the ability to define and agree our purpose and activities more easily
- being better organised and co-ordinated in our efforts
- having a clear focus on the users of our service
- efficiency at working together and communicating well as a team
- having a useful tool to use when reporting to funders.

Providing a child bereavement service means that much time is given to service delivery, fundraising, consulting with stakeholders, and strategic and operational planning. Quality assurance needs to be fully integrated into the planning cycle of an organisation. It is motivational to everyone to know they are getting good results from the effort they are putting in. Quality assurance is a natural and necessary ingredient to ensure organisations can plan a future that has longevity to fulfil its vision and offers value for money for all stakeholders.

The journey itself is the reward.

Figure 26: Guidelines for best practice

Childhood Bereavement Network

GUIDELINES FOR BEST PRACTICE

Safety

- Is there a documented policy to ensure the overall safety of children using your service/s? Does this policy encompass the whole range of work undertaken by paid/voluntary staff e.g. individual/group work, transport by volunteers, home visits?
- Does the policy incorporate a set procedure for the recruitment of paid staff and volunteers?
- Do paid and voluntary staff receive training and supervision to ensure the overall safety of children using your service?
- Do you work within the legislative framework and guidance, specifically the Children Act 1989, *Working Together to Safeguard Children* documents; *Safe from Harm* (Home Office), *Duty to Care* (DHSS Northern Ireland) and the Children (Scotland) Act 1995?
- Is there a documented policy on confidentiality? Is this reviewed on a regular basis and agreed with paid/voluntary staff?
- Is there a documented policy to ensure the personal safety of paid/voluntary staff? Is this policy reviewed and evaluated regularly in consultation with all staff?

Practice Context

- Are the principles embodied in the CBN Belief Statement incorporated into your practice and the service/s you provide? Do you regularly review your approach to your work? As an organisation, do you consult with paid/voluntary staff during this process?
- Is your documented policy on confidentiality fully discussed and agreed with the individual child, the parent/s, other family members and caregivers?
- Is there a documented health and safety policy?
- Are there procedures in place to ensure data protection?
- Are documented policies and procedures reviewed regularly to comply with legal requirements?
- Is your service appropriately resourced? Do you have reliable access to a safe space, room or premises? Do you have a budget to buy equipment?

Quality and Accountability

- Do you have procedures to enable you to monitor, evaluate and review the service/s you provide on a regular basis?
- Do you regularly undertake a needs assessment to review the appropriateness of your work or service/s? Do you liaise with users, key referral agencies, staff and other professionals working in your catchment area regarding any proposed service development? Do you have a procedure to ensure effective liaison with other local, regional or national organisations offering similar services?
- Is there a documented policy to ensure that all paid/voluntary staff are appropriately trained to work with bereaved children, their families and other caregivers? Are training needs regularly reviewed? Are all paid/voluntary staff offered regular opportunities to update their skills? Do you have a training budget?
  Is there a documented policy on supervision? Are all paid/voluntary staff appropriately supervised? Are paid/voluntary staff consulted on a regular basis to agree their supervision needs?
- Do you encourage feedback on your service from users, key referral agencies and professionals? Is there a documented and accessible complaints procedure for users, key referral agencies, paid/voluntary staff and the public?
- Do you have a statement of purpose or mission statement plus clear aims to define the remit of your service? Is there a business plan, including a funding strategy to ensure the sustainability of your service? Do you publish and circulate an annual report to key referral agencies and users?
- Is there a written definition of your service/s, which clearly sets out details of the information, guidance and support you offer? Is this regularly reviewed and updated? Within the remit of your service, is this information circulated to key referral agencies and potential users in the form of a publicity leaflet?

Equality

- Is there a documented and proactive equal opportunities policy?
- Do you regularly undertake a needs assessment to review the accessibility and appropriateness of your service/s in terms of equality of opportunity?
- Do you regularly review your service/s to identify and amend any anti-discriminatory practice?
- Are you able to respond to the needs of bereaved minority ethnic children, especially in terms of language?
- Are you able to respond to the needs of bereaved disabled children or those with learning disabilities?
- Do you liaise with other organisations to raise awareness of the needs of bereaved children, their families and other caregivers?

Organisational structure

Having grown in a relatively short space of time from a small local charity into a larger national one, we have needed to evolve structures and systems to ensure we are sufficiently robust to meet service demands. Staff and volunteers are organised into directorates for family services, external relations (fundraising and marketing), finance and administration, and quality assurance. The chief executive and directors form a Senior Management Team and take responsibility for the strategic direction of the organisation, linking closely with the Board of Trustees. A Management Group is responsible for the operational aspects of the organisation and is made up of the Senior Management Team and key managers from each directorate. A strategic plan and directorate operational plans are set, implemented and evaluated on a financial year cycle. Key performance indicators (KPIs) are an integral part of this process. Written policies and procedures ensure we work within sound guidelines. The Childhood Bereavement Network has produced a set of guidelines for best practice (see Figure 26) that we have found extremely useful, covering issues of safety, practice context, quality and accountability, and equality.

Recording, monitoring and evaluating all our data are becoming considerably easier and more reliable through the use of a bespoke database. While the stepping stones along the way to ensuring we are all competent and comfortable with using the database have been challenging (to say the least!), we are finally seeing the benefits in terms of access to records and data analysis for evaluation and research purposes.

This chapter has demonstrated the importance of service providers finding ways to measure inputs, outputs, outcomes and the overall impact these can make for the communities they support. The importance of implementing an effective quality assurance framework is also discussed. Are community-based child bereavement services on the right path? Perhaps the question needs to be reframed. Perhaps there is no one right path. Instead there are many routes to deliver services to bereaved children. The Clara E Burgess Child Bereavement Research Study has generated a wealth of data which are currently being analysed (Rolls and Payne 2003). The study is likely to make a significant contribution and will help clarify thinking on the conceptual issues inherent in understanding the diversity of models and practice in child bereavement services.

Conclusion

Then, now and always

The process of writing about the development of services at Winston's Wish has enabled some valued opportunities for reflection on why and how we seek to support bereaved children and their families. There can be few life events that have a greater impact on a child's life than the death of someone close; we are passionately committed to ensuring that all children are supported in their journey through grief.

It is over 10 years since the first small group of children came together to tell their stories, remember the person who had died, express their feelings and gain support from meeting each other. We have learnt so much in the intervening years from the families and colleagues we have met and worked with and we hope that we have succeeded within these pages in sharing some of that invaluable experience.

Children will continue to be bereaved of parents, siblings and important people. Sadly, we can't change the fact that death is a part of many children's lives. What can be changed is the way in which our society responds to these children and young people. We look to a time when there is an accessible, high quality service within reach of every bereaved child.

There will always be a place for services at the community level, backed up by national initiatives, such as the Childhood Bereavement Network and the Winston's Wish Family Line. While all of us who work with bereaved families are becoming more aware of their needs, it is encouraging to see the beginnings of recognition from policy-makers.

'The Children's NSF [National Service Framework] offers an opportunity to improve the lives and health of children and young people through the development of effective, evidence-based and needs-led services, and to improve their experiences and satisfaction with services. It sets out a challenging agenda, with three key objectives, namely, to put children and their families at the centre of care; to develop effective partnership working so that the needs of the child are always considered, and to deliver needs-led services.' (Department of Health 2003: p2)

Few people in the child bereavement world would disagree with this position. However, some level of government funding will be essential if the approach described in this book is to be developed for all local communities. Rolls and Payne (2003) have succeeded in mapping the location, range and type of childhood bereavement service provision in the UK. Their findings indicate that 85% of childhood bereavement services are located in the voluntary sector. The survey reported that the majority of services (73%) relied on both paid and unpaid staff. It also reported that 35% of the services included in the survey had started within the past five years and their findings show a diverse approach to organisational structure and delivery. The range of interventions was however broadly reflective of those described in this book.

In the National Service Framework for Children, the government has promised to 'set out ways of supporting the child through a number of journeys – the journey of growing up, of dealing with particular problems including injuries and illnesses, mental health problems and the journey that some families have to make in negotiating their way through a complex and bewildering web of apparently unlinked services' (Department of Health 2003: p4). Earlier on in this book we looked at the journey made by Tom following the death of his father. In closing, it is perhaps appropriate to look forward by looking back and reflecting on three letters that we received in the same week. Two were from children bereaved 12 years ago and one is from David, who began his bereavement journey over 65 years ago.

I feel I have a special interest in Winston's Wish having been orphaned at the age of 7 – in 1937... we went overnight from our home to the guardianship of an uncle and his childless wife who had disliked and disapproved of my mother. The then approved approach was to make a 'tabula rasa' of the past, no papers, books, toys etc went with us from the old to the new life, which included every luxury but without overt affection. None of us grieved openly, though I believe my behaviour, especially in the early days, left much to be desired. I have NO direct memories of my mother, father or eldest brother, nor did years of psychoanalysis remedy this. I am pleased to say that since then I have produced two excellent sons and six lovely grandchildren, *but* something vital died in me, in August 1937, which I dare say that such an organisation as yours might have helped to keep alive, or revived. I wish you every possible success, and I feel empathy with all the children you are helping in so many varied and admirable ways.

David, aged 73

June 2003

David's poignant letter is one of many we have received from adults – all essentially saying the same key message – 'I wish "this" could have been around for me …' Children are undoubtedly resilient, but resilience – like love – needs to be accompanied by an unconditional recognition that the death of a parent or sibling is one of the greatest challenges even the most resilient of children will ever need to face. Only then can we hope that letters like David's will be replaced by those of young adults like Gemma and Mandy who take joy in reminding themselves of a relationship that is important to them 'then, now and always'.

Gemma and her older sister Mandy were two of 14 children who attended a pilot group in September 1992. In June 2003 the sisters chose to make contact with Winston's Wish again, perhaps simply to touch base some 12 years after their mother's death from cancer. Now in their early 20s they arrived with two carrier bags full of photos, workbooks and letters. They remembered with tears and joy a journey in their lives that has left them with a respect for their own capacity to be resilient and a knowledge that they have successfully continued a bond which appears to have a genuine chance to be everlasting. After their visit each wrote a letter. With Gemma's and Mandy's permission we conclude by sharing extracts of their bereavement journeys.

I was 9 years old when mum was diagnosed with cancer in October 1990. During her stay in hospital Mandy (my sister, aged 11 at the time) and I were introduced to Julie. We talked about mum's illness, our hopes and fears and ultimately mum's death. These meetings were so important to me as I began to realise that I wasn't the only person going through something like this and that it's OK to cry and to show your feelings and emotions. In a way, I was being prepared for the worst. The worst came on May 9th 1991 at 2.42pm when mum died from cancer …

Just before mum died I rushed in to see her. I gave her a huge hug, deep down wishing that I could never let go as I knew this would be the last time to do so. I sat there for what seemed an eternity, talking to her about my school trip and helping her to drink some fluids. As I left her room to go downstairs I gave her a hug and kiss which are still very memorable to me as this was my very last time with mum.

Both Mandy and I continued our sessions; although we attended them separately. I was given a book that was designed to help children cope with grief, that I worked through. I drew pictures of my thoughts, feelings and favourite memories of mum. It was a nice way of extracting all my feelings that I could have so easily bottled up inside of me. We talked endlessly about mum too, which meant she was still alive in my thoughts.

My sister and I were one of the first people to actually take part in a Winston's Wish group. I remember we attended the group along with several other children who had lost a family member. This was such a good day for me as I realised that I was not alone, there were other people and other children who had been through the same as me … I still remember the boy I sat next to, he must not have been much older than me, and he told us about the experience of losing his dad. I was not alone and that was such a relief.

Now 12 years on, there is never a day that goes past where I don't think of mum. I feel her spirit is with me, guiding me through life. I talk to her in my subconscious all the time and I believe that I am able to do this as a result of my involvement with Winston's Wish. They encouraged me to remember mum and to keep her spirit alive.

At home, I have many photos of mum and one is kept beside my bed. I look at this every night before I go to sleep; it's my way of saying 'Goodnight Mum'. There are still times when I get upset and wish she was here, however, I now realise that she has gone to a better place and is no longer in pain. It's particularly hard when I see people around my age with their mums. I do get jealous, wishing I still had my mum, but I am proud to have spent the time that I did with her and remember that even though she isn't with me in body, she will always and forever be with me in memory.

Gemma, aged 22

July 2003

The day of Mum's death, I still remember as clearly as though it was yesterday. I was able to have a cuddle with mum, which I knew deep down would be my last one, and say goodbye in our own way. This is a memory, which will stay with me forever.

The visits after mum's death involved a lot of talking about how I felt, where I thought mum had gone, and my memories of mum – again helping me to understand more about death and bereavement, and that it was OK to cry. One of the first bits of 'work' was to write a biography of mum's life and I was encouraged to include lots of photos – which I did. This I still have today as a nice memento of my mum's life.

I do sincerely believe that being part of Winston's Wish has helped me to come to terms with the death of my mum. As a child it is a difficult thing to comprehend that you are never going to see this someone special ever again – but when all your questions, worries and fears are explained to you, it makes it that little bit easier. Realising you are not the only person to have lost your mum, and that you are not 'weird' was so important (in my opinion!). The encouragement I was given to talk about the person I have lost and to treasure my memories is the most important thing I learnt from all of those sessions.

I still have many happy, sad, good and bad memories of my mum, all of which I treasure. At home I have many photographs of her around the house. I am proud to wear various bits of her jewellery, including her wedding and engagement rings, and I take it as the biggest compliment when people tell me how much I look like her. My mum may be gone, but she is definitely not forgotten!

Mandy, aged 23
July 2003

On behalf of all bereaved children, Gemma and Mandy show us that, with care and support, their mother can be part of their lives ... then, now and always.

Afterword

10 action-packed years

Winston's Wish has travelled far in the last 10 years and is now poised for the next stage. Our future direction of travel will make sure that our service develops with a coherent mission and common purpose, rooted in clinical excellence.

We will continue to do this on six levels:

- **on a one-to-one level** – walking alongside children in their individual bereavement journeys
- **on a family level** – supporting families through the processes of grief
- **on a local level** – building a community network to support those who are bereaved and grieving
- **on a national level** – working in partnership to develop bereavement services for every child who is living with grief
- **on an international level** – improving services by sharing best practice, knowledge and research
- **on a global level** – raising awareness of the needs of bereaved children and their families.

By 2007, as part of our strategic plan to realise our vision for bereaved children, we want Winston's Wish to be known as an organisation which:

- continues to be at the cutting edge of developing creative approaches to supporting bereaved children and their families
- is valued by bereaved families and respected by professionals and researchers worldwide
- has worked in partnership with the Childhood Bereavement Network and other groups to change the world's understanding of the needs of bereaved children and their families.

The involvement of children in the processes of death and bereavement provides a significant challenge, but one that must be met if we are ever to take their needs seriously and create a system in which children are proactively offered support following the death of a family member.

Dame Janet Trotter *Chair, Winston's Wish Board of Trustees*

References

Achenbach TM and Howell CT. 1993. Are America's Children Getting Worse? A 13-year Comparison. *Journal of the American Academy of Child and Adolescent Psychiatry*; 32: 1145–1154.

Ayers TS, Kennedy CL, Sandler IN and Stokes J. 2003. Promoting Healthy Adaptation in Bereaved Adolescents. In: Gullotta TP and Bloom M (eds). *The Encyclopedia of Primary Prevention and Health Promotion*. New York: Kluwer Academic/Plenum Publishers: 221–229.

BBC. 1998. *Goodbye, God Bless*. An Everyman documentary produced for BBC Manchester. First shown on Sunday 6 December 1998, 10.45, BBC1.

Bentovim A and Bingley Miller L. 2001. *The Family Assessment: Assessment of Family Competence, Strengths and Difficulties*. Brighton: Pavilion Publishing.

Black D. 1991. Family Interventions with Families Bereaved or About to be Bereaved. In: Papadatou D and Papadatou C (eds). *Children and Death*. Washington DC: Hemisphere Publishing: 135–143.

Black D and Kaplan T. 1988. Father Kills Mother: Issues and Problems Encountered by a Child Psychiatric Team. *British Journal of Psychiatry*; 153: 624–630.

Black D and Urbanowicz MA. 1987. Family Intervention with Bereaved Children. *Journal of Child Psychology and Psychiatry*; 28: 467–476.

Bowlby J. 1980. *Attachment and Loss: Loss, Sadness and Depression*. Volume III. New York: Basic Books.

Buchsbaum BC. 1987. Remembering a Parent who has Died: A Developmental Perspective. In: Klass D, Silverman PR and Nickman SL (eds). 1996. *Continuing Bonds – New Understandings of Grief*. Washington DC: Taylor and Francis: 113–124.

Charities Evaluation Services. 2000. *PQASSO. How to Implement a Quality Assurance System. A Guide for Small Voluntary Organisations and Projects*. 2nd edition. London: Charities Evaluation Services.

Christ GH. 2000. *Healing Children's Grief – Surviving a Parent's Death of Cancer*. New York: Oxford University Press.

Clark SE and Goldney R. 2000. The Impact of Suicide on Relatives and Friends. In: Hawton K and Van Heeringen K (eds). *The International Handbook of Suicide and Attempted Suicide*. Chichester: Wiley: 467–484.

Cloitre M, Cancienne J, Brodsky B, Dulit R and Perry SW. 1996. Memory Performance Among Women with Parental Abuse Histories: Enhanced Directed Forgetting or Directed Remembering? *Journal of Abnormal Psychology*; 105: 204–211.

Collier J. 1997. Attitudes to Children's Pain: Exploding the Pain Myth. *Paediatric Nursing*; 9: 15–18.

Corr C. 2000. What Do We Know about Grieving Children and Adolescents? In: Doka KJ. *Living with Grief: Children, Adolescents and Loss.* Washington DC: Hospice Foundation of America: 21–32.

Corr C, Nabe C and Corr D. 2000. *Death and Dying, Life and Living.* 3rd edition. Belmont, CA: Wadsworth/Thompson Learning.

Cross S. 2002. *I Can't Stop Feeling Sad: Calls to ChildLine about Bereavement.* ChildLine Special Report: www.childline.org.uk

Crossley D. 1995. *Winston's Auntie Wina.* Gloucester: Winston's Wish.

Crossley D. 2000. *Muddles, Puddles and Sunshine: Your Activity Book when Someone has Died.* Stroud: Hawthorne Press.

Crossley D and Stokes J. 2001. *Beyond the Rough Rock: Supporting a Child who has been Bereaved through Suicide.* Gloucester: Winston's Wish.

Curtis K and Newman T. 2001. *Do Community-based Support Services Benefit Bereaved Children? A Review of Empirical Evidence.* City University London: Institute for Health Sciences.

Davies HTO, Nutley SM and Smith PC (eds). 2000. *What Works? Evidence-based Policy and Practice in Public Services.* Bristol: The Policy Press.

Department for Education and Employment. 2001. *Promoting Children's Mental Health within Early Years and School Settings.* Nottingham: DfEE Publications. www.dfes.gov.uk/mentalhealth/pdfs/mental.pdf

Department of Health. 1999. *National Service Framework for Mental Health.* www.doh.gov.uk/nsf/mentalhealth.htm

Department of Health. 2003. *Getting the Right Start: National Service Framework for Children – Emerging Findings.* www.doh.gov.uk/nsf/children/emergingfindingsindex.htm

Dobson S. 1989. Genograms and Ecomaps. *Nursing Times, Nursing Mirror*; December 26; 85 (51): 54.

Dyregrov A. 1991. *Grief in Children: A Handbook for Adults*. London: Jessica Kingsley Publishers.

Dyregrov A and Mitchell JT. 1992. Work with Traumatised Children: Psychological Effects and Coping Strategies. *Journal of Traumatic Stress*; 5: 5–17.

Freud EL. 1961. *Letters of Sigmund Freud*. New York: Basic Books.

Gal-Oz E and Field N. 2002. Do Continuing Bonds Always Help with Adjustments to Loss? *Bereavement Care*; 21 (3): 42–43.

Gersie A. 1991. *Story-making in Bereavement*. London: Jessica Kingsley Publishers.

Gersie A. 1997. *Reflections on Therapeutic Story-making – The Use of Stories in Groups*. London: Jessica Kingsley Publishers.

Gisborne T. 1995. Death and Bereavement in School: Are You Prepared? *Education*; June issue: 3–13.

Gisborne T, Stokes J, Crossley D and Elliot K. 1995. *Positive Responses to Death: A Strategy for Schools*. Gloucester: Winston's Wish.

Glaser D, Furniss T and Bingley L. 1984. Focal Family Therapy: The Assessment Stage. *Journal of Family Therapy*; 4: 132–177.

Gliori D. 1999. *No Matter What*. London: Bloomsbury Publishing Plc.

Goldman L. 1996. *Breaking the Silence: A Guide to Help Children with Complicated Grief – Suicide, Homicide, Aids, Violence and Abuse*. Washington DC: Accelerated Development.

Goleman D. 1998. *Working with Emotional Intelligence*. London: Bloomsbury Publishing Plc.

Greenhalgh T. 2002. Uneasy bedfellows? Reconciling Intuition and Evidence-based Practice. *Young Minds Magazine*; 59: 23–27.

Grollman EA. 1993. *Straight Talk about Death for Teenagers. How to Cope with Losing Someone you Love*. Boston: Beacon Press.

Harrington R and Harrison L. 1999. Unproven Assumptions about the Impact of Bereavement on Children. *Journal of the Royal Society of Medicine*; 92: 230–233.

Harris Hendricks J. 2002. Review of the Harry Potter Series. *Bereavement Care*; 21 (1): 11.

Harrison L and Harrington R. 2001. Adolescents' Bereavement Experiences: Prevalence, Association with Depressive Symptoms, and Use of Services. *Journal of Adolescence*; 24: 159–169.

Hawton K and Simkin S. 2003. Helping People Bereaved by Suicide – Their Needs May Require Special Attention. *British Medical Journal*; 327: 177–178.

Holland J. 2001. *Understanding Children's Experiences of Parental Bereavement*. London: Jessica Kingsley Publishers.

Howe ML. 2000. *The Fate of Early Memories: Developmental Science and the Retention of Childhood Experiences*. Washington DC: American Psychological Association.

International Working Group for Death, Dying and Bereavement. 1999. Children, Adolescents and Death; Myths, Realities and Challenges. *Death Studies*; 23: 443–463.

Janoff-Bulman R and Berg M. 1988. Disillusionment and the Creation of Value: From Traumatic Losses to Existential Gains. In: Harvey JH (ed). *Perspectives on Loss: A Sources Book*. Philadelphia: Taylor and Francis: 35–47.

Jones E. 2001. *Bibliotherapy for Bereaved Children – Healing Readings.* London: Jessica Kingsley Publishers.

Kagan J. 1996. Three Pleasing Ideas. *American Psychologist*; 51: 901–908.

Kent J. 1984. *There's No Such Thing as a Dragon*. London: Blackie and Son Limited.

Kiernan KE. 1992. The Impact of Family Disruption in Childhood on Transitions made in Young Adult Life. *Population Studies*; 46 (2): 213–234.

Klass D. 1988. *Parental Grief: Solace and Resolution*. New York: Springer Publishing Company.

Klass D, Silverman PR, Nickman S (eds). 1996. *Continuing Bonds – New Understandings of Grief*. Washington DC: Taylor and Francis.

Krauss F. In preparation. An Extended Warranty? In: Monroe B and Krauss F. *Brief Interventions with Bereaved Children*. Oxford: Oxford University Press.

Krupp G, Genovese F and Krupp T. 1986. To Have and Have Not: Multiple Identification in Pathological Bereavement. *Journal of the American Academy of Psychoanalysis*; 14: 337–348.

Malmquist CP. 1986. Children who Witness Parental Murder: Post-traumatic Aspects. *Journal of the American Academy of Child and Adolescent Psychiatry*; 25: 320–325.

Meltzer H, Gatward R, Goodman R and Ford T. 2000. *The Mental Health of Children and Adolescents in Great Britain*. Social Survey Division of the Office for National Statistics: www.statistics.gov.uk/downloads/theme_health/KidsMentalHealth.pdf

Muir Gray J. 2000. *Evidence-based Healthcare – How to Make Health Policy and Management Decisions*. Edinburgh: Churchill Livingstone.

Murphy J. 1998. *Five Minutes' Peace (The Large Family)*. London: Walker Books.

Nadeau JW. 1998. *Families Making Sense of Death*. London: Sage Publications.

Newman T. 2002. *Promoting Resilience: A Review of Effective Strategies for Child Care Services*. University of Exeter: Centre for Evidence Based Social Sciences: www.exeter.ac.uk/cebss

Newman T. 2003. Protection Racket. *Zero2Nineteen*; January issue: 8.

O'Connor M and Russell A. 2003. Working with the Legacy of Trauma. *Bereavement Care*; 22 (2): 22–24.

Papadatou D. 1997. Training Professionals in Caring for Dying Children and Grieving Families. *Death Studies*; 21: 575–600.

Parkes CM. 1998. Editorial. *Bereavement Care*; 17 (2): 18.

Parkes CM and Weiss RS. 1983. *Recovery from Bereavement*. New York: Basic Books.

Payne S and Relf M. 1994. The Assessment of Need for Bereavement Follow-up in Palliative Care and Hospice Care. *Palliative Medicine*; 8 (4): 291–297.

Pressley M and Schneider W. 1997. *Introduction to Memory Development during Childhood and Adolescence*. Mahwah, New Jersey: Lawrence Erlbaum Associates.

Pynoos R and Eth S. 1984. The Child as Witness to Homicide. *Journal of Social Issues*; 40 (2): 87–108.

Pynoos R, Steinberg A and Wraith R. 1995. A Developmental Model of Childhood Traumatic Stress. In: Cicchetti D and Cohen D (eds). *Development and Psychopathology*. Volume 2: *Risk, Disorder and Adaptation*. New York: John Wiley and Sons: 96–161.

Rando TA. 1993. *Treatment of Complicated Mourning*. Champaign, Illinois: Research Press.

Rolls L and Payne S. 2003. Childhood Bereavement Services: A Survey of UK Provision. *Palliative Medicine*; 17: 423-432.

Rosen, M. 2002. *Carrying the Elephant: A Memoir of Love and Loss.* London: Penguin Books.

Rowling JK. 1997. *Harry Potter and the Philosopher's Stone.* London: Bloomsbury Publishing Plc.

Rowling JK. 2003. *Harry Potter and the Order of the Phoenix.* London: Bloomsbury Publishing Plc.

Rowling L. 2003. *Grief in School Communities. Effective Support Strategies.* Bucks: Open University Press.

Royal College of Psychiatrists. 2003. As quoted in *Young Minds Magazine*; 65: 7.

Sanders C. 1999. *Grief: The Mourning After: Dealing with Adult Bereavement.* 2nd edition. New York: John Wiley and Sons.

Schneider W and Pressley M. 1997. *Memory Development Between Two and Twenty.* 2nd edition. Mahwah, New Jersey: Lawrence Erlbaum Associates.

Schuurman D. 2003. *Never the Same – Coming to Terms with the Death of a Parent.* New York: St Martin's Press.

Shapiro ER. 1994. *Grief as a Family Process: A Developmental Approach to Clinical Practice.* New York: The Guildford Press.

Shaw C. 2002. *Evaluation Toolkit: A Tailored Approach to Evaluation for Parenting Projects.* National Children's Bureau and Parenting Education and Support Forum: London: www.parenting-forum.org.uk

Siegel DJ. 1997. Memory and Trauma. In: Black D, Newman M, Harris Hendricks J and Mezey G (eds). *Psychological Trauma.* London: Gaskells.

Silverman PR. 2000. *Never Too Young to Know: Death in Children's Lives.* New York: Oxford University Press.

Silverman PR and Nickman SL. 1996. Children's Construction of their Dead Parent. In: Klass D, Silverman PR and Nickman SL (eds). *Continuing Bonds – New Understandings of Grief.* Washington DC: Taylor and Francis: 73–86.

Silverman PR, Nickman SL and Worden JW. 1992. Detachment Revisited: The Child's Reconstruction of a Dead Parent. *American Journal of Orthopsychiatry*; 62 (4): 494–503.

Silverman PR and Worden JW. 1992. Children's Reactions in the Early Months after the Death of a Parent. *American Journal of Orthopsychiatry*; 62 (1): 93–104.

Silverman PR and Worden JW. 1993. Children's Reactions to the Death of a Parent. In: Stroebe MS, Stroebe W and Hansson RO (eds). *Handbook of Bereavement: Theory, Research and Intervention*. Cambridge: Cambridge University Press: 300–316.

Slater A. 2003. Safety Net. *Young Minds Magazine*; 65: 24–25.

Smith SC. 1999. *The Forgotten Mourners: Guidelines for Working with Bereaved Children*. 2nd edition. London: Jessica Kingsley Publishers.

Smith SC and Pennells SM. 1995. *Interventions with Bereaved Children*. London: Jessica Kingsley Publishers.

Stokes J. 2000. *The Secret C: Straight Talking about Cancer*. Gloucester: Winston's Wish.

Stokes J and Crossley D. 2001. *As Big as it Gets: Supporting a Child when Someone in the Family is Seriously Ill*. Gloucester: Winston's Wish.

Stokes J, Pennington J, Monroe B, Papadatou D and Relf M. 1999. Developing Services for Bereaved Children: A Discussion of the Theoretical and Practical Issues Involved. *Mortality*; 4 (3): 291–307.

Stokes J and Wood L. 2003. *Service Evaluation Report: Parents' Feedback*. Gloucester: Winston's Wish, unpublished.

Stokes J, Wyer S and Crossley D. 1997. The Challenge of Evaluating a Child Bereavement Programme. *Palliative Medicine*; 11: 179–190.

Stroebe MS, Hansson R, Stroebe W and Schut H (eds). 2001. *Handbook of Bereavement Research: Consequences, Coping and Care*. Washington DC: American Psychological Association.

Stroebe MS and Schut H. 1995. Grief. In: Manstead A and Hewstone M (eds). *Blackwell Dictionary of Social Psychology*. Oxford: Blackwell: 260–262.

Stroebe MS and Schut H. 1999. The Dual Process Model of Coping with Bereavement: Rationale and Description. *Death Studies*; 23: 197–224.

Terr L. 1988. What Happens to Early Memories of Trauma? A Study of 20 Children under 5 at the Time of Documented Traumatic Events. *Journal of the American Academy of Child and Adolescent Psychiatry*; 27: 96–104.

Terr L. 1991. Childhood Traumas: An Outline and Overview. *American Journal of Psychiatry*; 148: 10–20.

Thompson F and Payne S. 2000. Bereaved Children's Questions to a Doctor. *Mortality*; 5 (1): 74–96.

Timimi S. 2003. The New Practitioner: The Emergence of the Post-modern Clinician. *Young Minds Magazine*; 62: 14–16.

Tonkin L. 1996. Growing around Grief – Another Way of Looking at Grief and Recovery. *Bereavement Care*; 15 (1): 10.

Traisman ES. 1992. *Fire in my Heart, Ice in my Veins*. Omaha, NE: Centering Corporation.

Wainwright S. 2002. *Measuring Impact. A Guide to Resources*. London: National Council for Voluntary Organisations.

Walter T. 1996. A New Model of Grief: Bereavement and Biography. *Mortality*; 1: 7–25.

Ward B and Associates. 1993. *Good Grief: Exploring Feelings, Loss and Death with Over Elevens*. London: Jessica Kingsley Publishers.

Ward B and Associates. 1993. *Good Grief: Exploring Feelings, Loss and Death with Under Elevens*. London: Jessica Kingsley Publishers.

Webb NB. 1993. *Helping Bereaved Children: A Handbook for Practitioners*. New York: The Guildford Press.

Weiss RS. 2001. Grief, Bonds and Relationships. In: Stroebe MS, Hansson R, Stroebe W and Schut H (eds). *Handbook of Bereavement Research: Consequences, Coping and Care*. Washington DC: American Psychological Association: 47–62.

Wertheimer A. 2001. *A Special Scar: The Experiences of People Bereaved by Suicide*. 2nd edition. Brunner-Routledge: East Sussex.

Winton P. 2002. *Bulletin 3*. Childhood Bereavement Network: www.ncb.org.uk/cbn

Wolfelt A. 1996. *Healing the Bereaved Child*. Colorado: Compassion Press.

Wolfenstein M. 1966. How is Mourning Possible? *Psychoanalytic Study of the Child*; 21: 93–123.

Word Centre, The. 2002. 117 *Easy Tips for Getting your Message Across Every Time you Write*. Sheffield: The Word Centre.

Worden JW. 1996. *Children and Grief – When a Parent Dies*. New York: The Guildford Press.

Wyer S. 1994. *A Service Evaluation Report of Winston's Wish*. Gloucester: Gloucestershire Royal Hospital NHS Trust.

Yendall D. 1996. *Bereavement Booklist – Stories and Information Books about Death for Children and Young People*. Schools Library Service: Gloucestershire.

Young B and Papadatou D. 1997. Childhood Death and Bereavement Across Cultures. In: Parkes CM, Laungani P and Young B (eds). *Death and Bereavement Across Cultures*. London: Routledge: 191–205.

Yule W and Gold A. 1993. *Wise Before the Event: Coping with Crises in Schools*. London: Calouste Gulbenkian Foundation.

Index

Picture credits and acknowledgements

Photography by Winston's Wish and Gettyone except for the following: BT (page 16, top); the *Gloucestershire Echo* and the *Citizen* (pages 244, 245, 246 and 248); *The Herald* (page 74); Veronica Jones (pages 40, 101, 137 bottom, 158 and 167); Chris Kelly (pages 152 and 287 top); and Pixel Studios, Cheltenham (pages 16 bottom, 80 top, 81, 112 bottom, 113, 131, 202 and 286 bottom). Photograph on page 89 courtesy of Jo. Photographs on pages 264, 266 and 288 courtesy of Gemma and Mandy. Website visuals on pages 219 to 223 courtesy of Nemisys.

The journey itself is the reward ... important steps along the way

Awarded the BT/ChildLine award for providing 'outstanding services to children'.

Published 'The Challenge of Evaluating a Child Bereavement Programme' (Stokes J, Wyer S and Crossley D. *Palliative Medicine*; 11: 179–190).

1992   **1993**   **1994**   **1995**   **1996**   **1997**   **1998**

Observational research of child bereavement services in Canada and the United States, funded by a Winston Churchill Travelling Fellowship.

'Winston's Wish' founded to meet the needs of bereaved children in Gloucestershire.

First residential weekend.

Launch of the service to schools. A resource called *A Positive Response to Death: A Strategy for Schools* circulated to all participating schools.

First residential group for families affected by suicide.

1,000th child referred.

Development of a national training programme for those who might be interested in setting up a grief support programme in their own locality, or for those who wish to enhance their own skills with bereaved children and young people.